QUEER ENCHANTMENTS

QUEER ENCHANTMENTS

Gender, Sexuality, and Class
in the Fairy-Tale Cinema
of Jacques Demy

Anne E. Duggan

Wayne State University Press   Detroit

17 16 15 14 13   5 4 3 2 1

Library of Congress Cataloging-in-Publication Data

Duggan, Anne E., 1967–
Queer enchantments : gender, sexuality, and class in the fairy-tale
cinema of Jacques Demy / Anne E. Duggan.
pages cm. — (Series in fairy-tale studies)
Includes bibliographical references and index.
ISBN 978-0-8143-3509-3 (pbk. : alk. paper) —
ISBN 978-0-8143-3854-4 (ebook)
1. Demy, Jacques—Criticism and interpretation. 2. Fairy tales in
motion pictures. 3. Sex role in motion pictures. 4. Social classes
in motion pictures. I. Title.
PN1998.3.D395D84 2013
791.43'6559—dc23
2013011385

To the queer and enchanting gang
of Le Carré Blanc, Strasbourg, 1987–88

CONTENTS

Acknowledgments

This book would not have been possible without the encouragement and support of Donald Haase. I have learned so much from him and from working with him on *Marvels & Tales* as well as on *The Greenwood Encyclopedia of Folktales and Fairy Tales* (2008). Moreover, his friendship, intellectual integrity, generosity, and, most importantly, sense of humor have made my day on more than a few occasions. I also have to give a special thanks to Donald Haase, Janet Langlois, Debra K. Peterson, and Anca Vlasopolos, with whom I collaborated for three years through our Wayne State University Humanities Center Working Group on the Fairy Tale, in which I first began to appreciate the work of Jacques Demy in relation to the fairy tale. While working on the book, I realized I also owe a great debt to Jack Zipes, who gave me the opportunity to develop a sound foundation in fairy-tale studies while working with him as a graduate student on *The Oxford Companion to Fairy Tales* (2000). And Tom Conley provided me with the example of an early modernist who could indeed write a book on film. In particular, I thank Donald Haase, Pauline Greenhill, and Elena Past for their responses to individual chapters and Victor Figueroa for patiently going over much of this manuscript at different stages and providing constant moral support. Much appreciation also goes to the two anonymous reviewers, whose feedback truly made this a stronger book, as well as to Annie Martin and the great team at Wayne State University Press, for all of their support for this project and their high level of professionalism. A special thanks goes to Walter Edwards and the Wayne State University Humanities Center for their support in the form of a faculty fellowship in summer 2010, which allowed me to carry out necessary research at the Cinémathèque française to be able to complete this book.

A shortened version of Chapter 4 appeared in *Marvels & Tales* 27.1 (2013) as "The Revolutionary Undoing of the Maiden Warrior in Riyoko Ikeda's *The Rose of Versailles* and Jacques Demy's *Lady Oscar.*" I thank Wayne State University Press for permission to reprint this material here.

Introduction

Queer Enchantments

I'm trying to create a world in my films.

—Jacques Demy

Perhaps less known today than his wife Agnès Varda, Jacques Demy has always held a tenuous place among directors of the French New Wave.[1] To the uninitiated, his films can seem strange, even laughable, in their use of sung dialogue. His color schemes convey a sense of gaudy artificiality that bears affinities with the films of John Waters, yet his films communicate a sweetness and melancholy not quite present in the American director's films. Demy's campy, fairy-tale aesthetics and melodramatic plots have influenced, since the late 1990s, a generation of queer filmmakers in France who demonstrate a new appreciation for Demy's cinema, an appreciation that earlier critics could not quite grasp.

Two essential aspects of the cinema of Jacques Demy have been understudied, overlooked, or ignored: the importance of the genre of the fairy tale, on the one hand, and the queer sensibility of his films, on the other. *Queer Enchantments* foregrounds both in an attempt to ask what Demy's cinema can tell us about the fairy tale and what the fairy tale can tell us about Demy's cinema. Such questions are intricately connected to how Demy unsettles conceptions of gender, sexuality, and class to open up the identity categories that often stifle his heroes and heroines as he broadens the possibilities of the genre of the fairy tale through his cinematic revisions. Thus it is specifically the "queerness" of

1

the enchanted worlds of Demy's films, as I will argue, that marks the distance between his cinematic oeuvre and the rest of the New Wave.

Although critics have often alluded to Demy's fascination with fairy tales, from those of Charles Perrault and the Brothers Grimm to the filmic versions of Walt Disney Studios, few have actually examined the extent to which the genre has influenced the shape of so many of Demy's films. Indeed, Demy was profoundly marked by the fairy-tale genre, producing films in which he explicitly drew from well-known tales, such as *Peau d'âne* (*Donkey Skin,* 1970) and *The Pied Piper* (1972), and others in which he integrated fairy-tale elements, including his Oscar-nominated *Les Parapluies de Cherbourg* (*The Umbrellas of Cherbourg,* 1964). This encounter between Demy's films and the genre of the fairy tale works to disarticulate the fairy tale from normative representations of gender, sexuality, and class often associated with it, resulting in the troubling of the values and identities such narratives can communicate.[2] Demy's films furthermore bring to the fore the inherent tensions and troubles that were always already present and never quite resolved in his source tales.[3]

Demy characterized his films as being "en-chantés," playing on the double meaning of the French word, which can signify both "enchanted" and "in song," referring to his unique use of sung verse in *The Umbrellas of Cherbourg* and, more generally, to his interest in the genre of the musical. The notion that his films are somehow enchanting reverberates with Demy's critics, who title their studies with reference to "dream," "enchanted cinema," "magical realism," and "other world" or "Demy-worlds."[4] "Enchantment," of course, brings to mind images of enchanted palaces in fairy tales as well as the idea of being under a magic spell. "To enchant" can mean "to attract, win over, compel, or induce," and, indeed, Demy hoped to draw his spectators visually and emotionally into his films through the use of elaborate sets, music, and recourse to melodrama. As his French biographers Jean-Pierre Berthomé and Camille Taboulay have made clear, Demy had been fascinated by fairy tales since his youth. At age seven Demy animated his own version of "Snow White" using a roll of toilet paper, which he illuminated using a flashlight (Taboulay 12). With the help of his father, Demy designed and built a puppet theater, where he presented tales by Perrault such as "Cinderella" and "Donkey Skin." Demy dressed his marionette princesses in fabrics found in the drawers of his grandmother, a seamstress in Nantes (Berthomé 30). In the early 1950s, just before apprenticing with the French animator Paul Grimault, Demy wrote "La Belle endormie" ("The Sleeping Beauty"), "the story of a princess bewitched by an evil genie, whom a young amorous poet dreams of saving" (Taboulay 16).[5] Demy in fact produced an excerpt of the projected film as a demo for producers and advertisers when he first started working in the industry.

As a filmmaker, Demy furnishes us with a particularly interesting example of an auteur who was extensively inspired by the genre of the fairy tale, which I use here in its broadest connotation to include folktales or märchen as well as marvelous tales.[6] In films such as *Donkey Skin, The Pied Piper,* and *Lady Oscar* (1979), Demy rewrites marvelous tales, legends, and folktales. Although not immediately evident, closer examination reveals that *Lola* (1961), *The Umbrellas of Cherbourg, Les Demoiselles de Rochefort (The Young Girls of Rochefort,* 1967), and *L'Evénement le plus important depuis que l'homme a marché sur la lune (A Slightly Pregnant Man,* 1973) either are structured around or make reference to folk- and fairy-tale motifs. Given Demy's youthful interest in and experimentation with fairy tales, it should come as no surprise that the genre made such an impact on his overall cinematic oeuvre.

The 1950s Hollywood musicals of Gene Kelly also left their mark on Demy's films. And like the fairy tale, the musical's fanciful aesthetic demands the suspension of disbelief as the spectator enters into the world of the marvelous. What Jessica Tiffin has said about the fairy tale and cinema is also true about the musical: "cinema, like fairy tale, is a form of illusion, its viewers willingly suspending disbelief in order to surpass reality and experience the magical" (182). Whereas the fairy tale, like film, carries the reader or spectator out of the world of the everyday into an "other" space, the musical transforms the everyday into a space of the marvelous through dance and song. In all cases, the world of the everyday is transcended, which opens up new possibilities of movement, sound, and sight. A film like *Donkey Skin*—a musical that is also a filmic rewriting of a fairy tale—truly highlights the affinities between these genres. The fact that Demy himself played on the double meaning of "en-chanté" suggests that he saw such connections between the tradition of the musical and the "enchanted" fairy tale.

However, Demy takes a very complicated view of the fairy-tale genre and the musical tradition, which are part and parcel of the Hollywood "dream factory." In his films, Demy constantly moves between different positions, one moment relishing the aesthetics of the marvelous, another moment reflecting on the often tragic consequences of conventional fairy-tale plots, the next teasing out what might already be subversive in these stories, and overall opening up the possibilities of the genre. Such tensions have always underscored folktales and fairy tales as well as Hollywood film. As Jack Zipes has noted, "From the very beginning folktales tended to be contradictory, containing utopian and conservative elements" (*Breaking* 140). And regarding the motion picture industry, Jane Gaines similarly remarks that the "dream factory" produces bourgeois hegemonic fantasies as well as utopian "hope-landscapes" (106–9). In his fairy-tale films, Demy takes what initially may appear to be utopian heterosexual fantasies and brings out their internal tensions, at times turning them into dystopian tales. As a queer director with working-class roots, Demy paints such fantasies with ironic distance and reveals the gut-wrenching disappointment that occurs upon fulfillment of these prefabricated dreams. The specific context of Demy's world, 1950s and 1960s France, was characterized by a renewed sense of material comfort and national identity after the humiliations of World War II, along with, according to Kristin Ross, "a new ideology of love and conjugality," which coincided with state natalist policy (126).[7] Life was reordered around "the consuming urban heterosexual couple" and "car ownership," with local economic practices and structures giving way to the "adoption of 'American' business practices" (Lindeperg and Marshall 99). Demy's films question the postwar economic and social order in France and the supposed fairy-tale ending this order was to bring.

Demy often blends nonheteronormative and working-class concerns into his films, which often results in the undermining of the traditional happy ending. In *The Umbrellas,* Cinderella may have married her wealthy bourgeois prince, but perhaps she would have been happier with her working-class lover. Donkey Skin may have evaded the advances of her incestuous father, but will she truly live "happily ever after" with her prince? At times Demy seems quite aware that what appear to be innocent tales for children are in fact mature stories that allow, even encourage, the exploration of questions pertaining to gender, sexuality, and class.

In so many respects Demy's "queer enchantments" set him apart from his New Wave contemporaries. As Richard Neupert affirms, Demy shared "in the stylistic and technical revival of the New Wave," yet he "has never fit comfortably in everyone's definition of the New Wave" (361, 360). It was with the help of Godard that Demy got Georges Beauregard to finance his first feature-length film, *Lola* (1961), in which Demy references Godard's *A Bout de souffle* (*Breathless,* 1960), and Demy worked with Godard collaborator Raoul Coutard on the shooting of *Lola.* Both directors were interested in the genre of the musical, but to different aesthetic ends. Regarding *Une Femme est une femme* (*A Woman Is a Woman,* 1961), Godard insists that "the film is not a musical. It's the idea of a musical" (qtd. in Monaco 127). In his films, however, Demy produces musicals that challenge generic boundaries, often by blending aspects of opera and operetta, with the result of creating an experimental, hybrid form of the musical.[8] One could argue that Godard's relation to the genre of the musical is based on "abstraction," a quality Geneviève Sellier has identified as a unifying concept among New Wave directors.[9] Demy, however, gives very concrete form—with a focus on costume, music, and color—to his singular conception of what a musical is and can do, simultaneously celebrating and destabilizing the genre and, as in the case of the fairy tale, hinting at the gender and sexual trouble that has always been a part of its history.[10]

Despite the fact that Godard expressed interest in the genre of the musical, New Wave directors predominantly drew from American film noir and the western, with some directors venturing into the domain of science fiction, such as Godard in *Alphaville* (1964) and François Truffaut in *Fahrenheit 451* (1966).[11] Sellier importantly emphasizes the gendered nature of the genres that most interested New Wave directors. American genres such as the thriller and the western—and one might add science fiction—"are actually addressed to a masculine public or constructed for a masculine gaze" (Sellier 28). New Wave critics and directors celebrated these masculine-gendered genres and removed them from their sociohistorical contexts, thus avoiding, according to Sellier, the political and ideological questions many of these films might have elicited. Regarding the group of critics–directors who were associated with *Cahiers du cinéma* and *Positif,* Sellier remarks, "The articles, all written by men, posit as an unquestioned *a priori* that the cinephilic gaze is necessarily male, heterosexual, and directed toward icons, fetishes, and female sexual objects" (29). Despite the fact that Sellier neglects to take into account the importance of irony in the representation of gender and sexuality in New Wave films, which might complicate her arguments, she rightly insists upon the masculinist and heterosexist tendencies underpinning the types of film upon which New Wave directors drew.

Although Demy also included references to more male-oriented genres in his films (Michel in *Lola* incarnates an idealized American cowboy type), his most significant influences were the fairy tale and the Hollywood musical, which typically have been gendered as feminine and, especially in the case of the musical, considered camp art forms. The use of color is an important aspect of both. Technicolor had been the process of choice for musicals since at least 1929, and after the production of *The Wizard of Oz* in 1939, the saturated hues of Technicolor came to be associated specifically with fantasy, whereas black-and-white was used for more "realistic" genres such as war and crime films.[12] In *Chromophobia*, David Batchelor discusses the devaluation of color in Western culture, arguing that "colour is made out to be the property of some 'foreign' body—usually the feminine, the oriental, the primitive, the infantile, the vulgar, the queer or the pathological" (22–23). Moreover, it is "relegated to the realm of the superficial, the supplementary, the inessential or the cosmetic" (23). Demy very consciously draws on color to emphasize the fantasy and artificial universes in which his characters materialize and to cite and pay homage to Disney fairy-tale films as well as the Gene Kelly musical. It is perhaps the devalorization of color, of "feminine" genres, of the cosmetic that explains in part the lack of critical attention to Demy's cinematic oeuvre in relation to other New Wave directors, despite the very self-conscious uses Demy makes of these aspects of his films.[13]

So what does this suggest about Demy's place within the New Wave? Numerous critics have pointed out Demy's "difference" from other New Wave directors but often fall short of words to describe it. For instance, Robynn Stilwell remarks, "He was of the Nouvelle Vague generation, yet never quite one of them" (23). For her part, Ginette Billard insists, "The thing that strikes one most in Demy's films is that they *are* fantasies, the fantasies of someone who does not belong to this world" (26). I would like to suggest that what makes Demy's unclassifiable, otherworldly films distinct from his New Wave contemporaries is precisely their "queerness."

Like the passing references to the fairy tale, studies of Demy's works make at best passing references to the ways in which his films communicate a queer sensitivity and aesthetic, with few exceptions.[14] Moreover, the implicit ways his own queer sexuality inflects his films, in part through autobiographical inscriptions, go almost completely unrecognized. However, his films have had wide appeal with gay audiences and directors in France. As Nick Rees-Roberts has noted, the demoiselles of *Les Demoiselles de Rochefort,* played by Catherine Deneuve and her sister Françoise Dorléac, "became something of camp icons in French gay popular culture" (109). French queer directors such as François Ozon, Christophe Honoré, Olivier Ducastel, and Jacques Martineau have all acknowledged their debt to Demy. In *8 Femmes* (*8 Women,* 2002), for instance, Ozon very consciously draws on Demy's color schemes and casts Deneuve, who starred in four of Demy's films, as an important celebrity intertext. Generally speaking, though, invoking the sexual orientation of a director, even when the director's sexuality influences the shape his or her films take, has been a taboo subject within French academic and intellectual circles. Alain Brassart expresses his frustrations with this situation in speaking about Agnès Varda's biographical film about Demy, *Jacquot de Nantes* (1991), in which "not a word is breathed about a homosexuality that was nevertheless known and that . . . decisively informs all of his works, enriching it against a resolutely 'normal' New Wave" (24).[15]

Throughout this book I will argue that Demy's films indeed are inflected by a queer sensitivity. Varda's pseudobiographical films of her husband, however, are of little help in our understanding of the ways in which Demy's films tie in with his own concerns about sexuality. They work instead, as Brassart suggests, to obscure a bisexuality or homosexuality—a queerness—that shapes his films in various ways. Adrian Danks characterizes Varda's *Jacquot de Nantes, Les Demoiselles ont eu 25 ans* (*The Young Girls Turn 25,* 1993), *L'Univers de Jacques Demy* (*The World of Jacques Demy,* 1995), and *Les Plages d'Agnès* (*The Beaches of Agnès,* 2008) as "somewhat chaste films about Demy," noting that "Varda's decision to only touch on specific aspects of Demy's personal life and even career in these films can be read as either an act of deep respect and solidarity—Demy himself was reluctant to discuss this part of his life—or a sign of her understandable inability to fully come to terms with the details and reality of Demy's sexuality, life and death" (161, 162). Although Demy's working-class background and its influence on his films are touched upon in the important biographies of Berthomé (1996) and Taboulay (1996), neither makes mention of Demy's sexuality, its importance to his work, or even his AIDS-related death in 1990, which Varda publicly acknowledged only very recently in *The Beaches of Agnès.*

Such issues, however, are central to this book. I foreground the ways in which Demy's fairy-tale films prove to be so many reimaginings of gender, sexuality, and class, reimaginings that are part and parcel of a queer sensibility. These "queer enchantments" destabilize binary oppositions such as feminine and masculine, queer and straight, lower class and upper class, and nature and culture, which uphold a heterosexist, bourgeois order in which capitalists, men, and heterosexuals are privileged over the working class, women, and queers.

Throughout this study, I use the term "queer" in its expansive meaning as critics such as Alexander Doty, Chris Straayer, and Steven Angelides have employed it. For Doty, queerness "is a quality related to any expression that can be marked as contra-, non-, or anti-straight" (xv). He opens up the notion of queerness to go beyond characterizing gay and lesbian practices in order to "challenge and confuse our understanding and uses of sexual and gender categories" (xvii). As such, Doty seeks to point out "the queerness of and in straights and straight cultures" and to carve out a space for "individuals and groups who have been told they inhabit the boundaries between the binaries of gender and sexuality: transsexuals, bisexuals, transvestites, and other binary outlaws" (xv–xvi). In her notion of queer, Straayer similarly includes nonnormative heterosexual practices, such as heterosexual sodomy and female ejaculation that challenge the notion of the "pure" heterosexual based on clearly demarcated and conventionally defined masculine and feminine roles (240–44).

Such redefinitions of "queer" work in part to deconstruct the dichotomy between gay and straight to include, in Angelides's words, "an umbrella category for the sexually marginalized" (165). For Angelides, "Instead of reifying sexual identity categories, queer theory takes as its project the task of exposing the operations of *heteronormativity* in order to work the hetero–homosexual opposition to the point of critical collapse" (168). Queer, then, refers to "that no-man's land beyond the heterosexual norm, that categorical domain virtually synonymous with homosexuality and yet wonderfully suggestive of a whole range of sexual possibilities ... that challenge the familiar distinctions between normal and pathological, straight and gay, masculine men and feminine women" (171).

These conceptions of queer are particularly useful in approaching Demy's films, which are often suggestive of homosexuality while troubling heterosexuality with the pairing of, for instance, a king and his daughter, a pregnant man with a woman, and a swashbuckling female cross-dresser with a stable boy. Demy's films carry out the queer work of challenging gender and sexual categories as well as that of social class. Although the genre of the fairy tale has often been accused of inculcating gender, sexual, and social norms—an over-generalizing and reductive view of fairy-tale history—Demy uses this fantastic genre to his advantage in his queer reimaginings of gender, sexuality, and class. Such reconceptualizations cannot be separated from Demy's own reconstruction of "self" through the references to his own life in his films. The ways in which Demy weaves these autobiographical references into his various films point to a thematic unity that very much goes against Varda's representation of a chaste and straight Jacques.

The unplanned son of a garage owner and a hairdresser, Demy is quoted as saying, "I wasn't a desired child" (qtd. in Taboulay 9). Interestingly, the rather melancholic Roland of *Lola* declares, "Only a child that's wanted is really happy."[16] It is perhaps due to this ambivalence regarding his own origins that Demy returns again and again in his films to "marvelous" beginnings. Historically, the fairy tale has often dealt with questions pertaining to conception and birth, including couples who cannot get pregnant and immaculate conceptions, the birth of princes and princesses, and monstrous births. Studies from Otto Rank's *The Myth of the Birth of the Hero* (1909) to Holly Tucker's *Pregnant Fictions: Childbirth and the Fairy Tale in Early-Modern France* (2003) have documented the rich history of conception and birth in the genre.[17] In several of his films, Demy invents almost "mythic" beginnings for his characters, many of whom bear traces of Demy's own past, although his concerns go beyond autobiography in his general preoccupation with legitimating marginal figures such as the artist and the cross-dresser.

In *Lola*, the title character, played by Anouk Aimée, is a cabaret dancer and single mother whose son Yvon never knew his father Michel. The film ends dramatically with an otherworldly Michel entering the cabaret Eldorado to reclaim Lola and his son, transforming the fatherless boy into the son of a modern prince. Not realizing that the unmarried Geneviève is pregnant with Guy's child, Roland remarks in *The Umbrellas of Cherbourg* that Geneviève resembles the Virgin with Child he saw in Antwerp. Such a remark pokes fun at notions of immaculate conceptions while it, nevertheless, suggests some kind of miraculous origins. Like the queen of "Snow White," who wishes for a child with lips as red as blood and skin as white as snow, Geneviève dreams about having a daughter named Françoise, just as Guy wishes for a son named François, and their desires eventually materialize, albeit not as the couple they had once imagined they would be. In the case of the tale and the film, the imagined portrait, gender, and name of the anticipated child precede and influence conception and birth in ways that recall the impact the imagination was believed to have had on the fetus in early modern folklore and medicine.[18] A Slightly Pregnant Man offers another kind of "miraculous" birth: Marco Mazzeti, a driving school teacher, informs his hairdresser wife Irène that he is pregnant. Such a story provides a modern example of a tale type whose history Roberto Zapperi traced from religious hagiography and Italian folklore to the Arabian Nights in his book The Pregnant Man (1991). In both The Umbrellas of Cherbourg and A Slightly Pregnant Man, "miraculous" births are clearly associated with Demy's own biography through characters who are auto mechanics and hairdressers. In all cases, different forms of "unwanted" or "irregular" pregnancies are transformed into something truly marvelous.

One area among others where Demy's queerness is foregrounded is precisely in these "miraculous" births. In The Umbrellas of Cherbourg, the fact that Guy and Geneviève, respectively, name their children "François" and "Françoise" suggests a certain gender ambiguity—feminine and masculine declensions of their child—that plays out fully in Lady Oscar. In this film, parental wish fulfillment with respect to a future child takes a twist. After fathering several daughters, General de Jarjayes expects his wife's last child to be a boy. When the nurse announces the child in fact is a girl, the general ignores her, declaring that his "son" will be called "Oscar François de Jarjayes." Although people at court are aware of her "true" sex, Oscar lives her life as a man, dressing in soldier's garb and serving as the personal guard of Marie Antoinette. Such films, including A Slightly Pregnant Man, suggest some kind of gender ambiguity at birth and could therefore be read as so many ways of imagining the marvelous origins of a queer identity. Drawing from the genre of the fairy tale to tell the story of queer origins, Demy thus invests marginalized forms of gender identity with extraordinary value. Taken together, Demy's films reiterate in different ways the story of the unwanted child with an ambiguous gender identity who proves to be a fairy prince(ess). Such a cursory overview of the ways in which the genre of the fairy tale inflects and provides a sort of unity to Demy's films only begins to hint at the importance of the genre within his cinematic oeuvre.

The lack of critical attention to the importance of the fairy tale within the work of Jacques Demy is symptomatic of the more general lack of critical attention to the fairy tale within film history, despite the overwhelming allusions to and explicit uses of the tale, starting with one of cinema's founding fathers, Georges Méliès, who drew heavily from the genre in his filmic experimentations. In his foreword to Pauline Greenhill and Sidney Eve Matrix's anthology *Fairy-Tale Films: Visions of Ambiguity* (2010), Zipes laments this state of affairs. He observes:

> In *The Oxford History of World Cinema* (1996) . . . there is not one word about fairy tale films. Even in the chapter on animation, the term "fairy tale" does not appear. All this is very strange, if not bizarre, given the fact that two fairy tale films—*Snow White and the Seven Dwarfs* [1937] and *The Wizard of Oz* [1939]—are among the most popular films in the world and have had a significant impact on cinema up through the present. The exclusion of fairy tale film as a category from *The Oxford History of World Cinema* is even stranger when one considers that the godfather and pioneer of film narrative, Georges Méliès, produced close to thirty films that were superb *féeries*. (ix)

Zipes goes on to mention the importance of the fairy tale in the era of silent film and in the work of filmmakers such as Lotte Reiniger, the Fleischer brothers, and, of course, Disney. He then applauds the editors of the volume for having put together one of the few anthologies that focuses on the impact of the fairy-tale genre on contemporary cinema, as seen in films from Andy Tennant's *Ever After* (1998) and Stanley Kubrick's *Eyes Wide Shut* (1999) to Guillermo del Toro's *Pan's Labyrinth* (2006) and films by Tim Burton.

Along with Greenhill and Matrix's important collection, there exists a handful of recent books that attempt to open up this understudied area of folk- and fairy-tale research. *Cinema and the Realms of Enchantment* (1993) brings together essays that provide a cursory view of the history of fairy-tale film from Méliès to Tim Burton. *Contes et légendes à l'écran* (2005), a collection of short essays, moves from early cinematic adaptations of Charles Perrault's tales to pieces on Terry Gilliam, Walt Disney, and Ridley Scott. *Folklore/Cinema: Popular Film as Vernacular Culture* (2007) is an anthology that looks at everything from ethnographic films about folk practices to folklore in Ingmar Bergman's *The Virgin Spring* and in *Tales from the Hood*. Most recently, Jack Zipes carries out a comprehensive critical survey of fairy-tale film from Betty Boop to Walt Disney in *The Enchanted Screen: The Unknown History of Fairy-Tales Films* (2011).[19]

Just as fairy-tale studies merit further consideration in the field of cinema, queer theory merits a larger place in fairy-tale studies. Feminist theory has had an important impact on the field, from the work of Zipes, Maria Tatar, Cristina Bacchilega, and Donald Haase to that, specifically in the area of the French fairy tale, of Lewis Seifert, Sophie Raynard, and Holly Tucker.[20] However, queer theory is a fairly recent and largely unexplored critical approach within folk- and fairy-tale studies. To exemplify this, upon doing a recent MLA International Bibliography search on "fairy tale" and "queer," "fairy tale" and "gay," "fairy tale" and "lesbian," and "fairy tale" and "homosexuality," a total of nine essays that actually dealt with the genre appeared.[21] The only book dedicated to queer theory and the fairy tale at the time of this writing was Kay Turner and Pauline Greenhill's edited volume *Transgressive Tales: Queering the Grimms* (2012), whose essays complicate our understanding of sexuality in the Grimms' corpus of tales.

Queer Enchantments: Gender, Sexuality, and Class in the Fairy-Tale Cinema of Jacques Demy thus contributes to scholarship both on film and on queer theory in fairy-tale studies. Modest in scope in its treatment of a single director, this book highlights the ways in which the fairy tale serves as a structuring device that facilitates a wide intertextual blending of literary and filmic references that include poems by Guillaume Apollinaire and Robert Browning, tales by Charles Perrault and the Brothers Grimm, Hollywood musicals and Walt Disney, Japanese manga, and, of course, French cinema. While fairy-tale plots hold together each film's playful intertextuality, queer identities and desires and a camp sensibility provide ideological and aesthetic unity to Demy's oeuvre.

In each chapter, I focus on how certain fairy-tale paradigms strategically unfold, how they are challenged, and how their subversive qualities are teased out in Demy's cinematic revisions. In chapter 1 I read *Lola* and *The Umbrellas of Cherbourg* through the lens of "Cinderella" and "Sleeping Beauty." I argue that Demy sets into play a dialectic, in the sense of "the existence or working of opposing forces, tendencies, etc." (Oxford English Dictionary [OED]), between fairy tale and melodrama, which destabilizes the heteronormativity of specific declensions of classical fairy tales. This narrative scheme works to challenge social and sexual norms and ideals of France in the 1950s and 1960s and to demythify the American dream. Chapter 2 explores Demy's re-vision of Charles Perrault's "Donkey Skin" from the particular angle of gay aesthetics. Drawing on the cinema of Jean Cocteau in particular and camp poetics in general, Demy uses the tale to explore alternative forms of sexuality and to denaturalize conceptions of gender.

Because chapters 3 and 4 deal with material that is not particularly well known to fairy-tale and cinema specialists, I spend more time developing the background to Demy's cinematic revisions. In chapter 3, I situate Demy's rendition of "The Pied Piper" in relation to a specifically Franco-American tradition of the legend, which thus far has not received critical attention. French and later French-inspired American iterations of "The Pied Piper" put into play tensions between bourgeois and Bohemians, commerce and art, which Demy adapts to his 1970s, post-WWII, and post-1968 audience. Although this chapter does not deal with "queer" as laid out in this introduction, it does deal with the marginalization of social and ethnic Others, who bear affinities with the sexually marginalized in his other films. Inclusion of *The Pied Piper,* moreover, conveys the breadth of Demy's sociopolitical engagement with questions of class and social justice in his films.

Finally, chapter 4 examines the ways in which Demy's *Lady Oscar* represents the undoing of the figure of the maiden warrior. The chapter traces the background history of the maiden warrior figure in China and France to its incarnation in Japanese manga and, specifically, *The Rose of Versailles* (1972–73) by Riyoko Ikeda, on which Demy's film is based. Although maiden warrior tales generally and necessarily problematize gender and sexuality through their cross-dressed heroines, questions related to class and political order often go unchallenged. By situating their maiden warrior tales within the context of the French Revolution, Ikeda and Demy end up challenging the very order that makes possible such tales. Especially conscious of class issues, Demy goes further than Ikeda in positing the people, rather than the aristocratic Oscar, as the vehicle for change. This film is also seminal in Demy's oeuvre. Whereas we can read *The Umbrellas of Cherbourg* in terms of the heroine not being able to come out of the closet, *Lady Oscar* proves to be a coming out narrative for both Demy's heroine and for Demy himself, who truly comes out as a queer director with this film.

Throughout the book I concentrate on how Demy draws from the fairy-tale genre to explore issues pertaining to gender, sexuality, and class in order to challenge gender, sexual, and social norms. What makes such a study particularly compelling are the ways in which it highlights Demy's creative uses of fairy-tale motifs to put forth liberating models of sociosexual relations through an aesthetic that moves between the visual and emotional pleasures of all things fairy, on the one hand, and the often tragic underseams that hold together conventional fairy-tale plots, on the other. Through his films Demy points to both the constraints and the utopian possibilities of the fairy tale.

1

Fairy Tale and Melodrama

Lola *and* The Umbrellas of Cherbourg

A knight (cowboy, ex-GI) dressed in white, on his white horse (Cadillac) seeks out the young princess (Lola) whom he loved. Innumerable evil spells (war, bad guys) separated them. For a long time the knight pursues his quest, regardless of pitfalls and bad luck. Finally, the lovers succeed in finding each other in a sort of enchanted grotto (the cabaret Eldorado) and forever reunited, they will depart together in a big white car for (the American) Eden.

—Paul Guimard on Jacques Demy's *Lola*[1]

Audiences wept, it was so sad. We'd planned it . . . we planned it well because Jacques and I, we wrote on the score: "First hanky, page 38. Second hanky . . ." So we had a score . . . a score full of hankies. [Jacques said] "There are too many of them." [I responded] "No, you'll see."

—Michel Legrand on *The Umbrellas of Cherbourg*[2]

At first glance, *Lola* (1961) and *The Umbrellas of Cherbourg* (1964) seem to be two very different types of films. Appearing in the wake of Jean-Luc Godard's *Breathless* (1960), Jacques Demy's first feature-length film, *Lola,* was filmed in black-and-white, and it centers on a moment in the life of a showgirl, whose lost love almost magically reappears at the end of the film. Visually striking in its use of saturated color, *The Umbrellas,* on the other hand, tells the tragic love story of a shopgirl and a mechanic, related through sung lines, as the film straddles the genres of musical and opera. Despite these apparent differences, the two films prove to be closely related, both structurally and thematically. As Jean-Pierre Berthomé has observed, "Many critics have noted the extent to which *The Umbrellas of Cherbourg* is a direct descendant of *Lola,* and they have remarked upon how the same themes of separation, waiting, and fidelity to a dream nourish the two films" (181).³ Furthermore, as Berthomé rightly insists, "More than the sequel to *Lola, The Umbrellas of Cherbourg* is the inverted reflection of it" (185).⁴ Read together, these two films explore what it means for the heroine to wait—or not—for her prince as well as the problematic nature of the "happy ending" premised upon such waiting.

Although *Lola* and *The Umbrellas of Cherbourg* do not draw directly from the genre of the fairy tale, as do Demy's later films *Donkey Skin* and *The Pied Piper,* critics such as Paul Guimard have remarked upon their underlining fairy-tale structure, evidenced in the passage that opens this chapter. Both films integrate motifs from "Sleeping Beauty" and "Cinderella," as articulated in particular by Charles Perrault and Walt Disney, whereby the suffering princess, made to carry out domestic chores and rendered passive, waits for and is finally rescued by the handsome prince, who promises the heroine a better life and with whom she is said to live happily ever after. Waiting for one's prince indeed is the stated moral of Charles Perrault's version of "Sleeping Beauty," a tale Demy had read in his youth. Perrault's moral equates the princess's sleeping with waiting:

> To wait so long
> To want a man refined and strong,
> Is not at all uncommon.
> But: rare it is a hundred years to wait
> Indeed there is no woman
> Today so patient for a mate.⁵

Much like Perrault's "Sleeping Beauty," Demy's *Lola* and *The Umbrellas* revolve around the heroine's ability to wait for her dream to come true. However, not only do Demy's cinematic rewritings of such tales question the underlying assumptions about gender and sexuality that these tales communicate, but they also problematize the nature of the dream that underpins the fairy-tale narrative.

In his account of his collaboration with Demy on *The Umbrellas of Cherbourg,* Michel Legrand makes clear that the film was meant to be a tearjerker. Thus, although Demy infuses *Lola* and *The Umbrellas* with fairy-tale motifs, both films can be characterized in terms of "melodrama," which etymologically denotes the combined use of drama and music and has narrative characteristics that elicit tears.⁶ Both *Lola* and *The Umbrellas* were to combine music and drama, but Demy could not get the financing to do a full-fledged musical in the case of *Lola,* which he nevertheless continued to consider a musical.[7] But the connection to melodrama in these two films goes beyond the combination of music and drama. In different ways, both films concern "the experience of loss," which, for Tania Modleski, "is at the heart of melodrama" (28). As opposed to the "happy ending" characteristic of many classical fairy tales, melodrama does not promise a better future. Rather, melodrama usually concerns a loss that is never recovered.

I would like to suggest in this chapter that Demy sets into motion a dialectic in *Lola* and *The Umbrellas* between the utopian promises of the fairy tale and the irrecoverable loss characteristic of melodrama to create films of disillusionment. The fairy-tale life promised in these films takes the shape of the American dream—itself shaped by Hollywood film—which served as the model for post-WWII modernization in France. Demy's films reveal the tragic underpinnings along with the illusions and the renunciations 1950s and 1960s Cinderella and Sleeping Beauty tales demand. Although the focus of this chapter will revolve around gender, I will also suggest ways in which both films elicit queer readings in part through their cinematic intertexts. In particular, it becomes evident that transgression of class and age markers can be read as transgression of heteronormativity, whereas renunciation can be related to the loss of a queer identity.

In the tradition of Charles Perrault and Walt Disney, Cinderella and Sleeping Beauty tales share the common underlying structure of an active hero, the prince, who saves the passive heroine, the princess, from malicious females, who are the social and sexual rivals of the heroine.[8] Walt Disney's cinematic refashioning of classic tales further reinforces underlying commonalities between, for instance, Snow White (*Snow White and the Seven Dwarfs,* 1937), who, like Sleeping Beauty (*Sleeping Beauty,* 1959), is awoken by a kiss, and Cinderella (*Cinderella,* 1950). As Jack Zipes has noted, Disney's Snow White "is at first depicted as a kind of Cinderella, cleaning the castle as a maid in a patched dress" (*Fairy Tale as Myth* 87). Likewise, Disney's Sleeping Beauty is first shown cleaning the humble cottage in which she lives with the three fairies, blending Perrault's "Sleeping Beauty" with elements from "Cinderella." Essentially, Disney makes of all three tales a female rags-to-riches story, infusing them with American values revolving around middle-class domestic bliss.[9]

For David Pace, what characterizes Cinderella stories is the overall narrative movement to establish a correspondence between internal virtue and external status. Whereas Cinderella is dressed in rags and given filthy tasks in her stepmother's home, her ugly and undeserving stepsisters enjoy cleanliness and luxurious clothes. Pace notes that in such tales, "the external, social signs of virtue [i.e., cleanliness, luxury] have not been assigned to the right persons"

(253). The work of the tale, then, is to correct this imbalance and appropriately reward—in other words, assign the proper social status to—the virtuous girl, which brings about the happy ending.

Part of what creates this imbalance is the absence of men, and specifically of the father figure. Cinderella finds herself in an oppressive situation upon the death of her father, which leaves her to the whims of her stepmother, a situation that improves only upon marriage with the prince, who performs the role of male rescuer. According to Pace, "The removal of a male at the beginning of the story (through the death of the father) created an initial imbalance which could only be rectified by the introduction of a new male (the prince)" (253). At the same time that the tale is about rewarding virtue, it also is about family structures and what makes those structures stable and able to function properly. Namely, it is about the reestablishment of heteronormative and patriarchal order, in which virtue is properly rewarded and vice—incarnated by unruly women—is punished.

Whereas the question of waiting to be saved is implicit in tales such as Perrault's "Cinderella" and "Sleeping Beauty," it is foregrounded in Disney films and is particularly evident in the films' songs. In essence, the heroine waits for her dream to come true, for the male hero to whisk her away to his enchanted palace, simultaneously saving her from her miserable environment and rewarding her for her true merit. The notion of waiting and dream recurs in the songs of *Snow White* ("Someday my prince will come. . . . Someday when my dreams come true"); *Cinderella* ("A dream is a wish your heart makes. . . . Have faith in your dreams and someday / Your rainbow will come smiling through"); and *Sleeping Beauty* ("If my heart keeps singing / Will my song go winging / To someone who'll find me" and "You'll love me at once / The way you did once upon a dream"). In all cases, the stationary heroine waits for the prince to come, to find her, and his (re)appearance and the couple's (re)union marks the actualization of her dream.

In her analysis of Walt Disney's fairy-tale films, Naomi Wood contrasts the dream vision of Disney with Freudian and Lacanian notions of desire. In the psychoanalytic model, true satisfaction of one's projected desires proves impossible after the Oedipal crisis and initiation into the realm of the symbolic. For Sigmund Freud and Jacques Lacan, entering the symbolic order, which entails submission to the law of the father—and, more broadly, adhering to socio-cultural and sexual norms and prohibitions—is a form of castration. However, in "Disney's dream theory . . . the Symbolic Order is benevolent. It supports wish fulfillment; all that is demanded is faithfulness to the dream" (Wood 34). Of course, underpinning Disney wish fulfillment is adherence to gender and sexual norms as well as class expectations. Just as the heroine is always patient, kind, and dainty, so the hero is chivalric, wealthy, and physically imposing. Disney films suggest that conforming to such heteronormative and middle-class codes and behaviors is effortless and painless, concealing the "castration" or repression—of singularity, of nonconformist gender and sexual traits and behaviors—such compliance requires.

It is precisely this sense of castration or loss that film melodrama engages. It is about what gets repressed or marginalized in the process of adhering to gender, social, and sexual norms. It is also about the inability to fully adhere to these norms. In many respects, we could read melodrama as the flip side of conventional Disney fairy-tale narratives. Melodrama is about the hero who could not fulfill the role of a prince, at least not without loss; it is about the heroine who could not be satisfied with the socially recognized prince; it is about heroes and heroines who end up betraying each other, either intentionally or unintentionally, often leading to the dissolution of the couple.

In his classic article on melodrama, Geoffrey Nowell-Smith argues, "In the American movie the active hero becomes protagonist of the Western, the passive or impotent hero or heroine becomes protagonist of what has come to be known as melodrama. The contrast active/passive is, inevitably, traversed by another contrast, that between masculine and feminine" ("Minnelli" 115). As Nowell-Smith suggests, then, melodrama gets gendered feminine because of the emasculation of male characters as well as the centrality of female characters, who often are victimized and rendered passive, "waiting at home, standing by the window" (Elsaesser 13). Although melodrama shares with the classical fairy tale the "fantasy" of "the union of an adult, heterosexual couple," as well as the "blockages" toward fulfillment of this fantasy, melodrama usually ends with the failure to realize that fantasy (Neale 12–13). Social pressures, class differences, and moral injustices often are not overcome at the end of a melodramatic film, although, as Steve Neale insists, this does not mean that such films completely eliminate "the possibility of fulfillment of a wish" (21).

Another aspect of melodrama relevant to films by Demy is "the claustrophobic atmosphere of the bourgeois home and/or the small-town setting" (Elsaesser 13), which heightens the pathos of melodrama by intensifying, like a pressure cooker, the social, sexual, or psychological tensions the film puts into play. Demy's films often take place in idealized, nostalgic versions of provincial cities such as Nantes (*Lola, Une Chambre en ville* [*A Room in Town*, 1982]), Cherbourg (*The Umbrellas*), Rochefort (*Les Demoiselles de Rochefort*), and Hamelin (*The Pied Piper*) from which characters nevertheless flee due to familial and social pressures or to their failure to achieve their dream. The claustrophobic atmosphere is emphasized by Demy in the use of iris-in and iris-out to open and close his films, which has the effect of containing the action of the film within a closed space. In fairy tales, insular spaces often translate into utopian ones, whereas the compressed space of melodrama is more suggestive of tragedy or, more precisely, tragedy's cousin, the *drame bourgeois*.[10]

Initially *Lola* and *The Umbrellas of Cherbourg* appear to tell the story of, in the first case, a successful Cinderella or Sleeping Beauty tale and, in the second, an unsuccessful one. However, through their filmic intertexts within and without his own cinematic corpus, Demy offers the realization of the dream only to undermine or problematize it, yet his characters continue to dream. In ways that recall Robert Bresson's *Les Dames du Bois de Boulogne* (1945) and Luchino Visconti's *Le notti bianche* (*White Nights*, 1957), Demy plays fairy-tale motifs off melodrama, with an increased focus on loss and disillusion and without ever letting the story completely slip into jaded cynicism: hope keeps one moving forward, despite the process of disillusionment.

LOLA, OR WAITING REWARDED

As critics have noted, Demy drew from several films to create his *Lola*. One narrative strand of the film involving the American sailor Frankie and his pals recalls *On the Town* (1949), starring Gene Kelly and Frank Sinatra, in which three sailors arrive in New York City, fall in love and have a good time, then return to their ship, only for a new crew of sailors to hit the town to start the cycle of love and fun all over again at the end of the film. Another fundamental reference in the film is Bresson's *Les Dames du Bois de Boulogne*, at both a structural and a thematic level. Bresson's Agnès—the fallen aristocrat-turned-showgirl played by Elina Labourdette, who plays the mother of Cécile in *Lola*—anticipates Demy's Lola, a showgirl from Nantes who returns for three days to her hometown to perform at the cabaret the Eldorado. Bresson's film is structured in many respects like a Cinderella or Sleeping Beauty tale, whose happy ending Demy problematizes in *Lola*. Although Demy dedicates *Lola* to Max Ophuls, whose *Lola Montès* (1955) clearly provides inspiration for his film, he also draws from Visconti's *White Nights* in significant ways. All of these filmic intertexts furnish Demy with material to create his own fairy-tale film about the princess who successfully waits for her prince and is rewarded—as least momentarily—with a happy ending. However, the Chinese proverb opening *Lola*, "*Cry who can, laugh who will*," announces the melodramatic undertones of the film.

The not-so-basic plot of *Lola* takes place, like Visconti's *White Nights*, over the course of three days. The film opens with a shot of Michel (Jacques Harden), whose white suit and white Cadillac give him the aura of an apparition; he drives into town after a seven-year absence, having left behind a pregnant Cécile—now the showgirl Lola—with a promise to return. For her part, Lola (Anouk Aimée) has come back to Nantes for three days to do a show at the Eldorado. Roland (Marc Michel), a disaffected, disillusioned young man, wants to leave provincial Nantes. In a bookstore he meets Madame Desnoyers (Elina Labourdette) and her adolescent daughter Cécile (Annie Duperoux), and Roland remarks that Cécile reminds him of a childhood friend, Cécile, whom he fondly recalls. Later he happens to bump into adult Cécile, now known by her stage name Lola, and they catch up on each other's lives. Lola explains that she had fallen in love with a man dressed as an American sailor, Michel, on her fourteenth birthday at a fair, and when he returned a couple of years later, she got pregnant with her son Yvon. Michel then left to make his fortune, but she has had no word from him in seven years. During these three days Lola has also met Frankie (Alan Scott), an American sailor she has been seeing. For his part, Frankie meets adolescent Cécile on her fourteenth birthday, and they go to the fair together, just before he leaves for Cherbourg. Roland believes he is in love with Lola, who thinks of him only as a friend, and when he realizes she will not marry him, he pursues a risky venture and leaves for South Africa. As Lola prepares to leave for another gig in Marseilles, Michel dramatically enters the Eldorado to whisk her and her son away to the new Eldorado, America.

From the beginning of the film, the notion of dream is foregrounded. Michel's mother, Jeanne (Margo Lion), thought she saw her son Michel earlier that day "in a dream car, an apparition, the Thousand and One Nights,"[11] but she cannot be sure. For his part, Roland is late for work because, as he puts it, "I dream," to which his boss retorts, "That's unhealthy."[12] Upon losing his job, Roland goes to the cinema and sees *Return to Paradise* (1953), starring Gary Cooper, who plays Morgan, an American who washes up onto the shores of the Pacific island Matareva and falls in love with an island woman, Maeva, with whom he has a child. After Maeva's death he leaves the island to return years later to discover that his daughter has fallen in love with an American pilot, as the cycle of life continues. We discover later in *Lola* that Michel was in fact stranded on the island of Matareva, whose name evokes the French word *rêve*, or "dream." But rather than returning to the island of Matareva like Morgan, Michel returns to the insular society of Nantes to reunite with Lola and his son.

Michel's apparition shares many affinities with that of the Tenant, played by Jean Marais, in Visconti's *White Nights*.[13] In the latter film, Natalia (Maria Schell), very much a Cinderella-like character, waits for her one true love, the Tenant, to rescue her from the grips of her grandmother, who continually pins Natalia to her skirt while they toil to repair carpets. One evening, while waiting on a bridge for the arrival of the Tenant, who had precipitously left a year earlier and who promised to return, Natalia encounters Mario, played by Marcello

Mastroianni. After Natalia finishes recounting the story behind her nightly visits to the bridge, Mario declares, "What an absurd story. . . . Are you telling me you've waited for a man for a year and you've had no word from him? You don't even know what he does?" Constantly questioning the veracity of her story, he asks Natalia, "Are you quite sure he exists?" Although he believes Natalia to be naïve, he is fascinated by her fidelity to a dream. Mario admits to her that "this is all so alien to me, to my way of thinking. . . . I didn't think there were girls like you left in the world. You might as well have told me you believe in fairy tales [*favole*]."[14] By the end of the third night, however, Mario has become more and more like Natalia: "I told you not to believe in fairy tales [*favole*]. Then I started to believe my own fantasy. I felt like you felt." Mario begins to dream about a future with Natalia, and now he is ready to do the waiting, hoping that someday she will forget the Tenant and marry him.

In a certain ironic twist, just as the realist Mario cedes to fantasy, fantasy is reaffirmed with the return of the Tenant, which, according to Nicolas Maille, "signals in some respects the victory of the imaginary over the real."[15] In fact, as Maille has argued, casting Jean Marais to play the Tenant was a deliberate move to enhance the character's fantastic aura: "The choice of Jean Marais to incarnate the mysterious handsome stranger is not innocent. Besides his charisma wreathed in a tragic lyricism, the actor conveys a Star image (thus object of fantasm)."[16] Visconti plays on the star image of Marais as well as the marvelous characters he had incarnated in other films, such as the Beast/Prince in Cocteau's *La Belle et la Bête* (*Beauty and the Beast,* 1946) and, most recently, Orpheus in Cocteau's *Orphée* (*Orpheus,* 1950). Dream triumphs over reality, just as the mysterious and otherworldly Tenant triumphs over the very real Mario.

Much like the Tenant in *White Nights*, whom he physically resembles, *Lola*'s Michel has an air of mystery about him. Like a mythic hero, Michel leaves his princess behind, only to return rich, as signaled by his white American convertible. Michel's mystique, however, does not arise from associations with traditional fairy-tale heroes, as was the case in Visconti's Tenant, whose incarnation by Jean Marais provided such allusions. Michel, instead, embodies the prince of the American dream, the self-made man who starts out penniless and becomes wealthy. He is the cowboy, the Hollywood movie star. Part of what attracts Lola to Michel is precisely his "Americanness." The film associates him with American sailors and, by extension, with sailors from Gene Kelly musicals, which Demy, a fan, discovered after the war.[17] Driving into town with his white cowboy hat, Michel also evokes the stars of cowboy movies and is associated in particular with Gary Cooper through reference to *Return to Paradise.* His quality as phantasm is underscored at the beginning of the film with his mother's remark about his almost marvelous apparition in Nantes, making it seem as though Michel had just materialized right out of a Hollywood film (Figure 1.1).

Just as Michel is invested with the mystique of all things American, so Lola is invested with layers of references to filmic showgirls and the divas who incarnated them. As a character, Lola could be described in the same way that Judith Mayne has described *The Blue Angel's* (1930) Lola Lola: "She is a pastiche, a collection of allusions" (33). Demy's Lola draws on a whole cultural fascination with the showgirl in cinema, from Lola Lola to the eponymous heroine of Max Ophul's *Lola Montès,* characters who, moreover, have become indelibly associated with stars such as Marlene Dietrich. In the 1950s Martine Carol, who played the role of Lola Montès, was the biggest sex symbol in France before Brigitte Bardot.[18] Dedicating *Lola* to Max Ophuls, Demy certainly had Ophuls's *Lola Montès* in mind, although Lola's costume and song clearly are so many winks to Josef von Sternberg's *Blue Angel* (Figure 1.2). It could be argued that both Lola and Michel are fantasy figures, incarnations of idealized characters from Hollywoodian films. However, *Lola's* 1969 sequel, *Model Shop,* would suggest that neither character can, in reality, live up to the image they appear to embody.

Like that of Visconti's Natalia, and for a much longer period of time, the

Figure 1.1. Jacques Harden, with cowboy hat and cigar, as Michel in *Lola.*

Figure 1.2. Lola (Anouk Aimée) performs "C'est moi, c'est Lola."

function of Demy's Lola is to wait. She explains to her childhood friend Roland that Michel is the only man she has ever loved and that, whatever happens, "I would have waited for him very sensibly."[19] When Michel finally materializes in a very theatrical entrance into the Eldorado through stage-like curtains, Lola runs to him and says, "Seven years, seven years, can you believe it? If you only knew how I waited for you, I only thought of you and sometimes I cursed you, because your memory poisoned my existence."[20] The film closes with an apparently happy ending, with Lola and Yvon driving in Michel's dream car on their way to America out into the sunset. However, the car passes the solitary and devastated Roland, who was unable to win Lola's love, as Lola looks over at him, and the film ends on a somewhat unsettling note.

Such moments destabilize the underlining fairy-tale plot through the sense of loss experienced by Roland. His dream did not come true. Other aspects of the film are further suggestive of a melodramatic story of loss without a fairy-tale ending. In particular, the film puts into play three generations of women whose lives together suggest both the possibility of dreams coming true and the disillusion brought about by loss and betrayal.

The film clearly makes a connection between the young Cécile, on the one hand, and Lola, whose given name is Cécile, on the other. Besides their common name and their relationship to the sailor Frankie, they share a common experience: their first true love occurs at fourteen with an older man who looks like (and in the case of Frankie is) an American sailor. It is through Cécile's experience with Frankie that we come to understand the almost fantastic experience of first love that keeps Lola hoping for Michel's return.

After meeting each other by chance in a tobacco shop, Cécile later runs into Frankie the day of her fourteenth birthday, and they go to the fair together. The scene is dreamlike, beginning with the pair climbing into bumper cars as Cécile lets her hair down, with the fast-paced music of Bach's well-tempered Clavier (Book 1: No. 2) playing in the background. The movement accelerates only to climax at the end of the second ride, which spins the couple round and round and closer together. Then everything decelerates, with Bach's slower prelude following, as Frankie lifts an enraptured Cécile out of the ride and they run off, all in slow motion. When Frankie explains he has to leave to take the train to Saint-Nazaire, then Cherbourg, before returning to Chicago, the film returns to a realistic representation of time, and Cécile and Frankie part ways. In many respects the scene's images, music, and rhythms evoke the act of lovemaking, with climax and afterglow, and depicts Cécile falling in love with Frankie in an idyllic, nonrealistic manner.

Through young Cécile's experience with Frankie, we come to understand Lola's affection for Michel and why she is willing to wait for him for seven years. She is attached to the myth of first love, which she hopes to reactivate upon reuniting with Michel, whereas Frankie, who resembles Michel, serves as a temporary replacement, an imperfect substitute. That Michel enters the Eldorado dressed all in white and as if walking onto a stage suggests the unreal nature of his reappearance and Lola and Michel's reunion. Indeed, the other dancers at the Eldorado begin to cry as if they are watching a play or a melodramatic film, which heightens the artificial nature of the scene, with a clear demarcation between "actors" (Michel and Lola) and "spectators" (the other dancers). Earlier in the film the character Claire says, "In cinema, everything is always more beautiful,"[21] and the scene invites the following question: Is this cinema or real life? Is this happy ending for real?

Whereas Cécile represents the young Lola and Lola the adult Cécile, whose dream appears to come true, Madame Desnoyers marks the age of disillusion. To play Madame Desnoyers, Demy cast Elina Labourdette, who incarnated the showgirl Agnès in *Les Dames du Bois de Boulogne*. In one scene, Madame Desnoyers's daughter Cécile emerges with a photograph of her mother as a showgirl, a frame from *Les Dames du Bois de Boulogne*. Through this filmic intertext, Demy integrates the story of Bresson's film into *Lola* in order to represent the past of Madame Desnoyers's character. As Camille Taboulay has remarked, "Demy thus truly prolongs her role, in short, inscribing Bresson's film into her living past."[22] The connection between Lola and Madame Desnoyers is further suggested through the overcoat Lola wears over her nightclub attire, which recalls the one Agnès wore in *Les Dames du Bois de Boulogne*. Daniel Millar notes, "It is easy enough to 'read' the cinematic meaning of Agnès's old raincoat thrown over her scanty black dance costume (Demy gives it exactly the same tarty significance, though a lighter tone, in his *hommage*, *Lola*)" (34).

Perhaps more explicitly than Demy's *Lola*, *Les Dames du Bois de Boulogne* is a 1940s fairy tale, a Cinderella story with a Sleeping Beauty ending. Agnès, a fallen aristocrat and a fallen woman, becomes a pawn in Hélène's (María Casares) plan of revenge against her former lover Jean (Paul Bernard). Used and abused by both Hélène and her mother, who is ready to prostitute her daughter to get by, Agnès the showgirl is eventually saved by Jean, who returns her to her former aristocratic status.

The film is based on the story of Madame de La Pommeraye from Denis Diderot's *Jacques le fataliste* (1796), which Bresson and Jean Cocteau, who wrote the dialogue, reshaped in part by infusing it with fairy-tale motifs. For instance, direct mention of "Cinderella" is made when Jean reads a letter he believes is from Agnès, which was in fact composed by Agnès and Hélène as part of the latter's ruse to get Jean to marry a "whore." Jean declares, "This is like Cinderella's slipper. If I found a letter like this in the street, I'd do everything in my power to find the girl who wrote it."[23] Like the prince in pursuit of the girl who lost her slipper, Jean pursues Agnès, finally marrying her in the end and loving her despite her past. References to "Sleeping Beauty" are also evident in the film. The "Bois de Boulogne" in the film's title, is not mentioned in Diderot's version. As such, the alliteration of the title, *Les Dames du Bois de Boulogne*, recalls that of the French title for Sleeping Beauty: "La Belle au bois dormant."[24] That the film is somehow a Sleeping Beauty tale is further evident at the end of the film, when Jean resuscitates a near-death Agnès with a kiss. Based on the alliteration of the title and the kiss at the end of the film, it would seem that Bresson and Cocteau were very consciously playing on references to "Sleeping Beauty."

Whereas *Les Dames du Bois de Boulogne* concludes with a "happy ever after," in *Lola* Demy undoes this ending, and in several respects. First, Agnès, now Madame Desnoyers, is a lonely widow and single mother who lost her husband in WWII. Second, we learn that her Prince Charming turned out to be a gambler with many vices. She proclaims, "May God save us from gamblers!"[25] His gambling and death financially ruined her, undoing the financial stability with which *Les Dames du Bois de Boulogne* implicitly concludes. Third, her daughter Cécile is the product of Madame Desnoyers's adulterous relationship with her brother-in-law, who lives in Cherbourg. The fairy tale turns out to be, in reality, a story about betrayal, loss, and disillusion, or, another way of looking at it, the fairy tale constitutes a moment or moments in a larger narrative that is essentially a melodrama.

As Charlotte Garson has pointed out, Demy wanted his films to be interconnected in the same manner as the novels constituting Honoré de Balzac's *Comédie humaine*. In a 1964 interview with *Cahiers du cinéma*, Demy stated, "My idea is to make fifty films that would all be linked together . . . through common characters."[26] This is particularly important with respect to *Lola* and its relation to the films that follow. Whereas *Lola's* Roland will continue to live on in *The Umbrellas of Cherbourg*, Lola will find herself in LA in the sequel to *Lola, Model Shop*. Just as *Lola* undoes the "happy ending" of *Les Dames du Bois de Boulogne*, so *Model Shop* undoes the "happy ending" of *Lola*. Now it is Lola who has been abandoned by her knight in shining Cadillac. Michel has left her for the gambler Jackie, a character from Demy's *La Baie des anges* (*Bay of Angels*, 1963), which further emphasizes ties between Lola and Madame Desnoyers. We also learn that Frankie was killed in Vietnam. Moreover, the fairy-tale world of America reveals itself to be a fiction: *Model Shop's* LA is an alienating landscape of strip malls and concrete, where Lola, appearing hopeless and desperate, literally is reduced to being the passive object of a camera. There is nothing left of the dream of *Lola*.[27]

In discussing melodrama, Thomas Elsaesser remarks, "What strikes one as the true pathos [of melodrama] is the very mediocrity of the human material, putting such high demands upon itself, trying to live up to an exalted vision of man, but instead living out the impossible contradictions that have turned the American dream into its proverbial nightmare" (15). Elsaesser points to a tension between the "exalted vision of man," which we could associate with the idealized characters of classical fairy tales and Hollywood film, and the "mediocrity of the human material," which is suggestive of the impotent heroes and heroines of melodrama. Lola, the seductive palimpsest of showgirls past and present, becomes a broken heroine in *Model Shop*. Michel, the idealized figure of American heroism associated with Gary Cooper, proves to be far from ideal in his abandonment of Lola and his attachment to gambling, which recalls Jean, the Prince Charming of *Les Dames du Bois de Boulogne*, who similarly disappoints, as we learn in *Lola*, his one "true love," Agnès/Madame Desnoyers. The heroines who waited to be saved by their heroes eventually end up abandoned and disillusioned.

The ways in which melodrama undermines the fairy-tale narrative results in the "demythologization" of the male rescuer, to use Carolina Fernández-Rodríguez's terminology. Like twentieth-century feminist authors of revisionist tales such as Sara Henderson Hay, Angela Carter, and Luisa Valenzuela, Demy questions the "mythical aura" of the male rescuer while also problematizing his function as "rescuing agent."[28] In *Lola* and its sequel *Model Shop*, the "mythical aura" of Bresson's Jean and Demy's Michel is negated by the revelation of both men's weakness for gambling, which destabilizes the financial security they implicitly promise as heroes, and in the particular case of Michel, by the revelation of his lack of fidelity, despite his earlier mythical return to his one "true love."

Moreover, due to the metaphorical connection between Michel and all things American, the demythologization of the male rescuer can be further related to the demythologization of the "American dream." Indeed, Demy's representation of Los Angeles is far from ideal. As Mark Shiel has observed about *Model Shop*, "The intense anomie generated by Los Angeles's synthetic surfaces is explicitly linked to the ongoing war in Vietnam and the antiwar movement then active in the city" (151). Rather than offer the promise of wealth, stability, and fulfillment, the American dream leaves Lola struggling to get by in an alienating landscape of social unrest and instability.

As scholars such as Kristin Ross and Brian McKenzie have demonstrated, in 1950s and 1960s France images prevailed that represented the "deprived France of the Occupation [that] could now be sated" (Ross 71). This satiation would take the form of modernization, which was inseparable from the concept of Americanization: "The Marshall Plan provided support for French modernization while U.S. public diplomacy simultaneously presented the American way of life as the most desirable outcome" (McKenzie 7). Along with the influx of American films, forbidden under the Occupation, French people were exposed to American culture and ideology through exhibitions that were held in dozens of cities, big and small, throughout the country. Attended by the thousands, these exhibitions were sponsored by the US government through Mission France and included such themes as "The True Face of the United States," which insisted upon Americans' high standard of living and purchasing power, and "The Future Is Yours," which anticipated the American-style modernization of France.[29]

From magazines of the period to cinema and even agricultural exhibits, the United States represented a fantasy world onto which the French people, encouraged by both US and French authorities, could project their hopes and aspirations for themselves and for their country.[30] Indeed, through the character of Michel, Demy's *Lola* plays on the fantasy of an American Prince Charming coming to take the French Cinderella off to a better place. However, *Model*

Shop reveals the underlying illusion—not to mention its politics of empire through allusions to Vietnam—behind this new Eldorado. Just as *Model Shop* illustrates that Michel and Lola cannot live up to their idealized images, so America falls terribly short of incarnating the blissful land where dreams come true.

Lola implicitly and *Model Shop* explicitly question the possibility of the realization of one's dreams in any enduring way. Nevertheless, *Lola* does end overall on a positive note, suggesting that one's dreams indeed can come true, even if only temporarily, and without having to sacrifice one's singularity, in other words, without having to undergo castration or repression. Whereas *Lola* may be characterized as a fairy-tale film hinting at melodrama, *The Umbrellas of Cherbourg* foregrounds melodrama, even as it draws on fairy-tale structures and motifs, and its aesthetics, especially its nonrealistic use of color, seem to take us into a marvelous realm. Read in light of *Les Dames du Bois de Boulogne* and Demy's own *Model Shop*, *Lola* undoes the myth of the male rescuer, revealing the figure's weaknesses, faults, and cracks. In *The Umbrellas of Cherbourg*, Demy similarly problematizes the role of the male rescuer as he examines more closely the ways in which adherence to certain versions of the dream of being saved by a Prince Charming results, tragically, in the repression of one's singular desires, that is, in castration.

GENEVIÈVE, OR THE IMPATIENT PRINCESS

One significant difference between *Lola* and *The Umbrellas* resides in the question of waiting. Whereas Lola manages to wait seven years for her prince, Geneviève fails to wait even four months for hers. Ironically, the theme song of *The Umbrellas* is "Je t'attendrai" ("I Will Wait for You").[31] The melody opens and closes the film, and lyrics are added in the scenes in which Guy announces his draft notice for Algeria, where he is to serve for two years, and in the scene in which he leaves the Cherbourg train station. In the first of these scenes, Geneviève sings,

Je ne pourrai jamais vivre sans toi!	I will never be able to live without you!
Je ne pourrai pas	I will not be able to
Ne pars pas, j'en mourrai	Don't leave, it will kill me
Mais mon amour, ne me quitte pas	But no, my love, don't leave me
. . . .	
Deux ans, non, je ne pourrai pas	Two years, no, I will not be able to

In the scene in the train station, Geneviève assures Guy that "I will wait for you all of my life" and that she loves him, all the while repeating, "I can't, I can't, I can't."[32] Geneviève both promises to wait for him and expresses her anxieties about her ability to do so. Although "I will not be able to" or "I can't" could be read in terms of the suffering and pain she cannot endure while Guy is away and that will kill her, after Geneviève's betrayal of Guy in the film, these words suggest instead her inability to wait for him: she simply cannot. The romantic promise of being faithful to a dream by waiting for the return of the hero is destroyed when Geneviève, ceding to maternal and social pressure, marries another man.

The plot of *The Umbrellas of Cherbourg* concerns Guy (Nino Castelnuovo), a mechanic in love with Geneviève (Catherine Deneuve), the daughter of Madame Emery (Anne Vernon), the owner of an umbrella shop in Cherbourg. Geneviève conceals her relationship with Guy from her mother, and when she finally announces that she wants to marry Guy, her mother disapproves, thinking Geneviève is too young—and Guy too poor. Because of her own debts, Madame Emery takes Geneviève with her to see a jeweler to whom she wishes to sell a necklace, and there they meet Roland Cassard (Marc Michel), the same Roland from *Lola* who has since struck it rich as a diamond dealer. He comes to Madame Emery's rescue and buys the necklace. In the meantime, Guy learns he has been called to serve in Algeria for two years, and Geneviève is devastated.

After Guy leaves for Algeria, Geneviève discovers she is pregnant with Guy's child, and as time goes by, she struggles with her feelings about Guy's absence. In the meantime, we learn that Roland is in love with Geneviève. Madame Emery encourages her daughter to pursue Roland, stirring up fears in Geneviève that Guy may not be faithful to her. Roland is willing to marry the pregnant Geneviève, and eventually Geneviève concedes, marries Roland, and leaves Cherbourg. When Guy returns, he is a broken man, who sinks further into depression when his aunt Elise (Mireille Perrey) dies. Madeleine (Ellen Farner), who took care of Elise, now takes care of Guy, with whom she clearly has been in love since the beginning of the film. Guy eventually buys an Esso gas station, marries Madeleine, and has a son with her. The film ends with Geneviève pulling into Guy's gas station with her—and Guy's—daughter, and the estranged lovers part ways during a beautiful snowfall.

That the film draws on the fairy-tale genre is evident in particular in two scenes. First, in the scene in the jewelry store, Roland shows the jeweler Monsieur Dubourg a beautiful necklace, which Roland describes as "the jewels of ... Sleeping Beauty."[33] Just as he pronounces these words, he gazes up at Geneviève entering the store with her mother. This line already suggests an ambiguity as to the nature of Sleeping Beauty's prince: although she will wait for the working-class Guy to return from Algeria, Geneviève ends up being "rescued" (depending on one's perspective) by the now wealthy Roland. Moreover, just like Michel in *Lola,* Roland is associated with a character from the Arabian Nights. When Monsieur Dubourg examines Roland's stash of gems, impressed, he refers to it as "Ali Baba's cave."[34]

The second scene in question takes place during Epiphany, which the French celebrate with *galette des rois* (kings' cake), in which a token is hidden; the person who finds the token is named king or queen for the day and chooses a partner to form a royal couple. In the film, it is Geneviève who finds the token in her piece of cake, and she places the paper crown on her head (Figure 1.3). Her mother tells her she must now pick a king and make a wish, and Geneviève, looking at Roland, responds, "I have no choice. You are my king."[35] Hardly the romantic response one would hope to find in a fairy tale, the scene is underwhelming in its designation of Roland as her Prince Charming.

Interestingly, it is as if fairy-tale references ("Sleeping Beauty," "Ali Baba,"

Figure 1.3. Geneviève (Catherine Deneuve) as Epiphany queen in *The Umbrellas of Cherbourg.*

references to kings and queens) work to push Geneviève toward embracing the socially acceptable prince, the wealthy Roland, although the structure of the narrative—Geneviève waiting for the return of her one true love—suggests that Guy fulfills, at least potentially, this function as well. Thus *The Umbrellas of Cherbourg* proposes two potential fairy-tale narratives: one in which Geneviève waits for Guy to return and save her from the grips of her petit bourgeois mother, who is willing to sacrifice her daughter's happiness for financial gain; and a second, in which the socially recognizable Prince Charming, this time with a black Mercedes, a black suit, and a stash of gems, "saves" Geneviève from social scorn and her mother's disapproval but ultimately proves unsatisfactory because the heroine cannot love him. The second fairy-tale narrative's triumph over the first results in melodrama, that is, in loss, in repressed or unfulfilled desires, in tears.

Demy divides the film into three clearly demarcated sections with section titles and an epilogue, whose themes are emphasized through Demy's singular use of color as well as time. The film is structured as follows:

1. *The Departure: November 1957*

2. *Absence:*
>*January 1958*
>*February 1958*
>*March 1958*
>*April 1958*

3. *Return:*
>*March 1959*
>*April 1959*
>*June 1959*

4. *Epilogue [my title]: December 1963*

Part 1 focuses on Guy and Geneviève's love, concluding with Guy leaving on the train, and it is the longest segment of the film—nearly forty out of ninety minutes. Part 2 is focalized through Geneviève and deals with the tensions she has with her mother as well as the pursuit of Roland for her hand. Part 3 tells Guy's story upon his early return, due to an injury, from Algeria, and the epilogue, which takes place a few years later, proves to be the melodramatic climax of love lost. Each of these sections follows a particular color and time scheme, which emphasizes the shifting moments of fantasy and realism, of fairy tale and melodrama, constitutive of the film.

The first part of the film is reminiscent of the scene in *Lola* where Frankie and Cécile go to the fair in its unrealistic cinematography, yet Demy uses different aesthetic techniques. Color is his tool in *The Umbrellas*, which is clear from the opening credits, in which well-choreographed and multicolored umbrellas dance in the rainy streets of Cherbourg. As scholars have noted, "The production literally painted large portions of the real city in the Easter-egg hues of the film" (Herzog 129). The film's saturated hues are reminiscent of Technicolor, the preferred color process for Hollywood musicals, which, especially after *The Wizard of Oz*, signified fantasy as opposed to reality.[36]

Much as Disney made use of Technicolor in films such as *Cinderella*, Demy associates specific colors with different characters and their spaces.[37] In the umbrella shop of Geneviève and her mother, bright pink hues peppered with pastel blues, dominate, whereas Aunt Elise's apartment, associated with Guy and Madeleine, tends to be green and a deeper blue. In scenes recounting Guy and Geneviève's love story, both characters wear pastel blues and pinks, and Geneviève's color scheme consistently jars with the bright reds associated with her mother. Toward the end of Part 1, when Geneviève accompanies Guy to the train station to see him off, fantastical colors give way to natural brown, green, and beige tones, just as fairy tale gives way to melodrama.

Over the course of Part 2, Absence, an interesting movement occurs: Geneviève's color scheme conflicts less and less with that of her mother's, until she finally blends into her mother's space like a piece of furniture.[38] In Part 1 Geneviève's pink and coral often clash with her mother's red, which symbolizes, as is clear in its use in the brothel scene, the loss of innocence. Significantly, Part 2 opens with Geneviève wearing red, just like her mother. Later when they dine with Roland, Geneviève wears a dark, almost reddish pink, whereas her mother dresses in black (Roland's color) and pink. In the following scene, Geneviève wears a washed-out pale blue, as she seems to be fading away, until finally, in the sequence of scenes leading up to her agreeing to marry Roland, Geneviève literally fades into the wallpaper, her dress being the exact same pattern and color (Figure 1.4).[39] The dress may signify springtime (she wears the dress in April 1958) and refer to her pregnancy (she shows quite a bit at this point) as well as mark her assimilation into her mother's worldview. Part 2 ends with Geneviève wearing her white wedding dress, having lost all singularity, all color distinction, through her conformity to her mother's desires.[40]

Whereas bright pastels and saturated hues dominate the first part of the film, the color scheme characteristic of Guy's return revolves around earth tones, especially browns, greens, and rust oranges. Guy is first seen in the brown jacket he wore upon departing from Cherbourg, and when he proposes to the down-to-earth Madeleine at the end of Part 3, they sit in a rusty orange

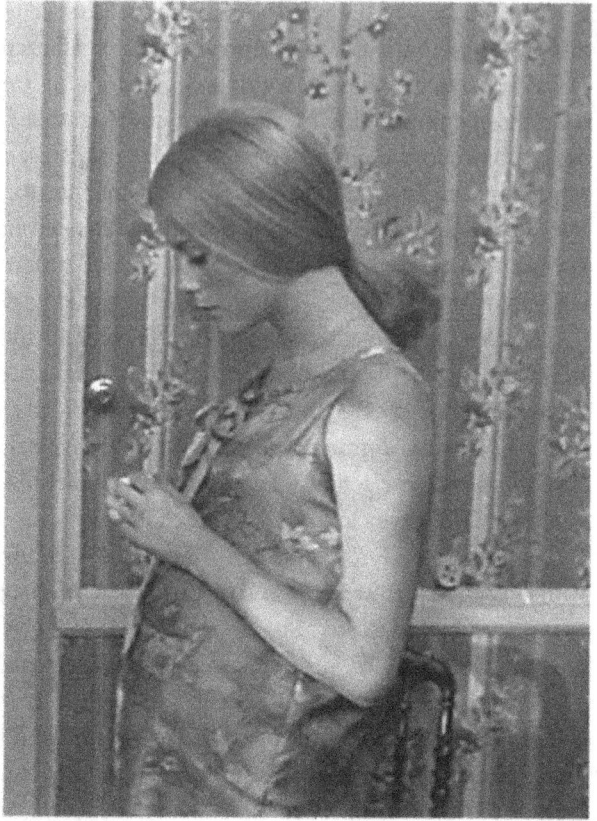

Figure 1.4.
Geneviève's dress
matches her
mother's wallpaper.

café, where Madeleine wears a dress of nearly the same color. For its part, the colorful umbrella shop has been taken over by the whiteness of a laundromat, almost as if it was erased right out of existence, its colors having washed away. With the exception of the scene in which Guy momentarily tries to escape the reality of having lost Geneviève by going to the sleazy red club where he encounters a prostitute, Part 3 provides a contrast to the rest of the film in its naturalistic use of color.[41]

Colors become less distinct, less saturated, until finally, in "December 1963," the whiteness of the snow takes over. The rain shower that opens the film, punctuated by a plethora of colorful umbrellas, contrasts with the cold absence of color in the film's finale. Paul Coates captures perfectly the significance of color in this scene when he talks about "the melancholy muting of coulour by the whiteness of snow in the finale's registration" as marking Geneviève's "definitive loss at Guy's petrol station" (125). Significantly, the scene also references the ending of Visconti's *White Nights,* whose white snow announces both the magical return of the Tenant and the final desperation of

Mario, who walks alone toward an Esso station in the film's final shot. (Figures 1.5 and 1.6). Pulling into the Esso station now owned by Guy, Geneviève emerges from Roland's black Mercedes in her black fur coat, wearing a black dress. Geneviève tells Guy she is in mourning over her mother's death, but black symbolizes another loss as well: that of Guy, her one true love. With the melody of "I Will Wait for You" playing in the background, we can only imagine how many hankies Legrand and Demy had written on the score as the music crescendos while Geneviève pulls out of the gas station. Indeed, the falling snowflakes foregrounded as the camera pulls out appear to be so many frozen tears.

As the use of color inflects the film's implicit tensions between fairy tale and melodrama, so does Demy's use of time. Part 1, the story of first love, is not broken down into time segments as are the other sections of the film. The longest part of the film makes of November 1957 a sort of eternal present. Just as the use of color transforms Cherbourg, the site of their love, into an unreal, fantastic space, so time is suspended. In contrast, Part 2 is broken down into four moments (January, February, March, and April 1959), which enhances the viewer's sense of Geneviève's anxious anticipation for the passage of time. She waits in January; she waits in February; she waits in March; then she gives up waiting in April, no longer able to bear the weight of waiting. The

Figure 1.5. The last shot of *White Nights*, in which Mario (Marcello Mastroianni) walks through the snow toward the Esso gas station.

Figure 1.6. The last scene of *The Umbrellas of Cherbourg* in which Guy (Nino Castelnuovo) watches as Geneviève (Catherine Deneuve) leaves his Esso gas station in the snow.

passage of time is further marked by Geneviève's ever-increasing belly. Part 3 is similar to Part 2 in its more realistic representation of time, this time revolving around Guy's return (March), his plunge into depression (April), and his rebirth (June), with the unrepresented May implicitly being the period of his recovery and courtship with Madeleine. The eternal present of love in Part 1 is thus contrasted with the passage of time and with change characteristic of Parts 2 and 3, as the plenitude of fairy tale gives way to the loss that is melodrama.

To return to Nowell-Smith's characterization of melodrama, loss is inseparable from the notion of "impaired masculinity" and more generally from the sense of impotence experienced by both male and female characters. In the eyes of bourgeois respectability, projected through the character of Madame Emery, Guy is a weak hero in his lack of social status, whereas Roland represents the chance for a better life and enhanced social status typical of fairy-tale plots. However, from another perspective Roland represents an impaired or impotent hero due to his inability to be loved by Lola or Geneviève. Geneviève, who opts for bourgeois respectability over true love, proves weak in her inability to make her singular dream come true.

That Guy somehow is a castrated character is symbolized, upon his return from Algeria, by his limp and, later, by the loss of his job. As a male rescuer, he fails due not only to his lack of social status but also to his powerlessness to avoid the draft, which prevents him from "saving" the pregnant Geneviève. As Neale points out, such forms of "blockages" are typical of melodrama: "Blockages, barriers and bars to the fulfillment of desire are constantly introduced as events change course. . . . These blockages are characterised and motivated in different ways. They may be specified, for instance, in social terms, as the product of family circumstances or the strictures of class and social propriety" (12). In *The Umbrellas*, questions of class and social propriety combine with the brutal imposition of the draft to impede Guy's ability to unite with Geneviève, which results in loss. Because of his impaired masculinity, Guy will depend on Madeleine to recover any sense of control over his life, as the true rescuer of this tale proves to be a woman who saves a man.

Although Roland appears to conform more closely to the traditional male rescuer, he fails to fully execute this role. *Lola* concludes with Roland's failure to "save" the showgirl from single motherhood (although one wonders if Lola really needed saving at all). This background is alluded to in *The Umbrellas* in a conversation Roland has with Madame Emery, in which music and footage from *Lola* is inscribed, thus integrating, in Tabouley's words, Roland's "living past" into the film, just as Demy did with the role of Madame Desnoyers in *Lola*.[42] Roland states very simply that "I loved a woman, she didn't love me."[43] Although he does not want to force Geneviève to marry him, *The Umbrellas* plays out what could have happened in *Lola* had Lola lost all hope of reuniting with Michel and had she felt desperate: she could have entered into a loveless marriage with Roland, as did Geneviève. Although in *The Umbrellas* Roland seems to follow a trajectory that recalls that of Michel in *Lola*—he leaves the provincial city and strikes it rich to return to France and claim a bride—he simply cannot live up to the ideal image and mystical aura that Michel embodies. Roland always falls short, except in the eyes of older women such as Madame Desnoyers and Madame Emery. Madame Emery in particular lives vicariously through her daughter: her desire for Roland ends up being consummated by proxy through her daughter's marriage to him. Nevertheless, Roland only appears to have succeeded and fulfilled his desires. Ultimately, he represents impotency in his inability to gain the love of a young woman with whom he believes he is in love.

For her part, and particularly when compared to Lola, Geneviève proves to be quite a weak character. Lola waits seven years for Michel; Geneviève cannot even wait four months for Guy. Lola has a child out of wedlock and she seems unconcerned about social perceptions of her position; Geneviève caves in to her mother's manipulation and concerns about what the neighbors might think. Madame Emery continually insinuates that Guy is probably betraying her in Algeria and tries to "sell" her Roland. Geneviève is quite aware of this: "You speak to me about him the way you talk about your umbrellas."[44] But her mother's intimations that Guy might abandon her and that she could end up alone with a child unless she agrees to marry Roland, along with her own inability to wait (she asks herself, "Why is absence so hard to bear?"), finally push Geneviève to renounce her love for Guy.[45]

It is in this sense that we can understand Geneviève's decision to marry Roland as the "acceptance of castration," which occurs "only at the cost of repression" (Nowell-Smith, "Minnelli" 115). The scene with the *galette des rois* is particularly revelatory of Geneviève's passive nature, which allows her to so easily surrender herself to the demands of her mother and, by extension, to French middle-class social and gender norms. When asked to choose a king, she claims she "has no choice" but Roland, which could be read as her failure to act, to affirm her singular desire for Guy. Elsaesser could very well be describing the dynamics at play in *The Umbrellas* in his characterization of the family melodrama:

> The family melodrama ... records the failure of the protagonist to act in a way that could shape the events and influence the emotional environment, let alone change the stifling social milieu. The world is closed, and the characters are acted upon. Melodrama confers on them a negative identity through suffering, and the progressive self-immolation and disillusionment generally ends in resignation: they emerge as lesser human beings for having become wise and acquiescent to the ways of the world. (9)

Geneviève's disillusionment begins with her own inability to wait or to die from love for the absent Guy: "Why did Guy go away from me, me, who would have died for him? Why am I not dead?"[46] Although Geneviève exemplifies the sense of disillusionment and resignation in the film, even Guy, who tries to create a new life with Madeleine, has lost the sense of joy and idealism that we see in the first part of the film. He remains, as does Roland in his own way, a broken man.

As opposed to the Disney fairy-tale film, with its "benevolent" symbolic order, Demy's *Umbrellas of Cherbourg* suggests that adherence to the fairy tale of middle-class bliss indeed involves castration. Castration takes the form of renunciation or blockage of one's singular desires and the impossibility—either self-imposed or imposed from without—to attain fulfillment of one's dreams. Whereas Guy is forced to momentarily abandon Geneviève by the French state through military service, Geneviève permanently abandons Guy by giving in to the demands and expectations of her mother and her social class. And for Geneviève, it is not just about giving up the individual Guy. Madame Emery fully recognizes that Guy furthermore stands for an alluring alternative lifestyle for Geneviève: "Guy might have represented a certain ideal for you, but what kind of future could he offer you?"[47] Guy, then, not only symbolizes "true love" but also a way of life, an ideal, and one that clearly does not conform to the petit bourgeois gender, social, and even sexual order to which Madame Emery adheres.

QUEER INFLECTIONS

In "L'Étrange Demy-monde" ("The Strange Demy-World"), Philippe Colomb asks why *The Umbrellas of Cherbourg* appeals so much to so many gay men in France. He compellingly shows the ways in which the film can be read in terms of the dynamics of the closet, involving denial and renunciation. He states, "This story is thus the story of a socially inadmissible love, a romantic and non-petit bourgeois love, which will be broken by the order of social proprieties. It is the story about a love opposed by a society that prefers couples without love to nonconformist couples" (40).[48] In his reading of *The Umbrellas* Colomb suggests that the condemnation of a relationship based on social class can serve as a figure for the condemnation of a relationship based on sexuality. In other words, the relationship between a petit bourgeois woman and a working-class man violates social codes in the same way that a same-sex relation violates heterosexual ones.

Whereas Colomb focuses on carrying out a queer reading of what may or may not be a queer film, I would like to propose that in both *Lola* and *The Umbrellas*, Demy hints at a queer subtext through the intertextual references made in these films. These intertexts suggest that at some level these films stage a sort of queer melodrama, particularly through the characters Geneviève and Roland, which exists in a relation of tension with the heteronormativity of the implicit fairy-tale narrative. It is precisely because of the queer subtext that the heteronormative fairy-tale narrative must give way to queer melodrama.

First of all, Demy's interest in the genre of the musical from the beginning to the end of his career (his last film, *Trois Places pour le 26* [*Three Seats for the 26th,* 1988], was a musical about making a musical) could be read in terms of Demy's longstanding interest in forms of gay aestheticism and camp, which will be treated at length in chapter 2. Several critics have noted the close associations between musicals, camp, and gay culture. John Clum remarks, "Musicals were always gay. They always attracted a gay audience, and, at their best, even in times of a policed closet, they were created by gay men" (9). Part of such associations, as Clum implies, has to do with the extent to which gay men influenced the very shape of Hollywood musicals. In his study of the largely gay Arthur Freed unit, which was responsible for many popular MGM musicals, including those of Gene Kelly of which Demy was so fond, Matthew Tinkcom convincingly argues that these "products" are marked by those who produce it. Tinkcom maintains, "Labors performed by particular subjects . . . can in some cases display the mark of the subject upon the product; the net effect of this claim is that some commodities are indeed . . . queer" ("Working" 29).[49]

Tinkcom points to aspects of the musical film that may have appealed to queer artists. Ostensibly, the musical, much like the classical fairy tale in the tradition of Disney, is a heteronormative genre: "The world in which a man and a woman meet and find initial attraction, in which their union is frustrated, and where ultimately the prohibitions to heterosexual bonding are overcome through the mediation of the song and dance number is typically the world of the musical" (Tinkcom, "Working" 33–34). However, the focus on spectacle—of both the male and the female body—and on performance destabilizes the "natural" order of gender and heteronormativity. Tinkcom argues that by integrating the musical numbers into the film instead of bracketing them off, an innovation of Minnelli, such films blur the distinction between realism and performance and emphasize "everyday life as performative, not least of which when it comes to thinking about gender" ("Working" 35).

Gene Kelly musicals in particular raise some interesting questions about gender and sexuality. Kelly sought to challenge stereotypes of the effeminate male dancer by donning a sailor suit, which accommodated the need to outline the dancer's body while masculinizing the dancer's appearance. But as Steven Cohan has remarked, "A man dancing immediately troubles normative masculinity, even if he does it in a sailor suit" by making his body a spectacle, an object of the Other's gaze (158). Moreover, the very reference to sailors destabilizes the heteronormative masculinity Kelly apparently was trying to project, for "sailor," much like "musical," was coded language for "homosexual."[50] Cohan points to the scene in *Anchors Away* in which Joe Brady (Kelly) pretends to be a "dame" to show the inexperienced result of all-boys schools, Clarence Doolittle (Frank Sinatra), how to pick up a woman. During their role-play on the street, a man in a suit walks by and gives them a funny look. For Cohan, "The scene alludes to homosexual gossip about sailors," who spent much time at sea without women and whose uniforms were particularly revealing of the male body (169). *On the Town* also provides an example of cross-gendered role playing, in which sailors Ozzie (Jules Munshin), pretending to be a woman, and Gabey (Kelly) play out a scene of "heterosexual" flirting and pickup.

Although I cannot address the extent to which "musical" would have served as a code word for homosexuality within a French context at the time Demy was producing films, sailors indeed were associated with homosexuality, as exemplified in the works, for instance, of Jean Genet.[51] Nevertheless, the queer inflections of these MGM musicals clearly appealed to Demy, who inserts similar types of inflections into his own films, most obviously through the inclusion of well-known gay actors whose sexuality in real life problematizes the homosocial and apparently heteronormative relations between characters in his films.

For instance, in *Les Demoiselles de Rochefort*—his homage to Gene Kelly, who appears in the film—Demy cast George Chakiris and Grover Dale as the two main carnies of the film. Both actors were gay and implicitly form, as Colomb has argued, a gay couple in the film. In the case of Dale, he was known for his relationships with men, and at the time of *Les Demoiselles,* his partner was Anthony Perkins, whom Demy had considered for the role of the prince in *Donkey Skin.* As Svea Becker and Bruce Williams have argued, the casting of Dale in particular "carries . . . weight in the creation of a gay celebrity intertext" (308). Jean Marais, whom we will discuss in more detail in the following chapter, also serves as a "gay celebrity intertext" in Demy's *Donkey Skin* as well as in his film *Parking* (1982).

Such examples only scratch the surface of queer intertexts in Demy's films. What I would like to suggest here, however, is that the implicit signifiers of queerness—for example, sailors in *Lola,* the musical aesthetics in *The Umbrellas*—hint at the possibility of reading the tensions in both films in terms of queer desire. Drawing from Colomb, I have already proposed that we can read the story of Geneviève in terms of the closet: her renunciation of Guy means the renunciation of her singular desire that goes against petit bourgeois social conventions. Another character who merits further attention within the optics of queer desire and melodrama is Roland.

Roland's character crosses both films, and in both cases, he never quite manages to find true love. His character is always located on the side of melodrama—of loss and lack—and can never claim any kind of real fairy-tale ending, despite appearances in *The Umbrellas.* In *Lola,* he proves to be the weakest male character: he is unable to gain Lola's hand, or even her bed. Although he seems to have "made it" in *The Umbrellas,* he presents a contrast to *Lola's* Michel in his less imposing appearance and his melancholic demeanor, which is made manifest in his association with black suits and cars as opposed to Michel's association with white.

Interestingly, in both films Roland believes he is in love with women who are passionately in love with other men and who show no amorous affection toward him. His love for Lola and Geneviève is completely misplaced, and the only reason he manages to marry Geneviève is the motherly and social pressures Geneviève experiences as an unmarried and pregnant woman. However, in both films it is the older women, Madame Denoyers and Madame Emery, who clearly are attracted to Roland. After recounting her life story to Roland and how she lost everything after the war, partly because her husband was a gambler, Madame Desnoyers declares, "What I needed was a husband like you."[52] For her part, Madame Emery tells her daughter, "It's amazing how nice he is,"[53] and throughout the film she gazes longingly at Roland. Both films hint at the possibility of a relationship between Roland and the older women, a possibility that is foreclosed upon with Roland's departure for South Africa in *Lola* and his marriage to Geneviève in *The Umbrellas*. One wonders, then, if Roland fails to act upon a form of forbidden love—a younger man and an older woman—in the same way that Geneviève similarly fails to marry the working-class Guy.

Reading *Lola* and *The Umbrellas of Cherbourg* together highlights the ways in which Demy creates a dialectic between fairy tale and melodrama. With its forceful and idealized hero and heroine who are reunited, thanks in large part to Lola's ability to wait, *Lola* proves to be a fairy tale in which dreams can come true. Yet read in light of the film's intertextual allusions to *Les Dames du Bois de Boulogne* and *White Nights* and in relation to its sequel *Model Shop*, *Lola* has melodramatic underpinnings. Through the representation of Cécile, Lola, and Madame Desnoyers, the film stages the cycle of romance from the fantastical foundations of first love to love's consummation to its final demise; in other words, it traces a movement from idealism to disillusion. "Matareva," then, not only signals "dream" (*rêve*) but also the death of that dream (*matar* means "to kill"). *The Umbrellas of Cherbourg*, on the other hand, foregrounds melodrama, as either the fairy-tale narrative is prevented from being realized—Geneviève does not marry her true love Guy—or it is problematized: marriage to the socially recognizable prince proves unsatisfactory. *The Umbrellas* starts off as a fairy tale whose movement toward wish fulfillment is blocked by war, social pressures, and the heroine's own weakness, and the film quickly moves into the melodramatic narrative about loss, impotence, and disillusion.

On one level, we can read the story of disillusion to be about France's romance with American culture. Both Michel and Roland represent different incarnations of the American dream and the American hero, and both characters fall short of being able to satisfy their princess. Just as the utopian promise of America is undermined in *Model Shop* by shots of LA that reveal its underlying empty and alienating landscape, so Michel and Roland prove to be empty and disaffected heroes. On another level, the story of disillusion is also the story about the queer subject who was unable to actualize his or her desires due to social pressures that make certain types of relationships untenable or even unthinkable. Cross-class and cross-generational couples can thus be read as figures for queer relationships, which are renounced in order to conform to the sociosexual and gender norms of middle-class French society.

Through recourse to fairy tale and melodrama, Demy creates films of hope and despair, idealism and disillusion. In different ways, *Lola* and *The Umbrellas of Cherbourg* point to the possibility of fairy-tale moments, those magical moments in life when time is suspended and the world is seen through Technicolor-tinted glasses. These films also deal with the reality of loss, repression, and feelings of impotence, which are sometimes the result of misplaced desires or personal weakness and sometimes the work of larger forces, such as the power of the state to draft young men into useless wars. Despite feelings of disillusion and despair, Demy's characters continue to dream and to struggle with the gender, sexual, and class tensions of their society from film to film. Sometimes they even come to terms with their queer desires, which still does not guarantee fairy-tale endings.

2 |

The Camping of "Donkey Skin"

Jacques Demy's Cinematic Re-Vision of a Classic Tale

One never marries one's parents
You love your father, I understand
Whatever your reasons may be
Whatever your feelings for him may be
My child, one doesn't marry one's mother either
It is said that traditionally
Questions of culture and legislature
Determined at one time that
Girls do not marry their daddy.

      —The Lilac Fairy's song to Donkey Skin[1]

Critics have noted Jacques Demy's longstanding interest in "Peau d'âne" ("Donkey Skin"), Charles Perrault's problematic tale about father–daughter incest. Jean-Pierre Berthomé claims that Demy "staged the tale by Perrault for his puppet theater, along with many other tales by Perrault and the Grimms."[2] Rodney Hill similarly maintains, "This classic fairy tale by Charles Perrault (1628–1703) fascinated Jacques Demy from his early childhood, and he had aspirations of filming it even as a teenager in Nantes" ("Donkey Skin" 40). Demy finally realized such aspirations with his full-length film *Donkey Skin*, starring Catherine Deneuve as the princess and Jean Marais as her incestuous father. Interested in the genre of the fairy tale in general, Demy was captivated by this tale of incest in particular. Indeed, the theme of incest returns in other films by Demy, including *Parking*—a version of Orpheus in which Hades (Jean Marais) is married to his niece Claude Persephone (Marie-France

Pisier)—and *Three Seats for the 26th*—in which the character Yves Montand, played by Yves Montand, unwittingly sleeps with his daughter Marion, played by Mathilda May.[3] Through his re-vision of this tale of incest, Demy represents queer desire in ways that denaturalize the normal and challenge the oppositions constitutive of the sociosexual order of postwar France. As I will argue, Demy essentially "camps" this classical tale, teasing out potentially subversive elements existing in previous versions of the tale and infusing it with elements characteristic of gay aestheticism, drawing in particular from the cinema of Jean Cocteau.

Whereas tales by Charles Perrault such as "Cinderella," "Sleeping Beauty," and "Little Thumbling" have frequently made their way to the silver screen since the origins of French cinema, few filmmakers have ventured to create a cinematic adaptation of Perrault's tale about an incestuous king who wishes to marry his beautiful daughter.[4] Before Jacques Demy, only the Pathé-Frères director Albert Capellani ventured to set "Donkey Skin" to film. However, his fifteen-minute silent film evades the theme of incest altogether by having the "ridiculous fiancé"—a terribly bowlegged nobleman—rather than the father propose marriage to the princess.

Many early French film directors drew from vaudeville to imagine their plots and scenes. Following in this tradition, Capellani blends into Perrault's tale elements from the popular vaudeville fairy-tale extravaganza, or *féerie*, *Peau d'âne* by Emile Vanderburch (or Vanderburck), Laurencin, and Charles Clairville. First staged in 1863, the *féerie* represents a revision of an earlier *féerie* by Vanderburch and Laurencin, and it remained popular in Paris and the provinces until at least 1878, when the stage designer Chéret sued his collaborators for not compensating him for his share of the profits.[5] Whereas the earlier version from 1838 hints at an incestuous attachment, or at least suggests the daughter loves her father too much (and perhaps for his overindulgence), the modifications made for the 1863 version downplay even further any allusions to incest. Instead, the writers play up the coquetry of the daughter, whose vanity leads to disaster. While the father is punished for his overindulgence, the daughter must wear a donkey skin for one year and one day in order to atone for her vain ways. Although Capellani reintroduced elements from Perrault's tale that were left out of the fairy-tale extravaganza, he clearly drew from the *féerie*, which is evident in the need to brush the donkey for it to emit gold coins (the coins fall off the donkey's coat) and in the avoidance of the question of incest.[6]

Based on the textual, theatrical, and filmic history of the tale, it would seem that reading about an incestuous father was less disturbing than seeing one represented on stage or screen. "Donkey Skin" as a tale fueled by a father's incestuous desire for his daughter circulated widely in book form in nineteenth- and early twentieth-century France. Although Amy Herzog suggests that "Donkey Skin" was one of Perrault's tales that was "reproduced the least frequently" and that "subsequent versions often downplay any illicit desire on the part of the father or excise this aspect of the narrative altogether," she seems to be making reference to its tradition in England (134). In France, however, the tale maintained the theme of incest even in editions aimed at younger children, and it saw wide distribution.[7] The tale was republished more than seventy times from 1850 to 1900 within fairy-tale anthologies and less often as an individual tale.[8] From 1901 to 1950, there were at least thirty-six collections that included the tale, with no fewer than nine reprints of the individual tale.

To pen his version of the tale, Perrault drew from the Italian writers Giovanni Francesco Straparola, whose Doralice flees to England in a chest to escape her incestuous father, and Giambattista Basile, whose Preziosa transforms into a bear to escape hers.[9] In Perrault's verse tale, first published in 1694, a dying queen requests that her husband not remarry unless he finds a bride as beautiful as she. Of course, the daughter alone can equal her mother in beauty, and the king requests the princess's hand. Troubled by her father's desire for her, the princess seeks out her fairy godmother, who advises the princess to ask for three extravagant dresses, thinking the king will not be able to produce them. Finally the princess asks for the skin of the king's donkey who defecates gold—an important source of his kingdom's wealth—and the king grants her outrageous wish. The princess flees the palace dressed in the donkey skin and is hired as a scullion. One day a prince spies her in her lowly cottage when she has donned one of her beautiful dresses, and he falls ill with love. When he discovers that this cottage is the abode of the scullion known as Donkey Skin, he requests a cake baked by her hands. Donkey Skin obediently prepares the prince a cake and accidentally—or not—drops her ring in the dough. When the prince finds the ring in his cake, he insists that he will marry no other than the woman who can wear the ring. After all the women in the kingdom from duchesses to servants have tried on the ring, Donkey Skin finally slips the ring on her finger. She then requests the time to change her clothes before meeting the royal family. She appears in one of her marvelous dresses, the prince and princess marry, and the princess reconciles with her father during the wedding festivities.

When compared with Straparola's and Basile's versions of the tale, Perrault creates a more passive and obedient heroine whose father's culpability is completely forgiven at the end of the tale. In Straparola and Basile, the incestuous father is completely expelled from the sociopolitical order that is reestablished at the tale's conclusion, because he is either killed or simply forgotten. In Perrault's version, however, the father is reconciled with his daughter and reintegrated into the sociopolitical order. In other words, rather than being punished, Perrault's father is rehabilitated.[10]

In 1781 a prose version of the tale was published and attributed to Perrault. This apocryphal version names the fairy godmother of Perrault's original the Lilac Fairy and, significantly, it lessens the father's culpability even more than does Perrault's tale, first, by having the queen insist that the king take a new wife after her death and, second, by having the ministers suggest to the king that he take his daughter as his new bride. Along with the 1694 tale, this apocryphal version saw numerous editions, especially in the nineteenth century, and it served as the basis for various adaptations, including the 1866 *Alphabet des contes des fées: Peau d'âne* (*The Alphabet of Fairy Tales: Donkey Skin*), in which the princess asks for her incestuous father's forgiveness at the end of the tale for having run away!

Demy's cinematic re-vision of "Donkey Skin" integrates numerous intertexts that destabilize Perrault's already unsettling classical tale. Drawing from Perrault's original, the apocryphal version, or printed versions that blend the two traditions, Demy also incorporates references to films by Jean Cocteau, most notably *Le Sang d'un poète* (*The Blood of a Poet,* 1930), *Beauty and the Beast,* and *Orpheus.* Although playful visual and thematic references are made to Disney's *Snow White* and to *The Wizard of Oz,* the allusions to Cocteau are most significant in that they can be read as so many inscriptions in *Donkey Skin* of gay aestheticism or camp, which undermines the apparent and disturbing heteronormativity of Perrault's fairy tale and the subsequent versions that grew out of it.

In what follows, I would like to consider the ways in which Demy camps Perrault's classical fairy tale to shape his film *Donkey Skin,* which will also bring to the fore what made this particular tale so fascinating to Demy. The process of camping, I contend, involves both reading camp into the tale as well as infusing the tale with camp aesthetics. My reading will highlight the ways in which Demy transforms a tale that traditionally has communicated, however problematically, heterosexual norms into one about alternative sexualities. He does so by denaturalizing cultural taboos and destabilizing the oppositions that uphold a sex–gender system in which women are construed as passive objects of the male gaze and are associated with the domestic sphere, and in which heteronormative sexuality reigns. Demy's *Donkey Skin* can be read as a queer and feminist critique of Perrault's tale, and through his film Demy celebrates the genre of the fairy tale and the court culture from which it emerged.

Drawing from the work of Susan Sontag, Jack Babuscio develops a definition of camp that I will be using here as an overall framework to think about gay aestheticism. For Babuscio, camp represents a response to sociocultural and sexual marginalization from the perspective of a gay sensibility. When discussing movie stars in particular, Babuscio states, "It [camp] is more a way of poking fun at the whole cosmology of restrictive sex roles and sexual identifications which our society uses to oppress its women and repress its men—including those on screen" (26). Babuscio identifies four features typical of works created or received as camp: first, irony, often taking the form of incongruity; second, aestheticism, or the emphasis "on sensuous surfaces, textures, imagery . . . not simply because they are appropriate to the plot, but as fascinating in themselves" (22); third, theatricality, particularly life-as-theater and the spectacle of the self; and fourth, humor, which relates back to irony and consists of a mix of comedy and pain, allowing us "to witness 'serious' issues with temporary detachment" (28). Finally, camp is interested in desires that subvert conventional heterosexual relations, which often play out in terms of incongruous couples: androgyny or cross-dressing in male–female couples or relations between, for instance, an older woman and a younger man in the tradition of *Sunset Boulevard* (1950).

For my purposes, I will focus on Babuscio's notion of camp (1) as subversive of heteronormative sexuality, (2) as aesthetic incongruity, and (3) as theatricality or self-as-spectacle. Throughout *Donkey Skin* Demy brings together each of these camp strategies in his use of incest as a trope for alternative sexualities; in the incongruous juxtapositions throughout the film between high and low, ancient and modern, nature and culture, which function to denaturalize accepted norms; and in the ways in which his heroines, like female dandies, are simultaneously works of art and desiring subjects. Together these camp strategies work to undermine or trouble apparent oppositions that uphold the sociosexual order of postwar France, which Rebecca Pulju characterizes as the "golden age of familialism," in which conservative notions of family and gender prevailed. A reaction to the chaos and loss of population during WWII, French familial policy turned back the clock on women's rights to focus on "the formation of nuclear families, with children, in which the father worked outside the home and the mother dedicated herself to the household" (99).[11] At certain moments in the film, Demy pokes fun at and implicitly criticizes associations between women and domesticity while also providing us with heroines who are agents of their own desire, another means of challenging the image of the passive, domestic housewife so touted in postwar France. Finally, as an homage to Jean Cocteau, *Donkey Skin* implicitly inscribes Demy within a genealogy of queer directors.

Let us start with the very pretext of the film: *Donkey Skin* is about a father who desires and wishes to marry his daughter. But, as the lines from the film opening this chapter make clear, Demy also makes it about a daughter who desires and wishes to marry her father. In one interview, Demy brushes aside the seriousness of the question of incest by stating, "Ask a little girl who she wants to marry and she'll say 'Daddy' if she's five or six and loves her father."[12] Several possible readings present themselves here. We could take Demy's words at face value and accept that the princess wanting to marry her father is "innocent." Another reading, suggested by the evolution of the tale since Straparola and Basile, could situate Demy's film with respect to Perrault's tale and the apocryphal version, which increasingly lessen the responsibility of the father for his advances toward his daughter. By having the princess desire her father, Demy could be said to be making the king even less culpable than in these earlier versions. For her part, Gwénaëlle Le Gras proposes a feminist reading of the incestuous relationship, in which she argues that Demy "reverses the hierarchy of the sexes in the couple, proposing here an all-powerful woman [the princess] and a non-patriarchal, castrated man [the king]" (30). I would like to propose yet another lens through which we can understand the theme of incest in the film not unrelated to Le Gras's feminist approach. Incest functions, albeit problematically, as a figure for queer forms of sexualities.

In his article "Homosexual Signs," Harold Beaver interestingly discusses homosexuality in conjunction with cannibalism and incest, the underlying connection residing in the apparent defiance such practices present to the Bible's injunction "Be fruitful and multiply." Beaver argues, "With cannibalism and incest, it [homosexuality] appears the very incarnation of social self-destruction, seeking whom it may devour. Like cannibalism, it threatens to turn abundance to sterility. Like incest, it irrevocably defiles [heterosexual] genital desire" (99). Later Beaver relates the taboo of homosexuality—which is seen to blend characteristics of male and female—to biblical law, notably that found in Deuteronomy and Leviticus, whose prohibitions institute and maintain delineations between woman and man, animal and human, and plant and animal, the mixing of which is deemed "unclean" (111). Thus what links incest and homosexuality in Beaver's view is their subversion of biblical (patriarchal, heteronormative) law and the categories and oppositions that uphold such law.

Commenting on *Donkey Skin*, Demy claims that the blue castle of the princess's father—the fifteenth-century fortified Château du Plessis-Bourré—represents Old Regime and conservative tendencies, and the red castle of the prince—the elegant Renaissance Château de Chambord—symbolizes something more "revolutionary."[13] Nevertheless, the blue castle blends nature and culture in ways that oppose its disorder to the more orderly Chambord. Berthomé notes, "Plant and animal life mount an attack on stone in the blue castle."[14] Much like Beauty's bedroom at the Beast's castle in Cocteau's *Beauty and the Beast,* that of the princess is covered with rose vines as if nature were taking over the space, and a figure of a stag stands next to her bed. Although Demy claimed to have had a different design for the princess's bedchamber, the stag cannot but evoke the one from the Beast's grounds in Cocteau.[15] The king's chambers likewise are strewn with vines, and he sits on a white cat throne.[16]

The blue castle, then, represents an "impure" site where nature and culture, human and animal, blend together—or in which these terms were never quite differentiated from one another in the first place. As it is not fully a space defined and claimed by "culture" (as opposed to "nature"), the blue castle is a space in which the prohibition of incest that enforces such oppositions can only be tenuous at best.[17] Here we might understand Demy's characterization of the blue castle as "conservative" to imply "primitive" in the sense of "earliest stages" (OED) of both society and of the individual and, in particular, of the princess who has yet to overcome her Electra complex.

The tenuousness of the prohibition of incest is highlighted in the scene in which the princess, after having learned of her father's intentions, goes to see her godmother the Lilac Fairy (Delphine Seyrig) at her woodland abode, another site where nature and culture, human and animal, mix and coexist.[18] Wishing to marry her father, the princess does not understand why she should not go forward with the wedding. The Lilac Fairy nonchalantly explains to her in a song that girls cannot marry their fathers: it is a question "of culture and legislature." In this scene, the princess desiring her father is presented in an amoral manner. It is as if the characters have not yet fully interiorized the law forbidding incest, and the law itself appears arbitrary: it is not based in nature but on human conventions. In fact, the only reason the Lilac Fairy invokes the law is that she herself wishes to marry the king. Unlike the figure of the fairy godmother in classic versions of fairy tales who support and come to the assistance of the heroine, in Demy's *Donkey Skin* the Lilac Fairy presents herself as the princess's sexual rival.

The fact that Jean Marais plays the incestuous king further complicates the signification of incest in the film. On the one hand, his presence in a fairy-tale film cannot but bring to mind his role as the Beast in Cocteau's *Beauty and the Beast.* In one interview, Demy explicitly commented on his desire to pay homage to Cocteau through this choice: "I wanted this wink to Cocteau ... because he was the only one in France to approach fantastic cinema. It is in memory of him, of *Beauty and the Beast,* that I so strongly wanted Jean Marais [for this film]."[19] As Berthomé has observed, Marais wears a cloak with broad shoulders in *Donkey Skin,* which recalls the costume he wore as the Beast (245; Figures 2.1 and 2.2). By using Marais to play the incestuous father, then, Demy could associate beastliness with the character's transgressive desire.

On the other hand, the presence of Marais in the film functions as a gay celebrity intertext, much like the casting of George Chakiris and Grover Dale in *Les Demoiselles de Rochefort* discussed in chapter 1. Marais, a gay actor, plays a man in love with a woman, who happens to be his daughter. As Le Gras has remarked, "Jean Marais was a well-known homosexual" (30), and he and Cocteau are considered one of the first out gay couples (as much as one could be out at the time) in French popular culture. For the informed adult viewer, then, such knowledge about Marais necessarily creates an aesthetic and even ironic distance between actor and role, which troubles the apparent heterosexuality of the incestuous relation between father and daughter as depicted in the film. Demy's use of Marais here makes the problematic heterosexual relation into something else: into something queer.

Since at least Jean-Jacques Rousseau's *Essai sur l'origine des langues (Essay on the Origin of Language,* 1781), incest has been associated with animality. Only amoral animals or preculture humans can freely engage in such sexual

Figure 2.1. Jean Marais as The Beast in Jean Cocteau's *Beauty and the Beast.*

Figure 2.2. Jean Marais as the king in Jacques Demy's *Donkey Skin*, with Catherine Deneuve as the princess. The structure of the king's costume recalls that of Cocteau's Beast.

practices.[20] As Rousseau and later Sigmund Freud and Claude Lévi-Strauss have maintained, the prohibition of incest marks the accession from a state of nature to a state of culture or the state of being animal to a state of being human. That the film's princess herself will be associated with beasts when she dons the donkey skin suggests, like father like daughter, she also has beastly (unhuman, nonnormative) desires.[21]

Critics have read the monstrous beast in film specifically as a figure for homosexuality.[22] With respect to Cocteau in particular, Irène Eynat-Confino contends, "As Cocteau's works repeatedly show, by using the monster as a trope or a concrete supernatural being . . . he was giving voice to an ordeal that he shared with the many whose sexuality was nonnormative and condemned as such by society" (93). Daniel Fischlin explains further:

> The Beast, depending upon the gaze constructing his or her presence, is thus an ambiguous sexual construct, a queer, especially in a reading that incorporates Cocteau's directorial eye into the context of the gaze constructing the beast as an object of desire. From that perspective the film's camera-work becomes a sensuous point of contact between Cocteau and his lover, a way of constructing their queer relationship in a visual code

driven by the passion of the lover's gaze. At that level of signification the Beast becomes the very signifier of queer presence in the film, despite the (not quite) conventional heterosexuality figured in the dénouement with which Cocteau was notoriously unhappy. (80)

If we accept Fischlin's notion that "the Beast becomes the very signifier of queer presence in the film," then Demy's casting of Marais as the beastly (incestuous) king can be seen as an inscription of queer sexuality in *Donkey Skin* through a gay intertext. Just as the love of Beauty for the Beast comes to signify a form of transgressive queer sexuality, so does the love of the princess (who becomes a beast) for her father (who references Cocteau's Beast).

Cocteau's *Beauty and the Beast* itself has somewhat of an incestuous subtext: Beauty refuses to marry Avenant because she does not want to leave her father's side. The only true substitute for her father is the Beast, and as critics have noted, Beauty appears disappointed when her Beast (*ma Bête*) transforms into a beautiful man.[23] In Cocteau's film, one form of transgressive love (incest) replaces another (bestiality). In *Donkey Skin,* the princess likewise seems disappointed at the end of the film. Her marriage to the prince, which she had indeed desired, seems anticlimactic, and the princess appears a bit miffed upon learning that the Lilac Fairy will be marrying her father. The Lilac Fairy remarks, "Oh, darling! I'm marrying your father. Try to look pleased."[24] The prince is only a substitute—imposed by an arbitrary law—who cannot fully replace the princess's original object of desire: the father. Like Cocteau before him, Demy associates monstrosity and incest with nonnormative forms of sexuality.[25]

In the period in which Cocteau and Demy (at least in the first part of his career) were active, male homosexual desire was viewed as being an anomalous realization of the Oedipus complex, in which the male child ends up desiring the father instead of the mother. Today such an approach to understanding male homosexuality is inadequate, not to mention extremely problematic. However, it was one of the dominant paradigms used to think about homosexuality until the 1970s, when the antipsychiatric work of Guy Hocquenghem put into question Freud's prevalent view on the subject, freeing up desire tout court from the Oedipus complex.[26]

In the Freudian scheme of things, male homosexuality is about desiring the father.[27] Steven Bruhm rather graphically sums up Freud's position: "The homosexual male . . . can both identify with and desire the father, thus giving rise to Leo Bersani's earlier discomfort that we might want to be the Father at the same time that we want to fuck the father; simultaneously, the homosexual male can identify with the mother out of his desire for her, thus adopting the 'negative axis' of desiring the phallus with her" (7). The gay male, then, can both identify with and desire the father, or identify with the mother and, through his identification with her, desire the father.

Despite its problematic nature, such a paradigm, because of its historical import, provides further insights into the possible significance of incest in Demy's *Donkey Skin*. Just as incest is represented as an arbitrary law based in culture and not nature, it can also be read in terms of the queer subject's desire for the father projected onto the heroine, who herself becomes a "beast," both animal and human, both male and female. Just as Cocteau's Beast (*ma Bête*) is both masculine and feminine (*bête* or "beast" is feminine in French), so Demy's Donkey Skin (Peau d'âne) is both feminine (she is a princess) and masculine (*âne*, or "donkey," is masculine in French). In Eynat-Confino's words, the monstrous is "the negation of binaries per se" (1). It is precisely because the monstrous (indefinable, queer) body of the princess is marked as both masculine and feminine that we can read her desire for the king in terms of male homosexual desire. That this may indeed be the case is suggested by Demy's obvious preoccupation with the question of incest in his films.

Demy makes reference to incest in *Les Demoiselles de Rochefort*—in which Monsieur Dame, the "stepfather" of Delphine, clearly desires her—and in *Parking*—in which Jean Marais again plays the role of an incestuous father figure.[28] Two years before his death, Demy made incest the primary focus of his last feature-length film, *Three Seats for the 26th*.[29] Like the princess in *Donkey Skin*, Marion in *Three Seats* is a desiring subject, and she in fact initiates the relationship with the man, Yves Montand, she later discovers is her father. Raphaël Lefèvre characterizes Demy's final film in terms of "calm audacity, absence of guilt and of moral judgment: Demy ends his career with a weak film but with an astonishing vision of love and taboos."[30] In all of these films, Demy makes light of incest, which for most spectators was a very heavy taboo—as was homosexuality. And just as he does in other films dealing with sexualities that go against the sex–gender system of 1950s and 1960s France, Demy neutralizes any moral condemnation, shame, or guilt characters would otherwise express or feel in more mainstream films.

This is not to suggest that Demy condoned incest. Rather, Demy used incest as a trope to talk about alternative, nonheteronormative forms of sexuality. It needs to be stated, however, that such a move is problematic and objectionable for at least two reasons. First, it fails to acknowledge the very real trauma that results from actual cases of incest.[31] Second, associating homosexuality with incest hardly does justice to queer desire, which becomes stigmatized as an abnormal, perverse form of sexuality.

Nevertheless we can understand Demy's lighthearted treatment of incest in terms of "denaturalizing the normal," to borrow Richard Dyer's expression. Dyer explains, "Normality passes itself off as naturalness; the gay perception of the literal superficiality of normality has the effect of denaturalising the normal. At the same time, gay aestheticism doubts that there is any such thing as a natural way of being and thus the honest way of proceeding is to acknowledge the artificiality of reality" (66). When the Lilac Fairy so casually states that incest is a question "of culture and legislature," she in essence denaturalizes the prohibition against incest, which does not represent for these characters some deep-seated taboo that brings shame and guilt. The same could be said about queer desire. Its apparent "incongruity" in the eyes of mainstream society is purely a matter of sociocultural convention.

Aesthetic Incongruities

When discussing camp irony, Babuscio characterizes it in terms of "any highly incongruous contrast between an individual or thing and its context or association" (20). Such incongruities are based on perceived oppositions, most notably between masculine and feminine but including as well sacred and profane, spirit and flesh, high and low status, youth and old age (Babuscio 20–21). Babuscio argues, "At the core of this perception of incongruity is the idea of gayness as a moral deviation. Two men or two women in love are generally regarded by society as incongruous—out of keeping with the 'normal,' 'natural,' 'healthy' order of things" (21). We might read the deployment of incongruities in terms, again, of denaturalizing the normal, of what we accept as normal in life—or in a tale. In *Donkey Skin*, Demy foregrounds what is already "incongruous" in the 1694 and the apocryphal versions of the tale and builds upon such incongruities to foreground the artificiality and the constructedness of the normal. Through such incongruities, the film also, in the words of Rodney Hill, "calls attention to and questions its artificial world and even its own status as fairy tale" ("Donkey Skin" 41). Demy constantly plays upon visual and temporal incongruities to deconstruct the heteronormative plot as well as to simply delight in an aesthetics of clashing colors and images.

Some incongruities become visible by the mere gesture of transferring the image onto the screen. For instance, in textual versions of the tale, the king's donkey expels gold coins instead of excrement.[32] However, to actually see the donkey doing so, accompanied by very loud braying and the sound of coins spilling down onto a plate as if one hit the jackpot, adds a layer of humor that textual representations and even illustrations of the tale cannot begin to convey. The scene mixes the scatological with signs of wealth, lower functions with higher ones, waste with revenue. Whereas I suggest elsewhere that turning shit into gold can be viewed as a figure for the abjectification and purification of Perrault's submissive heroines (Duggan, *Salonnières* 152), in Demy's film this same scene depicted on-screen functions instead in such a way that it literally explodes the order of reality that depends upon distinctions such as clean and unclean, high and low, money and feces.

Another moment in the written tale that takes on new dimensions by representing it on-screen is when the king first proposes marriage to his daughter and the princess goes to the woods to seek out the Lilac Fairy. Of course, Demy has his princess dressed like a princess, in a beautiful blue taffeta dress, which contrasts significantly with the wooded area through which she hastens. When the brush opens to let the princess into her godmother's woodland abode, a wink to Perrault's "Sleeping Beauty," contrasts are further accentuated. Characters dressed in refined garb clash with the natural setting as well as with each other, whose styles issue from different historical periods. What appears "natural" in the textual version of the tale—a beautifully dressed princess making her way through the woods—looks awkward on-screen as an unlikely juxtaposition of "nature" (the wooded area) and "culture" (the elegant and cumbersome gown). Demy's cinematic re-vision of Perrault's "Donkey Skin" seems to denaturalize the tale itself, foregrounding the incongruities that lay dormant in the classical tale.

As a character, the Lilac Fairy does not quite belong to this particular fairy-tale universe. She signals what Herzog has referred to as the "temporal anachronisms" (137) of the film, resulting from the blending of elements or temporal signs taken from different historical periods. For instance, the late medieval blue castle's princess dresses according to eighteenth-century norms, whereas the Renaissance red kingdom houses the prince wearing sixteenth-century attire.[33] Demy expressly requested such historical inaccuracies in order to create a sense of timelessness, an ahistorical past in which the tale is situated. However, with her 1930s Jean Harlow look, the Lilac Fairy presents a blatant contrast to all of the other styles represented in the film.[34]

With her references to "battery-operated" charms and her gift of poetry of the future to the king, the Lilac Fairy symbolizes modernity. The poems in question turn out to be penned by Guillaume Apollinaire and by Jean Cocteau, whose "Ode to Picasso" makes mention of such modern objects as telephones and gaslights, which get paired up with mythological figures such as Orpheus, Calliope, and Urania:

Ecoutant ta guitare fée	Listening to your fairy guitar
Tes objets te suivent Orphée	Your objects follow you, Orpheus
Jusqu'à la forme que tu veux	Letting you shape them as you like

Clio du zinc	Clio at the bar
Calliope téléphone les faits divers	Calliope phoning in a scoop
Et Uranie allume les becs de gaz	And Urania turning on the gaslights
Qui fardent les marroniers par dessous.	That powder the chestnut trees below[35]

The repetition of the sound "fée" (*guitare fée, Orphée, faits divers*), meaning "fairy" in French, associates the magic of modernity with all things fairy. Much in the tradition of Cocteau, Demy juxtaposes the ancient and the modern, which culminates in the film's conclusion, when the Lilac Fairy transports the king to the princess's wedding in a helicopter (Figure 2.3). Ironically, the helicopter, a realistic mode of transport, looks more bizarre in this fairy-tale film than would an imaginary flying coach. And like Cocteau's poem, the inscription of the helicopter creates a new sense of the magical, tied not to traditional forms of enchantment but to the marvels of modernity.

Through the figure of the Lilac Fairy, not only does Demy create an association with Jean Harlow, but he also implicitly makes reference to an even more modern princess: Grace Kelly. Demy served as "technical consultant for the official film of the marriage of Grace Kelly and Rainier de Monaco," which, importantly, foregrounded the use of helicopters (Taboulay 18–19).[36] Although the helicopters were not used to transport the royal couple, Demy may have drawn on his experience in the making of the short film in his conception of the fictive wedding of the king and the Lilac Fairy. With all of her links to

Figure 2.3. The Lilac Fairy (Delphine Seyrig) and the king (Jean Marais) arrive at the princess's wedding by helicopter.

modern texts and contraptions, the Lilac Fairy represents the future inscribed in the past, constantly reminding the viewer of the gap between our time and the no-time (the timeless past) of the tale represented, which makes evident and as such denaturalizes the artifice of the filmic medium.

As already suggested above, important allusions are made throughout the film to the work of Jean Cocteau. Although the blue men and horses from the princess's kingdom and the red ones from the prince's kingdom bring to mind the "horse of a different color" from *The Wizard of Oz*'s Emerald City, these colored men also recall in their statuesque postures the living statues of Cocteau's *Beauty and the Beast* and Orphic trilogy.[37] When the prince wanders through the forest after a village banquet, he comes upon a seeing and speaking rose, who leads him to the princess's cottage (Figure 2.4). As in *Beauty and the Beast*, the rose announces or makes happen the coupling of the two main characters. At the center of the rose we alternately see an eye or a mouth, as the rose gazes at and speaks to the prince. The feminine mouth recalls the one from Cocteau's *The Blood of a Poet* incorporated into the center of the painter's hand (Figure 2.5). Dressed in red and moving through green flora, the prince himself looks like a rose in the woods. Given the princess's beastly appearance and desire, the princess arguably plays the role of Beast in Demy's film, and the prince, through his association with the rose, that of Beauty.

In both Cocteau and Demy, dichotomies such as nature/culture, past/present, animate/inanimate, human/animal, human/plant, and feminine/masculine are problematized through such incongruous juxtapositions. They function to denaturalize conventional perceptions of "reality," including sexuality. Challenging such oppositions constitutive of the sociosexual order of postwar France functions in such a way as to undermine the logic of gender that underpins it. This is highlighted in particular in the scene in which the princess carries out the order of baking the lovesick prince a cake.

In Perrault and in the apocryphal version of "Donkey Skin," the princess bakes the cake in "a beautiful bodice of bright silver, with a skirt to match" (*Complete Fairy Tales* 225). Demy exaggerates this image by having his heroine wear her extravagant sun-colored gown as she sinks her hands into flour and kneads the dough, thus superposing woman-as-beauty onto woman-as-domesticity (Figure 2.6). Demy further foregrounds the incompatibilities of the traditional gender roles women were supposed to embody by juxtaposing the beautiful princess to her thoroughly domestic alter ego Donkey Skin, who reads the princess the recipe for the "love cake," sweeps the floors of the cottage, and makes the bed (Figure 2.7). The scene consists of a doubling of contrasts, with the image of the elegant princess baking (doing domestic work), on

Figure 2.4. In *Donkey Skin*, the prince (Jacques Perrin) comes upon a speaking and seeing rose.

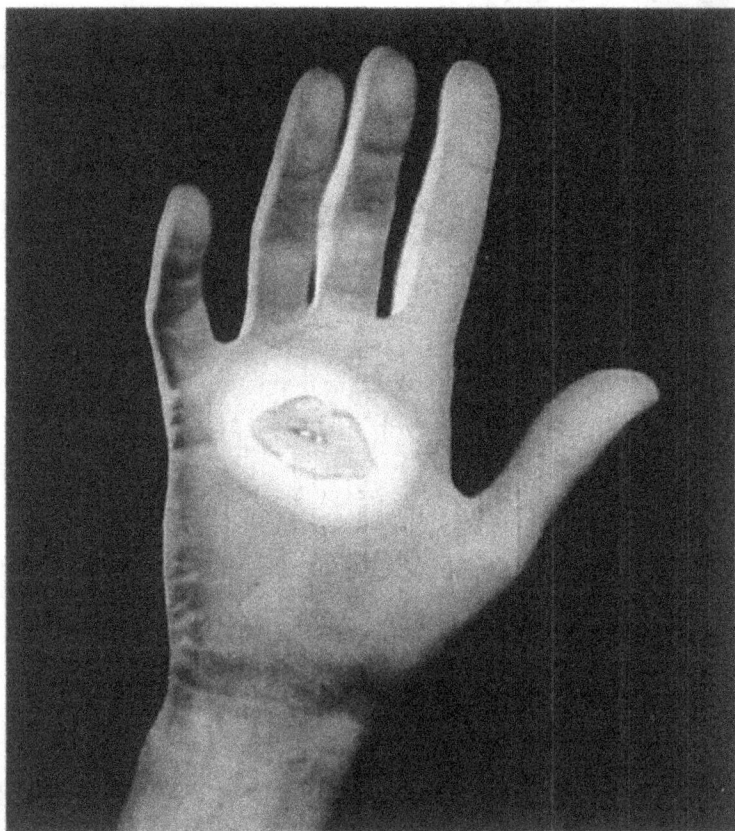

Figure 2.5. A mouth appears on the hand of the Poet, played by Enrique Rivero, in *Blood of a Poet*.

the one hand, and the refined princess opposed to her domestic and animal-like double, on the other.

Kristen Ross has argued that after World War II, when France's colonial empire was collapsing in the 1950s and 1960s, a new emphasis was placed on domesticity and the political economy of the household, whose "cleanliness" was to support a new distinction between France and the colonies, symbolizing France's move toward modernity. She explains, "An efficient, well-run harmonious home is a national asset: the quality of the domestic environment has a major influence on the physique and health of the nation. A chain of equivalences is at work here; the prevailing logic runs something like this: If the woman is clean, the family is clean. If the French woman is dirty, then France is dirty and backward" (Ross 78).

Such an ideology of domesticity was not foreign to American culture in general and Walt Disney in particular. This is evident in the modifications Disney made to "Snow White" by the Brothers Grimm to produce his first feature-length animated film in 1937. Even more than his nineteenth-century precursors, Disney foregrounds in his version of *Snow White* notions of domesticity and the nuclear family. For instance, Disney transforms his Snow White into a scullery maid and has her dress in rags, which, as M. Thomas Inge suggests, is an image borrowed from "Cinderella" (136). Inge furthermore insists that "allegiance to the home and family" was an important value instilled in this

Figure 2.6. The princess (Catherine Deneuve) bakes the prince a cake in her dress that is the color of the sun.

Figure 2.7. The princess's double, Donkey Skin (Catherine Deneuve) reads the recipe to the princess and sweeps the cottage while the princess bakes a cake.

and other Disney films (140). Like the emerging ideology of domesticity in France, which cannot be separated from modernization-as-Americanization, the "Disney Doctrine" valorized "the nuclear family, with its attendant rituals of marriage, parenthood, emotional and spiritual instruction, and consumption" (Watts 326). Disney's Snow White incarnates the modern mother, preoccupied not only by the cleanliness of the home but also by the personal hygiene of her "seven little children," the dwarfs.[38]

We might therefore read the scene in which the princess bakes a cake for the prince as a parody or camp version of the cleaning scene in Disney's *Snow White*. In an interview for *Télérama*, Demy explicitly states, "When I wrote the scene where we see Donkey Skin kneading the dough and singing the song of the love cake, I saw Snow White, assisted by birds, preparing a pie."[39] However, Demy's juxtaposition of the princess with her beastly double, along with the incongruity of the image of the princess baking a cake in a formal, elaborate, and cumbersome dress, renders the scene rather ridiculous—or foregrounds what can already be read as camp in the Disney film, whose depiction of domesticity itself borders on parody.

Demy playfully highlights the incompatibilities and tensions between the two principal functions of women in bourgeois society: woman-as-spectacle or object of desire (woman as exchange value) and woman-as-domestic-worker (or woman as use value).[40] The scene, furthermore, plays on representations of woman as ethereal beauty, perfectly incarnated by Catherine Deneuve as the princess, which contrasts with the representation of woman as animal, represented by the princess's double, Donkey Skin. This mixing of low and high, animal and human, ironically could be said to render "unclean" (in Beaver's sense of the word) this scene of domesticity. As is the case in the other scenes of the film, incongruity undermines bourgeois heteronormative order through its denaturalization.

SELF-AS-SPECTACLE

In her celebrated "Notes on Camp," Susan Sontag chooses an apt quote from Oscar Wilde to characterize camp aestheticism as it manifests itself in the individual subject: "One should either be a work of art, or wear a work of art."[41] This statement implies that the self becomes spectacle, set before "the public gaze," to borrow the language from the Oxford English Dictionary, "as an object either (a) of curiosity or contempt, or (b) of marvel or admiration." In *Donkey Skin*, Demy makes his characters into so many objects of contempt, in the case of the scullion Donkey Skin, and, more often, of marvel or admiration who display themselves as works of art. The mirror plays an instrumental role in the construction of the self-as-spectacle, not only in its function as a support for the making of the self into a work of art but also in its ability to aestheticize the objects reflected in it. As Dyer explains, "Mirrors aestheticise because they frame sections of reality and render them on a shimmering, one-dimensional surface: they make reality into beautiful pictures" (66). One cannot speak of spectacle and mirrors without considering the different functions of the gaze. Demy constantly stages the narcissistic gaze of the self contemplating its mirror image and the voyeuristic gaze of the Other, neither of which marks a stable object or subject position in the film, as we shall see. Like the dandy, Demy's female characters in particular mark a site where narcissism, exhibitionism, and voyeurism intersect in complicated ways.

To some degree Demy contextualizes Perrault's tale by integrating into his film elements taken from the time of the court society of Louis XIV, the period in which the fairy tale emerged as a literary trend, referred to as the fairy-tale vogue of the 1690s.[42] *Donkey Skin* makes mention of such worldly seventeenth-century figures as la princesse Pioche de la Vergne, an allusion to the novelist Madame de Lafayette (who was actually a countess); "la Clève," a reference to the heroine of Lafayette's celebrated novel *La Princesse de Clèves* (1678); la marquise Marie de Rabutin Chantal, or the renowned epistolary writer Madame de Sévigné; and la comtesse d'Escarbagnasse, the title character of a play by Molière. Even "la Segur," or la comtesse de Ségur, the famous nineteenth-century writer of children's tales, has a place in Demy's pantheon of aristocratic divas.

None of these references are present in Perrault's original tale or in the later apocryphal version. In *Donkey Skin* and later in *Lady Oscar*—situated at the court of Louis XVI—Demy demonstrates at least an aesthetic appreciation for seventeenth- and eighteenth-century aristocratic culture, which can be characterized in terms of performance (at court or in salon circles) and self-fashioning. Antoine Watteau's "L'Enseigne de Gersaint" ("The Shop Sign of Gersaint," 1720–21), for instance, epitomizes the early modern notion of "aristocratic figures as aesthetic objects." Surrounded by elegant portraits, three aristocratic patrons gaze at themselves in a mirror as they examine "the materials that will enhance their beauty: brushes for grooming their hair and boxes to contain the powders, perfumes, or jewels that serve to adorn them" (Vidal 188). Gersaint's shop provides the props that support aristocratic performance. In *The Aristocrat as Art* (1980) Domna Stanton traced affinities between the *honnête homme* of Louis XIV's court and the more rebellious dandy of post-Revolution France, who, like his early modern antecedent, valued performance and self-fashioning.

In an early modern culture preoccupied by the self-as-art, it should come as no surprise that mirrors played an important supporting role. Unlike Perrault, the apologist for domesticity, Perrault's contemporary Marie-Catherine d'Aulnoy celebrated the aristocratic culture of her period in her works.[43] In several of her tales, including "La Belle aux cheveux d'or" ("Beauty with the Golden Hair"), "L'Oiseau bleu" ("The Bluebird"), "Le Prince Lutin," "Le Mouton" ("The Ram"), "Babiole," and "Le Nain jaune" ("The Yellow Dwarf"), characters admire themselves—or deplore their magical disfigurements—in mirrors. Beauty with the Golden Hair adjusts herself and approves her appearance in her hall of mirrors before meeting Avenant; the princess Florine is amused by magical mirrors in which women and men gaze at themselves, for these mirrors have the power to depict people as they wish to be, not as they are; the Prince Lutin gazes at his own image in a mirror in order to draw his portrait for the princess, as he doubly turns himself into art through the frame of the mirror and the reproduction of his mirror image on canvas; and when the monkey Babiole is transformed into the beautiful princess she really is, she revels in the beauty of her own image. D'Aulnoy's interest in mirrors resides in their status as fashionable luxury items, as a prop in the construction of the self, and in their function of celebrating the superficial, external, and powerful beauty of worldly, aristocratic women and men.

Whether or not Demy was familiar with d'Aulnoy's tales, he shares with this seventeenth-century *conteuse* the preoccupation with characters whose self has become spectacle—for others as well as for the characters themselves.[44] The mirror symbolizes the celebration of superficiality and appearances, or what Christine Jones calls an "aesthetic of frivolity" ("Poetics" 71).[45] When the film's princess goes to see her fairy godmother about the serious issue of her father wanting to marry her, the Lilac Fairy reprimands her for having interrupted her toilette, or the preparation of her self-as-spectacle: she is not yet ready to be seen, even by her goddaughter the princess. The fairy exclaims, "You, at this hour! You know how I abhor it when I'm surprised like this. I'm not ready yet!"[46] The princess begins to cry, and in an effort to console her, the Lilac Fairy tells her, "Don't cry, my child. Tears ruin the face and make it look gaunt." Appearances must be maintained, and she tells the princess she needs another minute to complete her toilette, looks at herself in the mirror, and declares, "Frankly yellow isn't very becoming on me." She changes into a lilac dress and looks at herself in the mirror again, saying, "Yes, that's better" as she primps her hair.[47]

In his representation of the Lilac Fairy's coquettishness, Demy may in fact have been drawing from Vanderburch's fairy-tale extravaganza. In the 1838 version, Lilia seeks out the fairy to help her find her father, whom Medinazil has taken away to punish for his overindulgence. The fairy replies, "Did you think about it? In this négligé! . . . I was still resting when your cries of distress troubled my sleep . . . my hair is such a mess . . . I have to get ready."[48] In the 1863 version, at the same point in the féerie, the fairy counsels Lilia, "My dear Lilia, keep this in mind: whatever grief a woman might have, she must never neglect her appearance. . . . First one must make oneself up, and then one can cry, and not too much. Nothing dulls the luster of one's eyes like tears."[49] The proximity of the dialogue between féerie and film and the fairy's and princess's preoccupation with their image would suggest that Demy indeed was familiar with the fairy-tale extravaganza. Unlike the stage version, however, which punishes princess and fairy alike for their coquetry, Demy values their artistry.

Although he draws from the féerie, Demy plays down the seriousness of incest present in Perrault's tale by focusing on the frivolity of the Lilac Fairy, who will not listen to the princess until after she has finished her toilette. Demy's representation of this scene weighs the apparently superficial toilette more heavily than the apparently serious question of incest. The construction of the self must take precedence over all other matters. As such, the Lilac Fairy embodies Oscar Wilde's aphorism: "In all unimportant matters, style, not sincerity, is the essential. In all important matters, style, not sincerity, is the essential" (Miscellanies 176).

Like her fairy godmother, the princess is associated with mirrors. As in Perrault's tale, the princess asks her father for three dresses in order to postpone the wedding. The first dress is "couleur du temps," or color of the sky; the second "couleur de la lune," or color of the moon; and the third dress is "couleur du soleil," or color of the sun. With the donning of each dress, each of which truly is a work of art, the princess gazes at her image in a mirror and is gazed upon. Even her transformation into the scullion Donkey Skin does not occur without the mediation of a mirror: it is before a mirror that she deplores her transformation. When she first occupies the lowly cottage as Donkey Skin, the princess uses her magic wand to give herself a bed, a chair, a table, a chest, and, of course, a mirror, thus re-creating for herself the proper setting for the performative self. She then begins to sing, "Love, love, I love you so" while looking at herself in the mirror.[50] Like Belle's mirror in Jean Cocteau's *Beauty and the Beast*, the mirror allows the princess to see the reaction of her father to her departure. At the same time, it emphasizes the princess's relation to her own image.

In the next scene, Donkey Skin runs into the woods and, like Narcissus, fixes upon her image reflected in a pond. The scene makes reference to Albert Capellani's 1908 film, in which Donkey Skin also contemplates her image in a pond as she tends sheep, and it further recalls Cocteau's *Orpheus,* in which Jean Marais's character similarly gazes at his image reflected in a large puddle. Significantly, in 1968, two years before the premiere of *Donkey Skin, Look,* one of the most important American magazines of photojournalism after *Life,* featured Catherine Deneuve on the cover, with the heading "She just might be the world's most beautiful woman."[51] Demy was known for playing on the "real-life" images of his actors, and here he exploits Deneuve's worldwide reputation in his choice to have her play the singularly beautiful princess. In addition, his use of mirrors clearly references the films of Cocteau, who equated "mirrors, narcissism and homosexuality" in almost all of his works (Dyer 67).

The mirror both serves as the support for and the glorification of the self-as-art and functions as a site of conflict. For instance, in the very first image we see of the Lilac Fairy, she sits before her mirror casually filing her nails. However, the viewer sees the reflection of the princess in the mirror, not that of the fairy. Later, when the Lilac Fairy becomes fully aware of the princess's charms upon her father, the older woman mentions that her own charms are weakening like a battery. The mirror reflecting back the princess's image and not that of the fairy recalls the mirror in Disney's *Snow White,* which informs the wicked stepmother that she no longer is the fairest one of all but that Snow White now has this honor. The connection to the stepmother in *Snow White* is further emphasized by the Lilac Fairy's fanlike collar and color scheme.[52] In the final wedding scene the princess wears a similarly styled collar, perhaps suggesting that in the conventional order of things into which the princess has entered upon renouncing her incestuous desire, she inevitably will be challenged by younger women as her own charms diminish.

Like Charles Baudelaire's dandy, Demy's princess and Lilac Fairy appear to "live and sleep before a mirror."[53] The Lilac Fairy and the princess make extensive uses of mirrors in their self-conscious fashioning of their respective selves, which they present to others as well as to themselves as works of art. As such, we might consider these characters to be female dandies.[54] As in the case of the male dandy, both characters remain desiring subjects even as they are presented as objets d'art.

This is perhaps best demonstrated in the scene in which the prince first sees the princess. In Perrault, when Donkey Skin returns to her humble cottage, she regularly puts on the elegant gowns given to her by her father. One day, the prince is hunting and comes across Donkey Skin's cottage. He gazes at her beauty and falls ill with love, but she does not see him, or at least this remains unclear. In Demy, the dreamy, fairy-believing prince wanders through the forest, and when he comes upon Donkey Skin's cottage, he is not at liberty to choose the position from which he can look upon her. An invisible wall obstructs his access to the cottage and limits his visual scope (Figure 2.8). The shot references Cocteau: it strikingly resembles the scene from *Orpheus* in which we see the title character from behind the mirror as he tries to find a way to go through it (Figure 2.9). Blocked by the invisible wall, Demy's prince is forced to climb up a lean-to and contemplate the princess from a specific window, which only gives him limited access to her—her back is turned toward his position. The princess, however, has a perfect view of the prince through her handheld mirror.

It is as if the princess set up the spectacle of herself to make the prince fall in love with her and to gaze upon him, which leads the viewer to wonder if she has a few fairy powers of her own. The distinctions between narcissism, voyeurism, and exhibitionism get blurred in this scene, for the princess gazes at herself and at the prince and knowingly makes herself the object of his gaze.[55] Just as camp aesthetics disturb such dichotomies as nature/culture, feminine/ masculine, animal/human, so the camp gaze destabilizes the opposition between subject and object, self and Other by simultaneously making oneself into spectacle while desiring oneself and the Other. Earlier in the film the princess expresses her intention to meet the prince, and it is her desire to see him that leads her to control his positioning. By controlling his gaze, she is the one in a position of power, not the prince. It is the princess who plays the role of predator or hunter, setting the trap for her prey. As the forest-dwelling beast, Donkey Skin thus recalls the wolf of "Little Red Riding Hood," with the prince dressed in red playing the title role.

Figure 2.8. The prince is prevented from looking into the lower window of the princess's cottage by an invisible wall.

Figure 2.9. In *Orpheus* Jean Marais attempts to go through a mirror.

In effect, the Lilac Fairy and the princess revel in their own images while also working at making themselves the object of desire for an Other whom they themselves desire (or whom they desire because their true object of desire has been prohibited).[56] They are connected to the dandy through what Sima Godfrey refers to as the dandy's "self-conscious celebration of style and personal elegance" (23) and, relatedly, through the self-as-spectacle (for oneself as much as for others). Their image is a powerful one, for although they appear to be caught up in frivolous matters, they exercise an uncanny power over men and their world. By waving a magic wand, they are able to turn a forest into a boudoir and a humble cottage into the chambers of a princess, thus transcending the limits and constraints of a sometimes harsh reality to create the props and contexts necessary for their aesthetic performances.

Nine years after the premiere of *Donkey Skin*, Demy drew from his construction of the princess and the Lilac Fairy to develop his version of the character of Marie Antoinette in *Lady Oscar*. Like the female characters from *Donkey Skin*, Marie Antoinette represents a figuration of the self-as-spectacle, both being and wearing works of art. As in the case with the Lilac Fairy, the first image we have of Marie Antoinette is before her mirror, with the royal coiffeur sculpting her hair and integrating a silver replica of a ship into its folds. Like *Donkey Skin*'s princess, Marie Antoinette receives three extravagant dresses, each one a breathtaking piece corresponding to natural phenomena: the first dress is referred to as "the pounding of the restless heart," the second dress as "spring's first blossom," and the third as "sunset's silent song." And like *Donkey Skin*'s princess, Marie Antoinette marks a site where narcissism, voyeurism, and exhibitionism intersect: while she gazes at her own image, the count Fersen gazes up at her apartment. Then Marie Antoinette, Lady Oscar, and Madame de Polignac all return the gaze, admiring Fersen's beauty. The queen is both object of the Other's gaze and desiring agent gazing at the Other.

The notion of Marie Antoinette as art and as spectacle is reiterated in several other scenes. Marie Antoinette as object of beauty is foregrounded when the character Elisabeth-Louise Vigée Le Brun paints her famous portrait of Marie Antoinette. In the scene in which Marie Antoinette is on a swing, it appears as if she emerged right out of Jean Honoré Fragonard's 1767 painting "L'Escarpolette" ("The Swing"). Marie Antoinette is associated with theatricality when she incarnates Rosine from Pierre-Augustin Caron de Beaumarchais's *Le Barbier de Seville* (*The Barber of Seville*, 1773) in the theater she has constructed at Le Petit Trianon. Unlike at Versailles, however, where Marie Antoinette is constrained by court etiquette and the gaze of scheming courtiers and ministers whom she distrusts, at Trianon—much like at Donkey Skin's cottage—it is Marie Antoinette who can masterfully control the gaze of the Other, in part by choosing those who can look upon her.

Marie Antoinette is not only a work of art but also a creator and admirer of it. She works with her architect to design the Petit Trianon hamlet. The marvelous nature of the hamlet is exemplified in the following exchange with her architect:

> MARIE ANTOINETTE: The dung heaps! They won't smell, will they?
>
> ARCHITECT: Of course not, your majesty.
>
> MARIE ANTOINETTE: Good. I'd rather nothing smelled . . . and I'd prefer that none of the peasants be old. The milkmaids should have rosy cheeks.

In the same manner that Madame d'Aulnoy populated her utopian "Island of Felicity" with young and beautiful nymphs, Marie Antoinette makes her hamlet into a pastoral utopia inhabited by young and beautiful peasants, with the budget of the French Crown fulfilling the role of magic wand.[57] Demy interestingly paints a sympathetic picture of Marie Antoinette, even though he is quite critical of the abuses of the aristocracy in the film. Although the film implicitly condemns Marie Antoinette's total blindness to the state of France and of actual peasants, Demy appreciates Marie Antoinette the work of art and the artist, who, stifled by life at court, creates her own little paradise, of which she says, "I could sit here forever looking at beauty."

That Demy endowed his Marie Antoinette with specific qualities borrowed from the princess and the Lilac Fairy emphasizes his preoccupation with the self-as-art. The Lilac Fairy, the princess, and Marie Antoinette are all beauties who admire beauty, including their own. The mirror in particular and dandy ways in general aestheticize these characters, who function simultaneously as objects and as agents of desire. Mirrors as well as dandyism come together in the figure of Narcissus, a figure often deployed in the works of queer artists, from Oscar Wilde's version of the myth in "The Disciple" and André Gide's *Traité du Narcisse* (*Treaty of Narcissus*, 1891) to the work of Demy's artistic mentor, Jean Cocteau, himself often listed among the ranks of modern dandies.[58] Through such characters Demy inscribes himself in a genealogy of queer artists who appropriated the problematic association of Narcissus with homosexuality to celebrate a self viewed as socially and sexually aberrant by bourgeois society.[59]

We might read Demy's representation of these three female figures as a form of "diva worship," which, according to Brett Farmer, is part of the "reparative" survivalist dynamics of queer culture (167). By this Farmer refers to the investment the queer subject makes in a cultural text or object, bestowing it "with almost talismanic properties to repair or make good a damaged *socius* [or social bond]" (168). Diva worship is a way for the stigmatized subject, through identification with the diva, to feel believed and adored, performing, in Farmer's words, "the transcendence of a limiting heteronormative materiality and the sublime reconstruction, at least in fantasy, of a more capacious, kinder, queerer world" (170). Whether we think of the ostracized Donkey Skin embellishing her simple cottage or Marie Antoinette creating her fantasy world of Le Petit Trianon to overcome constraints at court, Demy's fairy-tale films indeed perform such transcendence. Much like the *conteuses* of the 1690s, Demy invents fairy characters who delight in pleasure and beauty in utopian worlds, transcending the limits of gender and sexuality imposed by their respective societies.

In one interview that took place during the period of *Donkey Skin*'s release, Demy insisted that France "is a very closed, self-censuring country with old structures, where a film like *Trash* [1970] by Paul Morrissey [film director associated with Andy Warhol] is finally unthinkable. . . . If in Warhol's film, actors are admirable in their improvisation, it's because they know each other, I mean biblically as well, and that permits them to move out of themselves, to overcome their sense of modesty and their shame."[60] That Demy cites such an icon of camp cinema in conjunction with his film *Donkey Skin* is significant.[61] Despite Demy's apparently naïve statement cited earlier about the film simply representing a daughter's love of her father, here Demy indeed situates his film within a larger cinematic movement that challenged not only traditional aesthetic standards but also heterosexual norms. Fascinating him ever since his youth, Demy effectively deployed the classical tale as a vehicle for questioning heteronormative forms of sexuality in the tradition of gay writers and filmmakers, most notably Jean Cocteau, using incest as a trope to explore alternative sexualities.

Demy's camping of Perrault's tale involves both foregrounding what could already be read as camp in the tale—teasing out potentially subversive elements already present in the classical version—and investing the tale with camp signs. Such narrative and cinematic strategies work in such a way as to, first, destabilize oppositions such as nature/culture, animal/human, woman/man and, second, denaturalize our perceptions of "reality," (hetero)sexuality, and gender. In fact, through its visual and temporal incongruities, Demy's film denaturalizes the tale itself, a tale that in written form has enjoyed popularity among French children and adults even up to the present but whose lack of cinematic representations hints at its problematic nature. A tale penned by Perrault that reinforced, however disturbingly, patriarchal and heterosexual norms becomes, under Demy's guidance, a camp film exploring alternative sexualities and gender identities that undermined the sociosexual order of postwar France.

3

Artistic Freedom and Grotesque Satire

Bohemians and Bourgeois in The Pied Piper

It's the end of a scandal. We can finally see in France this delicious film shot four years ago by Jacques Demy, adapted very freely from the legend of "Hans the Flute Player."

—*France-Soir,* February 22, 1975[1]

Persuaded that this beautiful film was not commercial enough, they [French distributors] preferred to postpone the verdict of the public, forgetting at the same time about the popularity of Donovan among the young generation and that of Jacques Demy since *The Umbrellas of Cherbourg.*

—Henry Chapier, *Quotidien de Paris,* November 5, 1976[2]

Released in 1972 in England and in the United States, Jacques Demy's *The Pied Piper* did not make it to France until December 31, 1975. Many film critics lamented the lack of confidence French film distributors showed in Demy's latest film, which was produced by the British duo Sanford Lieberson and David Puttnam. It was not until *The Pied Piper* received a standing ovation at the Festival de Paris in November 1975 that French distributors decided to circulate this film by the celebrated French auteur.[3] Despite such an enthusiastic reception by festival audiences and critics, *The Pied Piper* never achieved the kind of acclaim attained by *Donkey Skin,* and the film has largely been forgotten within French popular culture.

Unlike Charles Perrault's "Donkey Skin," perhaps the story of the pied piper was not familiar enough to French audiences for them to appreciate the film, although the German legend indeed has a history within French folklore and literature. Moreover, the film differs in tone from Demy's earlier films, which constantly move between nostalgia for the provincial city one left to "make it" in Paris and criticism of the malaise of bourgeois life within the closed environment of such cities as Nantes (*Lola*), Cherbourg (*The Umbrellas of Cherbourg*), and Rochefort (*The Young Girls of Rochefort*). In *The Pied Piper*, Demy takes a darker, satirical approach to depict the insular society of Hamelin, whose authority figures repress all forms of freedom of thought, which ultimately leads to the town's demise. There is no nostalgia left for this corrupt and plague-ridden provincial town.

Lacking the popularity of Demy's earlier films, *The Pied Piper* nevertheless represents an important film within Demy's cinematic oeuvre. Although Demy cowrote the screenplay with Andrew Birkin and Mark Peploe, his signature can be seen, first, in the overall structure of the film, whose errant artists recall the traveling carnies of *Les Demoiselles de Rochefort*; second, in the celebration of the artist; and, third, in his critique of stifling social norms and political exigencies that repress creativity and curb his characters' freedom to love and even to live. In his earlier films this critique is rather subtle and includes a focus on sexual mores. In *The Pied Piper*, however, Demy uses black humor to caricature in less than subtle ways the sociopolitical and religious authorities of Hamelin. The film's medieval décor conceals a very modern allegory about the blind obedience to power that results not only in the exploitation of the people and the failure to embrace Otherness but also and quite significantly in mass destruction. Finally, Demy's *The Pied Piper* anticipates his more overtly political films, *Lady Oscar* and *A Room in Town*, in which characters actively participate in effecting change in their respective worlds at the risk of their very lives.

Demy's film also provides a unique perspective on the legend of the pied piper. He draws from a specifically Franco-American tradition, which thus far has not received critical attention, and builds upon it to create a truly 1970s countercultural tale. The German and English traditions of the legend tend to present us with a piper whose nature is somewhat ambivalent. Sometimes associated with the devil, as in Jobus Fincelius's 1556 rendition, sometimes taking on, in the words of the Brothers Grimm, "a terrifying countenance," the piper can even appear to have emerged from a tomb, as in Robert Browning's poem.[4] In the hands of French authors and composers such as Prosper Mérimée, Théophile Gautier, and the team of Maurice Vaucaire, George Mitchell, and Louis Ganne, however, the story of the piper takes on new meaning. Growing out of nineteenth-century Romanticism and the cult of the artist, the legend of the piper gets reshaped to tell the story of the tensions between, on the one hand, the Bohemian artist, associated with love, freedom, and Otherness; and, on the other, the town's bourgeois authorities, who repress everything the artist represents. This French tradition of the piper made its way to the United States, evident in the filmic versions of Walt Disney and Bretaigne Windust, both of whom foreground the exploitation of the people by town authorities in ways that anticipate Demy's rendition of the legend.

Demy's film marks a continuity with French and French-inspired versions of "The Pied Piper" while also taking a much more pessimistic view of the possibility for reconciliation between the ideals of the artist and bourgeois social and political structures. The versions from which Demy draws prove critical of the money-driven culture of the town's burghers but suggest that a market economy can indeed make a place for love and art. Demy exaggerates the parodic representations of town authorities present in earlier versions, depicting them as grotesque in ways that visually recall, as we will see, Alfred Jarry's *Ubu roi*. The only variant of the legend to explicitly associate the Black Death with the story of the infamous rat catcher, Demy's film turns "The Pied Piper" into an allegory about the violence and cruelty of modern, post-WWII society, a violence and cruelty that modern Bohemians—the hippies of the 1960s and 1970s—rejected in hopes of a better world.

Although this chapter does not deal with queerness as defined in the introduction of this book or as discussed in the previous chapters, it does deal with a film by a queer director who is interested in Otherness generally, whether in relation to sexual, social, ethnic, or political Others. Indeed, *The Pied Piper* is unique among Demy's films in that it does not deal much at all with sexuality, although it does take aim at traditional Catholic representations of women, evident in the bishop's misogynous speech during the wedding of the young and innocent Lisa to the baron's malicious son, Franz. It also hints at the possibility of a prelapsarian society freed from sin, which indeed has implications for sexuality. Moreover, the pied piper and the characters associated with him could be characterized as "queer" in the term's connotation of "strange, odd, peculiar, eccentric" (OED). From the perspective of Hamelin's political, social, and religious authorities, these Bohemians indeed appear "queer" or eccentric in their belief systems, creativity, and errant way of life. As such, the piper and his friends represent Otherness within the space of the same; their very existence challenges normative values, which threatens the hegemonic hold town authorities have over the economic, political, and religious spheres of Hamelin. These "queers," or Bohemians, must leave or be extirpated from the body politic, although the actual threat attacking this body, which takes the metaphoric form of the plague, issues from the authorities themselves, who are ultimately responsible for bringing destruction upon their insular world.

The Franco-American Tradition: The Bohemian Piper

As we have seen in the previous chapters, Demy's films often work to subvert or tease out already present subversive elements of classic tales such as "Cinderella," "Sleeping Beauty," "Snow White," and "Donkey Skin." Demy's rendition of "The Pied Piper" builds upon a specifically French tradition of the piper, which tended to question bourgeois mores through the figure of a piper who takes on traits emblematic of the Bohemian. Wolfgang Mieder has carried out seminal work on the origins and history of "The Pied Piper," most notably in *Tradition and Innovation in Folk Literature* (1987) and *The Pied Piper. A Handbook* (2007). Although Mieder covers an extensive amount of terrain, he only very briefly mentions a very small slice of the French tradition of the piper: Charles Marelles's 1888 French rendition of the legend, which was a source for Andrew Lang's version of "The Ratcatcher."[5] Because the French tradition of "The Pied Piper" has not received critical attention and because its history is relevant to Demy's filmic adaptation, I would like to lay out its principal characteristics below.

The first printed version of "The Pied Piper" that appeared in France was published by Prosper Mérimée in 1829.[6] Interpolated into his *Chronique du règne de Charles IX (A Chronicle of the Reign of Charles IX, 1829)*, Mérimée has the beautiful "Bohemian" (here signifying gypsy) Mila, who has come to France from Germany, recount the story of the pied piper to a group of German and French protestant soldiers. Mila's narrative begins with mention of the stained-glass window of Hamelin's Market Church that depicts the piper leading the children away, which the German soldier Fritz also has seen, providing proof of the authenticity of the legend.[7] The legend is further authenticated by Mila's claim that her grandmother, who had supposedly witnessed the events, told her the story. Basically following the standard plot of the legend, except that it is only boys who are lured away, Mérimée introduces two elements not present in earlier versions that will persist in the French tradition of the tale: (1) when the piper begins to play the flute to rid the town of rats, he turns his back to the church; and (2) an old white rat strays and is the last to be drowned in the river.

Moreover, by having Mila recount the legend, Mérimée creates an association between Bohemians and the legend. Initially "Bohemian" was a term used to designate gypsies, whose place of origin was believed to be in Czechoslovakia. In the 1830s, young artists who similarly lived in poverty and enjoyed an errant lifestyle also were dubbed "Bohemians." Associated with Romanticism, Bohemia represented an opposition to classicism as well as to "bourgeois society," which "was also just being formed and defined" (Seigel 5). Jerrold Seigel,

Elizabeth Wilson, and Mary Gluck all emphasize that the Bohemian was "the 'Other' of bourgeois society, that is to say, it expressed everything that the bourgeois order buried and suppressed" (Wilson 240). Emerging at a time when, in Seigel's words, "patronage gave way to the market" (13), the Bohemian is inseparable from the important socioeconomic shifts of post-Revolution France, which led to an oppositional rather than complementary relationship between art and society.[8] The notion of the artist-as-Other is exemplified in the ethnic connotations of the term "Bohemian," and Bohemians such as Théophile Gautier even donned ethnic garb to reinforce their status as Other.[9]

Gautier, who frequented the same circles as Mérimée, drafted a libretto for a ballet based on "The Pied Piper," which would never come to fruition. Just before his death in 1872, Gautier met with Jules Massenet, who was going to compose the music for the ballet, but the project died with the celebrated author.[10] However, Gautier's son-in-law and Massenet's friend, Emile Bergerat, published the libretto in 1879. Gautier transforms the legend into a fairy tale, creating an underground, magical world accessible through a well into which the gypsy-like rat catcher lures all of the young women of Hamelin after the burgomaster refuses to pay him for ridding the city of rats. When the lovers Hermann and Vanda (the burgomaster's daughter) are finally reunited at the end of the ballet, the rat catcher reveals himself to be the prince Udolph, in true fairy-tale style. Although quite different from Mérimée's version, Gautier seems to be familiar with it: the rat catcher turns his back to the church when he begins to play, and an old white rat is the last to plunge into the river. Moreover, Gautier further develops associations between the piper and the Bohemian. Described as being "a character of a singular demeanor, half traveling entertainer, half musician"[11] Gautier's rat catcher bears signs associated with Bohemia: "art, youth, the underworld, the gypsy life-style" (Seigel 3).

Although Gautier's plan to produce a ballet about the pied piper never materialized, there was one important theatrical production based on the legend: the operetta *Hans, le joueur de flûte* (*Hans the Flute Player*, 1906) by composer Louis Ganne, with libretto by Maurice Vaucaire and George Mitchell. In the late nineteenth century, Ganne was a well-known composer who conducted at the Paris Opéra and directed the Louis Ganne orchestra at the Monte Carlo Opéra, a popular venue at the time, where *Hans the Flute Player* premiered.[12] The operetta attained such acclaim that Oscar Hammerstein, grandfather of the famous lyricist, brought it to the Manhattan Opera House in 1910, where it was well received.[13] *Hans the Flute Player* was performed at the Apollo in Paris in 1910 and at the Parisian Gaîté Lyrique in 1928 and 1937. Ganne's operetta remained popular, such that Jacques Demy—born in 1931—was able to see it performed as a child at the Théâtre Graslin in Nantes (Berthomé 261).

Significantly, Ganne was a student of Massenet. One wonders if Ganne was inspired by his teacher's aspirations to set to music the story of the pied piper, and it certainly is possible that Vaucaire and Mitchell consulted Gautier's libretto, given that it had been published in 1879. But comparing the two librettos, it would appear that the only element Vaucaire and Mitchell might have borrowed from Gautier is the love interest and the apparent threat the pied piper seems to present to the lovers, only to better unite them. At the beginning of Gautier's ballet, the burgomaster Pyrkmayer refuses to allow his daughter Vanda to marry Hermann. When Vanda finds herself in the underground world with the other girls of her town, she appears to be pursued by the rat catcher, who tells her he wishes to marry her. But when Hermann jumps into the well to find his Vanda, the rat catcher reveals that he was only testing their love, and the ballet ends with the marriage of Vanda and Hermann.

Vaucaire and Mitchell's rendition of "The Pied Piper" also contains a love interest, which is not found in versions before Gautier. In the operetta, Yoris, the socially marginal artist, is in love with Lisbeth, the daughter of the burgomaster. In a manner similar to Gautier's rat catcher, Hans, the pied piper figure, pretends to claim in this case a simulacrum of Lisbeth—a doll created by the artist Yoris—but only as a ruse to trick the burgomaster into marrying Lisbeth and Yoris.

Demy had a strong interest in *Hans the Flute Player,* which possibly influenced American versions of "The Pied Piper" from which Demy also likely drew. It is therefore worth pausing a moment to lay out in more detail how Vaucaire and Mitchell reshaped the story. Although all versions of "The Pied Piper" concern the avarice of the townspeople in general and the burgomaster in particular, all of whom refuse to pay the rat catcher, in *Hans the Flute Player,* the mentality of the bourgeois town (here a Dutch-Flemish town called Milkatz) is more developed. Vaucaire and Mitchell create a clear opposition between money and commerce, on the one hand, and art and love, on the other; in other words, the operetta very clearly revolves around the opposition between bourgeois and Bohemian.

The first act of the operetta opens with the night watchman waking the town at six in the morning and the townspeople chanting, "Everyone to their shops! / Everyone to work!"[14] Angry with Guillaume, who has failed to show up to open the doors of the town hall (leniency is not granted to Guillaume, who was just married the night before), the burgomaster Pippermann declares to his councilmen, "May I remind you that we have no time to lose. Time is gold! . . . Within a year, we will have cornered, monopolized the world grain market! . . . We amass, Sirs! We pile up! We accumulate!"[15] Petronius, the only councilmember with interests beyond commerce, reminds the other men that today is the festival of Saint Gregorius, which traditionally had been celebrated by artists who presented beautiful dolls that the entire duchy came to admire. Petronius's proposal to reinstate the festival is mocked, as Pippermann complains about useless artists.

In the following scene Yoris the artist enters and is greeted by Pippermann's insults: "Lazy, vagabond! good-for-nothing!"[16] The council even threatens to arrest him. Yoris insists on holding the festival of dolls and decries the council's scorn for art: "Your mercantile administration killed all of these beautiful works. Art is dead! The ideal has taken flight!"[17] Yoris later shows his doll—which Pippermann threatened to break into pieces—to the newlyweds Guillaume and Ketchen, a servant who works for and is mistreated by Madame Pippermann. The doll is a perfect replica of the beautiful Lisbeth, whom Yoris loves but who is engaged to the smug burgher and councilman Van Pott. As Yoris pines away in his hopelessness of ever gaining Lisbeth's love and hand, Hans the flute players appears before him. After telling Hans about his impossible love, Yoris informs the stranger that he is in a city that lacks generosity: the people of Milkatz sell, they do not give. Hans then asks Madame Pippermann for charity, who responds, "Begging is forbidden in the duchy of Milkatz!"[18] Hans, who "come[s] from a land / Where love and art go hand in hand," punishes a town that scorns love and art.[19] He initially plays his flute not to lead the rats away but to drown the cats that protect Milkatz's hoards of grain, after which he releases his mice.

When the town council members approach Yoris to ask the artist to steal Hans's pipe, thinking they will then be able to retake control of the situation, Yoris refuses to betray the piper, for Hans "let me speak of love!"[20] Van Pott and Pippermann then accuse the piper of witchcraft; Pippermann goes further, accusing Yoris of witchcraft through his association with the piper and consequently has the poet–artist imprisoned: "That is witchcraft, and the accomplice of a witch is burned like a bundle of wood!"[21] It is when Van Pott and Pippermann make light of burning Yoris—referring to him as a "roasted rival"—that Lisbeth's love for Yoris is revealed to her father.[22] After a few bungling attempts to outwit Hans, the council ends up calling him back, and Hans agrees to rid the town of mice on three conditions: first, they must release Yoris; second, they must hold the festival of dolls; and, third, Hans will be given the doll of his choice. After a brief misunderstanding between Hans and Yoris, there is a happy ending, with the union of Yoris and Lisbeth, and Hans, the "merchant of ideals," leaves Milkatz to save other lovers.

Hans the Flute Player foregrounds several pressing issues on the minds of politicians and intellectuals of France's Third Republic. As had been the case since the 1830s and 1840s, artists and critics were concerned about the place of the artist in a commercial culture that privileged practical, utilitarian knowledge over art.[23] As we have seen, one form such concerns took was the myth of the Bohemian, which, according to Gluck, had conservative as well as utopian variants. In her discussion of Henry Murger, whose *Scènes de la vie de bohème* (*The Bohemians of the Latin Quarter*, 1855) inspired Giacomo Puccini's *La Bohème* (1896), Gluck identifies one of the dominant trends of this myth: "Murger's bohemian stories had two central themes that were of equal fascination to contemporary audiences: the artist's life as an alternative to bourgeois norms of respectability and conformism; and the artist's calling as a counterpart to modern commercial and professional identities" (16). Whereas representations of Bohemia proved more subversive, Gluck contends, in the hands of Théophile Gautier, Murger's Bohemia only "superficially challenged notions of bourgeois propriety and convention, but on a deeper level it was in essential harmony with the aesthetic values and epistemological categories of middle-class life" (21).

We can place *Hans the Flute Player* within this latter trend, given the fact that the operetta ends with Yoris the artist—who in fact escaped from jail to study math and commerce to please Lisbeth's father—reconciled with the bourgeois community that initially marginalized and condemned him. The operetta raises the question of the place of art and artist within a commercial society, and indeed a place is carved out for both in Milkatz, but only through the magical intervention of Hans. By the end of the operetta, art and bourgeois commercial life are able to coexist. The harmonious ending represents a compromise: Yoris opens himself up to learning about commerce, and the townspeople open themselves up to art.

Hans the Flute Player can be situated in relation to a second issue of equal importance in the 1890s and early 1900s: vagabondage and the related issue of mendicity. With the decline of French agriculture since mid-century and a significant fall in grain prices in the 1890s, many small farmers became destitute and began migrating to wealthier regions. To give a sense of the urgency of the problem, Timothy Smith cites the example of Poitou, which by 1890 had "seven to eight times more beggars . . . than fifty years earlier" (824). Rather than view the problem "as the result of socio-economic crisis," authorities "presented vagabondage as a problem of poor behavior or eugenics" (822). Consequently, vagabondage and mendicity were criminalized as France "engaged in a ruthless crackdown on beggars and vagabonds" (823). Smith notes that "larger French cities now went out of their way to make migrants feel unwelcome, they encouraged migrants to return to their home towns, or they simply expelled them" (835).

Interestingly, at the beginning of the operetta, the artist–Bohemian Yoris is referred to as "lazy" and a "vagabond." Described as an "errant Jew" in the prologue, Hans likewise is associated with vagabondage as well as with mendicity when he asks Madame Pippermann for charity. Both Yoris and Hans are threatened for their actions and for their very beings by the bourgeois council, who wishes to remove them from Milkatz. Given this second context, the opposition between bourgeois and artist might also be viewed in terms of an opposition between grain merchants and the vagabond "have-nots" (or, in Pippermann's words, "good-for-nothings"), viewed as threatening by bourgeois authorities. That they indeed are construed as being a threat is made clear when Lisbeth mentions that her father believes Yoris to be "a dangerous dreamer" (Vaucaire and Mitchell 33). The operetta works to relieve the townspeople's fear of these artistic and social Others: Lisbeth ends up falling in love with Yoris, and the wives of the councilmen learn that Hans is neither a two-horned nor a three-horned devil: in fact, he has no horns at all!

Although "The Pied Piper" by the Brothers Grimm and by Robert Browning have been regular American fare, it is possible that the French tradition informed to some degree American versions of the German legend. In particular, *Hans the Flute Player,* which was a popular operetta in the United States in 1910, may have contributed an important frame to both Walt Disney's *The Pied Piper* (1933) and director Bretaigne Windust's *The Pied Piper of Hamelin* (1957), both of which may have informed Jacques Demy's 1972 film. Ganne's operetta revolves in part around tensions between the imperative to constantly carry out utilitarian work, on the one hand, and the impulse toward art, love, and leisure, on the other. Disney and Windust build upon this underlying opposition to create their own versions of "The Pied Piper" in ways that anticipate Demy's film.

Disney's *The Pied Piper*, directed by Wilfred Jackson, appeared in the series "Silly Symphonies," which often drew from the European folk- and fairy-tale tradition (Allan 27). As one might expect with a Disney film, the violence of the legend is toned down. For instance, rather than drown the rats, this pied piper makes appear a giant piece of Swiss cheese full of holes into which each of the rats plunges; then the piper simply makes the cheese disappear, sparing the rats any suffering. And unlike Browning's poem, in which the lame boy laments the fact that he has been left behind, Disney's film has the boy on crutches makes it to the "joyous land," where his lame foot immediately heals as he throws aside his crutches to run and join the other children.

Three elements in particular point to possible borrowings from the French tradition and specifically from Ganne's operetta. First, when Disney's piper rids the town of rats, there is one rat who strays, but he finally leaps into the cheese and disappears with the other rats. Browning is one of the sources for the Disney short, but Browning's lone rat survives to tell his story. In Méri-mée, whose version is the first to make mention of a trailing rat, the rat joins the others in their terrible fate. Of course, it is possible that Disney modified an element borrowed from Browning or that Disney had read Lang's transla-tion of Marelles's version, which also casts a lagging rat.[24] Second, Disney's *The Pied Piper* is sung in verse; it is itself an operetta of sorts. Although other Silly Symphonies include some singing, they do not share the structure of having a chorus (the townspeople), with two main characters—the pied piper and the burgomaster—singing their lines.[25] Third, as in *Hans the Flute Player,* the town's emphasis on work is criticized, which seems out of place for a Disney film. Whereas Ganne's operetta questions the town's focus on work in general, only hinting at the exploitation of servants such as Ketchen, Disney's film con-demns the townspeople, whom we do not see working, for exploiting their own children, depicted as carrying out grueling, backbreaking chores.

The connections between *Hans the Flute Player* and Disney's *The Pied Piper* may seem tentative, but the structure and themes of Bretaigne Windust's *The Pied Piper of Hamelin* suggest a close affiliation between Ganne's oper-etta and Windust's film. Moreover, the film develops the notion of exploitative work present in Disney's animated short that clearly anticipates Demy's ver-sion of *The Pied Piper.* Although Windust's film initially was created for NBC, airing on November 26, 1957, it was released in theaters in the United States in 1961 and later in West Germany and Venezuela. It also regularly aired on television during holiday seasons, possibly making it accessible to Demy, who went to Los Angeles in November 1967 to film *Model Shop,* which premiered in February 1969 in New York City.

Born in Paris and fluent in French, German, and English, Bretaigne Win-dust "was one of the most successful and celebrated directors on Broadway" in the 1930s and 1940s (Eder). After several Broadway hits, Windust made his way to Hollywood, launching a career in film. *The Pied Piper of Hamelin* was the sixth feature film he directed or codirected, and it starred Van Johnson as Truson and the pied piper and Claude Rains—best known for his role as Cap-tain Louis Renault in *Casablanca* (1942)—as the mayor of Hamelin.

Like *Hans the Flute Player,* Windust's *Pied Piper* is structured around the doubling of the piper character. Yoris and Hans, the piper figure, could be read as doubles, for like the flute player Yoris is associated with witchcraft, both are described as being "errant" or "vagabond," and both defend the causes of art and love. This doubling becomes more obvious in Windust's film, in which Van Johnson plays both Truson—who protests the mayor's policy of mak-ing the entire town, including the children, slave away to build an exquisite clock tower—and the pied piper—who, like Truson, is an advocate of children, beauty, and love. As in the case of Yoris, Truson is imprisoned on trumped-up charges for his relationship to the piper as well as for his love of the burgomaster's daughter Mara.

After the opening scene, in which we see a man (the pied piper) sliding down a tree like a snake performing beautiful feats of magic, we are quickly introduced to Paul, a lame child, and his adult friend Truson. Then the camera moves to shoot a group of children gathering straw, women working in mud, and men making and laying bricks. The mayor of Hamelin and his council have forced the entire town to work to build a spectacular clock tower, which they hope will bring the town prestige; the king's emissary is visiting the town shortly, and the mayor hopes their town will be rewarded with the king's banner. A representative from the neighboring town of Hamelot—a competitor for the king's favor—requests Hamelin's assistance when their town is flooded by the River Weser. The mayor and his council cynically agree to assist the people of Hamelot: they will help by sending their regrets. Hamelot destroyed, the rats of Hamelot invade Hamelin, to the mayor's and townspeople's despair. Then appears the pied piper, who agrees to rid the town of rats for 50,000 guilders, just the amount the mayor has saved to make the bells for the clock tower. As the legend goes, the mayor refuses payment, and the children are led away to a land that in fact resembles the joyous land in Disney's short. As in Browning's rendition of the legend, however, Windust's lame boy does not make it into the mountain cavern with the rest of the children. In the spirit of *Hans the Flute Player*, Windust's film maintains the opposition between work and greed, on the one hand, and play, love, and beauty, on the other.

As previously noted, several versions of "The Pied Piper," especially within the German tradition, depict the rat catcher as an ambivalent character. However, from Gautier and Ganne to Disney and Windust, any assertions that the piper is evil or terrifying prove to be ruses on the part of town authorities to discredit the piper and his claims against the town and its council. By the end of the spectacle, the piper proves to be an unambiguously good fellow. In each of these versions, the piper (and sometimes his double) reveals himself to be the champion of children and lovers alike, who protects beauty and love from the gluttonous, avaricious hands of a corrupt city government. In all four of these versions of the legend, there is some kind of reconciliation: the story does not end as badly as in Fincelius or the Grimms. In Gautier and Windust, the girls/children are returned to the town, whereas in Ganne they are never taken away. Although Disney's children are not returned home, it all seems for the best, given their apparent exploitation by adults and the wonderful land they will inhabit. In Gautier, Ganne, and Windust, a love interest shapes the plot as the story moves from a serious of oppositions—between piper/his double and town council, between art and commerce, between play and work—that are resolved in the end, with the union of the couple representing the synthesis of apparent opposites. Bohemian and bourgeois reconcile as the town accepts the artistic Other within its market-driven public space.

Demy's Revision of "The Pied Piper"

Drawing from the Franco-American tradition outlined above, in which the pied piper is associated with art, love, and the social Other, Demy likewise depicts the piper from the very beginning of his film in an explicitly positive light. Demy incorporates a love interest, and he plays on the opposition between bourgeois and Bohemian, between the town council's greed and the generosity of lovers of art and knowledge. However, Demy's film presents a more jaded view of power, evident in his grotesque representations of figures of authority. In his Hamelin, the insular townspeople never overcome their fears of the Other. Performing the function of the piper's double, the Jewish alchemist Melius—like Yoris and Truson—represents the internal Other, the voice of reason coming from a marginalized member of the town, who is scapegoated for his opposition to city authorities. Yet whereas the town council never makes good on its threat to burn or hang Yoris or Truson, Demy's municipal, political, and religious authorities have Melius burned at the stake at the end of the film. In Demy, there is no possibility for the social or ethnic Other to be reintegrated into the social body, which is so corrupt it ends up bringing about its own demise. As one might thus expect, the characters fulfilling the function of the lovers are never united; there is no resolution of the underlying conflicts.

The film opens with the ambulant actors Matteo and his family traveling across Germany; they are later joined by a pilgrim and the pied piper, played by the pop music star Donovan, whom they picked up along the way. These vagabond types make their way to Hamelin, which has completely closed itself off from the rest of Germany in order to protect itself from the Black Death. Although the plague poses a potential threat to the city, the true menaces to Hamelin include the burgomaster Poppendick, a social climber who sells his daughter off to improve his own social standing; the baron, so obsessed with his own personal salvation that he spends all of his wealth and resources on building a cathedral instead of fighting the plague; and an unscrupulous and superstitious clergy, who condemn the Jewish alchemist Melius for believing the plague has natural causes and is not a punishment sent from God. Although Demy complicates the opposition between Bohemian and bourgeois, given the tripartite structure of medieval society, his burghers, nobles, and clergymen come together in their exploitation of the people and the persecution of Otherness, all for personal financial and social gain. The tale ends tragically when the authorities of Hamelin, out of self-interest and social prejudice, refuse to pay the man who rid the city of rats and burn at the stake Melius, who nearly found a cure for the plague. In Demy's *Pied Piper*, the plague becomes a metaphor for the ills of Hamelin society. In the end, it is not the rats or bubonic plague that destroy the town but the people themselves.

GROTESQUE AUTHORITIES

Inspired by Ingmar Bergman's *The Seventh Seal* (1957), Demy introduces into his version of the legend a plague narrative, often hinted at in late medieval versions of "The Pied Piper" but never directly referred to.[26] By integrating the Black Death into his adaptation, Demy can emphasize the tragic consequences of the decisions of Hamelin authority figures: their combined actions help bring about the film's apocalyptic conclusion. In effect, Demy draws from the caricatures of town authorities present in Ganne, Disney, and Windust and renders them more dangerous, more troubling, and—given the context of the plague—more grotesque.

Theorists from Wolfgang Kayser and Geoffrey Harpham to Mikhail Bakhtin have attempted to delimit the notion of the grotesque, an unstable concept indeed.[27] For my purposes, I would like to foreground what I think is pertinent to Demy's representation of Hamelin's authority figures. Harpham notes that "grotesque forms are material analogues or expressions of spiritual corruption or weakness" (*Grotesque* 6). In essence, they mark the sinful nature of humanity after the Fall, in the spirit of, for instance, Hieronymus Bosch. This notion of the grotesque intersects with Bakhtin's concept of the grotesque body, characterized by excess, a body that continually moves beyond its own confines, that "swallows the world and is itself swallowed by the world" (317). Among other bodily functions to be associated with the grotesque body, Bakhtin mentions eating and, in particular, the "gaping mouth [which] is related to the image of swallowing, this most ancient symbol of death and destruction" (325). Whereas Bakhtin emphasizes the creative or productive forces of the grotesque, through his *Pied Piper*, Demy focuses on its destructive, darker side.

The grotesque functions at the level of the body or the microcosm as well as at the macrocosmic level, as Bakhtin's comments would suggest. Just as grotesque representations of the body highlight the body's disordered or chaotic form due to its protrusions and tenuous boundaries between inside and outside, so grotesque representations of the body politic depict it, in Harpham's words, as "falling apart," evident in common grotesque themes such as the plague and the Apocalypse ("Grotesque" 462, 467). In his discussion of the modern grotesque, John Clark similarly suggests that the grotesque concerns "a universe gone awry" (23), in which "unworldly upheavals and transformations and near lunatic disarray threaten to overturn the bourgeoisie's own world of sanitary and sanctimonious normalcy" (25). These two levels of the grotesque—the grotesque body and the grotesque body politic—come together in Demy's film to characterize Hamelin's authority figures and their destructive effect on the town.

Demy wanted his film to be realistic in its depiction of the Middle Ages, evident in the ways he used color in the film. As opposed to the saturated colors of *The Umbrellas of Cherbourg*, *The Pied Piper*'s tones are more naturalistic and earthy. However, Demy's representations of Hamelin's authority figures are not entirely faithful to mid-fourteenth-century style.[28] For instance, the horned headpiece the burgomaster's wife Frau Poppendick wears to her daughter's wedding exaggerates what was actually more of a fifteenth-century style (Figure 3.1). Given Frau Poppendick's unrestrained desire for her daughter's future husband Franz, we could view her red horns as a manifestation of her barely controlled sexual impulses pushing forth out of her body and into the world. The horns mark her excessive sexuality, which seeks to "devour" what is not hers: her future son-in-law, who will gladly comply. Signaling her diabolical nature and the fact that she is and will continue to make a cuckold of her husband, her headpiece functions in such a way as to render her body grotesque. Although Demy supports subversive forms of desire elsewhere, here we might understand his use of traditional medieval and Catholic misogynistic symbolism as a means to exaggerate Frau Poppendick's unscrupulous behavior toward her daughter in particular, whom she is willing to sell off to her own lover, and toward her servants in general, whom she continually mistreats, much as Madame Pippermann does in Ganne's operetta.

The baron's costume throughout the film and that of the burgomaster at his daughter's wedding recall the grotesque image of King Ubu from Alfred Jarry's eponymous play of 1896, and they share a similar function. For his revolutionary fin-de-siècle play, Jarry adapted Shakespeare's *Macbeth* to the modernist age and the symbolist stage in such a way as to transform the tragedy into a black or grotesque comedy that takes all glory and dignity away from the pursuit of power. As Maria Delaperrière explains, "Jarry wrote a sort of canvas where tyranny was seized in its pure state, so to say, in its terrifying monstrosity—so terrifying that one can only react with bursts of laughter.... [The use of] derision, the grotesque, and triviality revealed power at its lowest and most absurd."[29] Significantly, the iconic Ubu is round with a phallic headpiece (Figure 3.2). Such protrusions pushing their way outside of Ubu's

Figure 3.1. Frau Poppendick (Diana Dors) dresses for her daughter's wedding.

body signify his insatiable appetite for food and domination, and the pairing of the two serves to trivialize yet depict as quite unsettling Ubu's will to power. The simplicity and vulgarity with which Jarry represents King Ubu denies him an interiority—a troubled conscience, a complicated psychology—that might lead to audience identification and a level of sympathy, which one can experience while watching *Macbeth*. Jarry's grotesque caricature serves instead to underscore the monstrous and absurd nature of dictatorial violence.

Visually, the baron and the burgomaster Poppendick resemble King Ubu with their phallic hats and their round bodies (Figures 3.3 and 3.4). The name "Poppendick" itself has phallic connotations. It plays on the name of the bur-

Figure 3.2. Alfred Jarry's
Ubu roi (King Ubu).
From *Ubu roi: Drame
en cinq actes* (Paris:
Librairie Charpentier et
Fasquelle, 1922).

Véritable Portrait de Monsieur UBU.

gomaster from *Hans the Flute Player*, "Pippermann," as well as the expression "Poppycock," and contains a reference to the male organ. The grotesque forms of both characters operate as signs of their appetites for power, which lead them to transgress the traditional limits of their respective functions. The baron, political leader of Hamelin, leads the way to the construction of a cathedral, a seat of religious power, in order to purchase a salvation he so fearfully desires. For his part, the burgomaster, center of economic power and city administration, hopes to attain social prestige by sacrificing his daughter to the baron's son Franz. Their almost childlike (one might argue Id-like) desire for salvation and social prestige only emphasizes their cruelty.[30] Demy presents us with a grotesque caricature of authority figures prepared to indiscriminately sacrifice human beings—the townspeople and even their own children—in order to

Figure 3.3. The burgomaster (Roy Kinnear) looking particularly Ubuesque for his daughter's wedding.

attain their vain and selfish goals. As Jarry does in *Ubu roi*, Demy represents Hamelin's authority figures in their most blatant cruelty, without the cover of psychological complexity to elicit any kind of compassion or understanding for their final tragic fate. Moreover, their desire to exercise authority beyond their traditional functions contributes to the overall chaos that Hamelin experiences when faced with the plague.

Their hunger for power and influence is nowhere more evident than in the baron's desire to build a cathedral. The building of the cathedral in Demy parallels the building of the clock tower in Windust, both constructions involving oppressive means of exacting work and money from the people to build monuments glorifying the wealthy and powerful (Figures 3.5 and 3.6). We learn at the beginning of the film that the baron has already run out of funds for the

Figure 3.4. The Ubuesque baron (Donald Pleasence).

construction of the cathedral, funds acquired through the exploitation of serfs, and the masons refuse to work without pay. The baron laments the situation, declaring that he will be dead before the cathedral is completed. Also invested in the completion of the cathedral, Hamelin's bishop responds to the baron's concerns most crudely: "Then they must be made to work faster, my lord." It occurs to the baron to use the money from the dowry he will receive from his son Franz marrying the burgomaster's daughter Lisa. However, Franz contests his father's claim to the money, for he intends to use the money himself to wage wars of glory, which, as his father reminds him, he usually loses. Franz comes up with a novel idea: "Anyway your cathedral can be built for nothing. Your masons don't have to be paid. They can be whipped." Franz's blunt statement only foregrounds what remains veiled in the baron's and the church's approach to the workers: ultimately they are slaves to Hamelin's sociopolitical and religious authorities. The grotesque overstatement shocks the spectator; the simplistic language employed to express domination is itself violent and

Figure 3.5. Workers forced to build a clock tower in Bretaigne Windust's *The Pied Piper of Hamelin*.

only begins to hint at the actual violence of the oppressive socioeconomic relations underpinning Hamelin society.[31]

Like the baron, members of the clergy also appear in phallic garb, particularly evident in the trial and execution of the Jew Melius (Figure 3.7). Their phallic appearance corresponds to their own will to power to control the lives and even the thoughts of Hamelin's people. The bishop and his fellow clergymen push forward the construction of the cathedral, regardless of the cost to the town or its people. Whereas the baron desires its construction for his own salvation (or rather, as he clarifies, to avoid going to hell), Hamelin's clergy claims to believe that the cathedral will prevent the plague from entering the city. But it also provides the bishop and his men with a pretext to control the baron and his money through their ability to threaten him with eternal doom, and they seem to enjoy the power they are able to exercise over him. When Franz and the baron argue over possession of the dowry, the baron declares in a childlike manner, "It's my money, I shall spend it on my cathedral." Then the

Figure 3.6. Workers slaving away to build a cathedral in Demy's *The Pied Piper.*

bishop, in a paternal manner, corrects him: "*Our* money, my lord," to which his man cynically adds, to attenuate the greediness of the bishop's claim, "for the reparation of sin, and the glorification of God." In the film, the discourse of the clergy proves to be nothing more than a ploy to position themselves advantageously in a struggle for power over the body politic.

While Hamelin's clergy pressures the baron to continue work on the cathedral, the pope demands troops from the baron to wage war against the emperor. When he arrives in Hamelin, the papal nuncio explains the irony of the situation to the baron: "The pope wants a new emperor because the emperor wants a new pope." Just as Franz wishes to raise troops for wars of personal interest, so does the pope, who is prepared to militarily interfere in secular affairs to maintain his own prestigious position as head of the Catholic Church. Like the secular authorities in the film, members of the clergy, from pope to bishop, covet the very worldly objects of money and prestige, thus moving beyond the supposed boundaries of their prescribed roles and functions within the body politic. What the film underscores, then, is a very Foucauldian understanding of how various institutions—through their discourses, subjects, and other resources—vie for power to control the body politic.[32] Their ostensible differences, representing economic, political, and religious power, only conceal what binds them: their desire to maintain hegemonic control over Hamelin.

Besides costume, the insatiable greed of city authorities is also signaled in the film through the consumption of food, which can be linked to the protrusions of the grotesque body. Already Windust creates such an association in his film in the scene in which the king's emissary is offered a sumptuous

Figure 3.7. Clergy at the execution of Melius.

feast including Arabian plums, Beaujolais grapes, Persian melon, and roasted suckling pig. Demy further exaggerates the gluttony of the rich in his film by having the burgomaster's kitchen resemble a slaughterhouse and by including not only swine but also swan at Lisa and Franz's wedding feast.[33] Whereas the juxtaposition in certain shots of the pig's head with the burgomaster and with members of the clergy provides an imagery that needs no explanation, the consumption of swan points to a sacrificial symbolism. Demy often used white to depict positive or idealized characters in his films. For instance, in *Lola*, Michel drives a white convertible and wears a white suit, and Lola dons a white dress. Demy also may have been familiar with tales about "swan maidens," in which the swan proves to be a princess metamorphosed.[34] Because the burgomaster's daughter is dressed in white, we might read this scene in terms of Lisa being sacrificed, much like the white swans, to the appetites of those in power.

Hamelin's authority figures—with their gluttonous, grotesque bodies— who devour the town's resources and its people in their hunger for power end up bringing about the destruction of the town itself. It is because they refuse to see or because they cannot see the importance of mustering their resources to protect the town from the plague that the Black Death spreads to Hamelin.

Warned by Melius that the rats arriving in town carry the plague, city authorities—much like those of Albert Camus's *La Peste* (*The Plague*, 1947)—ignore the warning as the rat infestation grows.[35] Forbidding Melius's working on a cure, Franz instead forces the alchemist to concoct fool's gold to lure naïve children into his projected army. Although the piper will rid the city of its rats, it is too late, for the Black Death has already spread to the population.

Although the menace was pointed out to authorities earlier in the film, the extent to which the rats pose a problem becomes evident during the morally corrupt wedding banquet. As wedding guests prepare to indulge in dessert, rats begin to emerge from the cathedral-shaped wedding cake, which collapses upon itself as the vermin take over and wreak havoc in the banquet hall (Figure 3.8). During a feast emblematic of the grotesque appetites of the burgomaster, the baron, his son Franz, and the clergy, it seems only appropriate that the rats—symbolic of disease in the film through their association with the plague—overrun the festivities.[36] The scene prefigures the ways in which the town itself will be destroyed by the plague. Hamelin will implode just like the cake, collapsing upon the very authority figures that ushered in the Black Death due to their fanaticism and vainglory pursuits of grandeur.

At the level of the macrocosm, the grotesque plays out in the film's apocalyptic finale, which reveals the consequences of "the Sleep of Reason," when those forces that threaten our "essential humanity" are unleashed upon the body politic.[37] It is the grotesque body that knows no limits, and not the plague, that brings corruption and leads to the decay of Hamelin. Curiously, although Demy could not have known what the future would hold for him personally

Figure 3.8. Rats begin to emerge from the wedding cake.

at the moment he was filming *The Pied Piper*, his version of the legend reveals something about the way in which the modern plague of AIDS has been dealt with: the lack of will to act for moral reasons and out of a sense of humanity on the part of political and religious demagogues only serves to fan the epidemic's flames.[38]

HAMELIN'S OTHERS, OR MODERN BOHEMIANS

Whereas Hamelin's authority figures appear inhumane in their grotesque bodies, humanity is located in those characters who come to represent Otherness in their Bohemian lifestyles and philosophical perspectives. In the film, the family of traveling performers, the pilgrim, and the musician–piper who enter Hamelin from the outside become associated with Melius the Jew and the young artist Gavin, who are located within the city's walls. What connects them is their literal and figurative errancy, which allows them to move in and out of closed spaces and ways of thinking. They represent freedom of movement and of thought in a city that is held hostage, evident in the scaffolding that fits like a straightjacket over the cathedral and in the camera's emphasis on Hamelin as a closed space under careful guard.[39] As such, their errancy bears affinities with Gilles Deleuze and Félix Guattari's notion of "nomad thought," which puts into question fixed identities and celebrates difference and heterogeneity. Associated with "smooth spaces," nomad thought is opposed to the immured, striated space of the state that limits physical, intellectual, and artistic movement.[40] In the film, Church orthodoxy and sociopolitical order incarnate this striated space—the rigid and fixed state structures—that Demy's Bohemians challenge through their physical, artistic, and intellectual errancy, an errancy that both embraces and generates difference.

This tension between Bohemian and bourgeois, between nomadism and a repressive sociopolitical order, reveals itself in the very structure of *The Pied Piper*. At the beginning of the film, we see the actors Matteo, Helga, and their family moving within an open, "smooth," apparently boundaryless space until they are stopped by the city walls of Hamelin. The film concludes with the opposite movement: the actors, along with the artist Gavin, leave the walled city to regain open spaces, making their way toward the Netherlands, where Gavin intends to continue his artistic studies, in other words, where he will continue to engage in nomad thought, this time through painting.[41] As the actors and Gavin travel toward the Netherlands, the pied piper, along with Hamelin's children, similarly moves away from the closed space of the city out into open fields; however, the piper has no clear destination in mind. This way of structuring the film, opening with errant artists who enter the closed city only to exit the insulated space at the end of the film, is reminiscent of Demy's *Les Demoiselles de Rochefort*.[42] In this film, the aspiring painter Maxence and the dancer Delphine leave the constraints of the provincial city with the caravan of performers who entered the city at the beginning of the film. Demy structures both films around the implicit opposition between errant artists, associated with free movement (through travel, through dance, through thought) and the close-minded inhabitants of the ordered, constrained space of the insular city. Spatially as well as ideologically, then, Demy creates an opposition between Bohemian and bourgeois.

With the casting of Donovan as the pied piper, the film asks us to make connections between Bohemians of the past and present, whereas inclusion of the character Melius suggests that we might read the film allegorically, in light of recent European history, specifically, the Holocaust. The piper and Melius can be viewed as doubles or in complementary terms; they incarnate variations of the Other, representing different modes of resistance to Hamelin's authorities. Whereas the piper is associated with children and a certain carefree attitude, Melius proves to be a figure of wisdom who engages directly in his world to transform it. For his part, the artist and scientific apprentice Gavin unites both tendencies, perhaps pointing the way toward a better future or more effective forms of resistance.

Expanding upon what Vaucaire, Mitchell, and Ganne do in *Hans the Flute Player*, Demy revisits the question of the place of the artist in a society riddled with greed, war, and narrow-mindedness. Although Demy celebrates the artist in all of his films, nowhere is the artist more oppressed and marginalized than in *The Pied Piper*. Even though art is not completely despised in Hamelin, those in power subject art to their narcissistic desires: they only appreciate art insofar as it glorifies them. For instance, the baron has a beautiful cathedral built, which he views as his ticket to heaven; the baron's son Franz despises Gavin but envisions that one day Gavin could become his official painter. The theater troupe and pied piper are forbidden entry into the city until they become useful to those in power: the pied piper is called upon to heal the burgomaster's daughter, and the theater troupe is commissioned to entertain at Lisa's wedding to the baron's son Franz. But when the pied piper sings to common children in the streets of Hamelin, town authorities threaten the pied piper, declaring, "Stop that noise. . . . We've burned three witches this year on less evidence than we've got against you!" The case of the inventive alchemist Melius is the most blatant example of the persecution of creativity: he is burned at the stake at the end of the film.

The character of the young artist Gavin blends aspects of Yoris from *Hans the Flute Player* and of Maxence, the aspiring painter from *Les Demoiselles de*

Rochefort. Like Yoris, Demy's Gavin is in love with the burgomaster's daughter Lisa, whose name recalls Ganne's Lisbeth. Each of the three characters creates a simulacrum of his true love: Yoris designs a doll perfectly resembling Lisbeth, Maxence paints the portrait of his true love whom he has never seen but who turns out to be Delphine, and the adolescent Gavin makes an imperfect but loving attempt to paint the young Lisa.[43] Lisbeth finally is united with Yoris and not Van Pott, and Maxence, it is understood, will find his true love Delphine; but Lisa is forced to marry the cruel Franz and then is lead away with the other children by the pied piper. The failure of the young lovers to unite at the end of the film is symbolic of the impossibility, in Demy's Hamelin, for art and love to exist within a society driven by money and selfish ambition.

Gavin is the apprentice of Melius, a character Demy and Mark Peploe developed more fully after they got a hold of Andrew Birkin's initial draft of the screenplay.[44] In many respects Melius's character recalls that of Windust's Truson but without the love interest and with a more philosophical demeanor. Throughout the film, Melius's reason is opposed to the superstitious and orthodox ways of the clergymen. When Lisa is sick and the bishop is ready to administer the last rites, Melius insists she is fighting the fever and simply needs rest. He suggests that music might help, and the bishop declares, "These superstitious philanderings are being denounced by Pope Clement himself, and by our Holy Mother the Church!" Later, Melius appears before the court of inquisition and refuses to agree that the plague is a punishment from God. He maintains instead that the plague has natural causes and is carried somehow by the rats. In his ability to conceptualize outside of orthodoxy and accepted forms of knowledge, Melius embodies nomad thought; he is able to envision other ways, other paths, with the goal of healing both Lisa and the community around him.

In an ironic turn, the clergy accuse Melius of bringing plague and heresy to Hamelin and sentence him to be burned at the stake. *Hans the Flute Player* already introduces into the plot of "The Pied Piper" the threat of being burned at the stake for witchcraft, but in Demy's film, that threat comes to a head.[45] Melius eloquently responds to the accusations of the inquisition with a call to embrace Otherness. He declares, "I commend myself to your mercy in the hope that future generations may learn, at least by your mistakes, if not by my discoveries, and I hope also, my lords, that they may learn not only to tolerate each other's differences, but even to rejoice in them." Such a call is all the more imperative in that it will be sealed by Meluis's death. Demy's film communicates a sense of urgent need to accept the Other that is not present in his sources, which in part has to do with the sociohistorical context in which his film was produced.

Significantly, Demy's version of "The Pied Piper" is the only one to give as the date of the action 1349. In the Brothers Grimm, the date is 1284; in Browning, 1376; and Gautier sets the action in the sixteenth century. One reason Demy might have set the action in 1349 is that this is precisely the year in which Jews were massacred in Germany, scapegoated by Christians who blamed them for the plague: "The massacre began in northern Spain in the summer of 1348. It spread to Switzerland, Bavaria, and in January 1349 along the Rhine, then to Magdeburg and Berlin, and finally to Nuremburg" (Pasachoff and Littman 154).[46] The film closes with the epilogue running over the final images, reading in part, "The Black Death ended four years later, having killed an estimated 75,000,000 people. The religious persecution that followed was to remain without parallel *until this century*" (my emphasis).

These lines ask us to reflect upon the persecution of the alchemist Melius, who happens to wear a Star of David on his cloak, not only with respect to the obscurantist thought of the distant past but also in light of the Holocaust of the recent past. Melius's lines at the end of the inquisition trial that ask us to embrace Otherness, then, can be resituated within a contemporary context. Through *The Pied Piper*, Demy warns his viewers about the potentially tragic consequences that irrational fears of the social or ethnic Other can engender.

The period in which Demy was working on *The Pied Piper* marks the emergence of a new anti-immigrant far right in France. After World War II, the extreme right collapsed due to its associations with the Vichy government and collaboration with Germany (Starzmann-Gaillard 177). With the rise in North African immigration and the process of decolonization in the late 1950s and early 1960s, "anti-Algerian sentiment ran high in metropolitan France. It culminated in the violent October 1961 Paris marches that resulted in thousands of arrests and scores of dead and wounded" (Bleich 116). During this police attack of peaceful Algerian immigrant protesters, "50 Algerians were to die or 'disappear' that night, while a further 11,538 men were savagely beaten and herded into sports stadia" (House and MacMaster 267). The decolonization of North Africa was an important factor in the revival of the far right, and the very year Demy's *Pied Piper* was released in England, the National Front, headed by Jean-Marie Le Pen, was created, "bringing together those who were nostalgic for Vichy, antigaullists, Poujadists, neofascists, intellectuals, and activists" (Mayer 12). The year 1973, which saw the National Front's first anticommunist, anti-immigrant electoral platform, was the year of the "murderous summer," when "more than fifty Algerian male workers were attacked and fifteen killed in separate acts in and around Marseilles."[47] With pressure from the extreme right and rising unemployment, "the French government halted immigration in 1974; Algeria had in fact already suspended emigration by its own citizens in September 1973" (Hargreaves 5).[48]

A second development regarding the transnational movement of people in relation to France is also noteworthy. As Richard Ivan Jobs argues, "Travel became the foundation for a youth identity that emphasized mobility and built a shared political culture across national boundaries" in Western Europe in the 1960s (376–77). Looking at the popular media of the period, Jobs finds evidence that these youthful "vagabonds" were being construed as subversives, and their movement was viewed as a contagion that needed to be controlled (383). National governments, including those of Great Britain and France, sought to control and even bar so-called provocateurs from entering their countries. Jobs sums up the overall situation with respect to migration and the circulation of European youth as follows: "On the one hand we have the migration of mostly non-white, non-European poor for economic reasons, while on the other we have the travels of mostly white Western European middle-class young people for political reasons" (381). Both the external and internal Others were viewed as threats to national identity and order. Indeed, Demy's *Pied Piper* recalls the sociohistorical context of *Hans the Flute Player*. Ganne's operetta similarly was produced during a period of mass displacement and relocation. In the period of *Hans the Flute Player*, however, French peasants were considered the "outsiders" and troublemakers, co-existing with the Bohemians who challenged the dominant political and cultural order of turn-of-the-century France.

Demy may not have been explicitly or intentionally addressing issues related to the circulation of migrants and counterculture youth in *The Pied Piper*. However, it is notable that a project about a town that closes itself off to outsiders and persecutes those of a different ethnic or social identity was conceived and produced at a time when racism, limiting immigration policies, and efforts to control the circulation of transnational youth were on the rise in France and other European countries. The fact that Demy worked to develop Melius's character in the film and has Melius implore his audience to learn from the past suggests that Demy may indeed have had such concerns in mind.

Although the doubling of characters in *Hans the Flute Player* and Windust's *The Pied Piper of Hamelin* is tighter than in Demy's film—Yoris is punished for Hans's "witchcraft," and Truson and the piper are played by the same character—Demy develops an affinity between Melius, the internal Other, and the pied piper, the external Other. Significantly, both characters are healers. Both Melius and the pied piper are called to Lisa's bedside to care for her, and both characters attempt in their own ways to "cure" the townspeople and its children of the moral corruption plaguing Hamelin. However, whereas the pied piper leads the children away in either an escapist or utopian gesture, Melius is committed to changing the town from within in ways that are engaged and practical but that lead to his death.

Melius is well aware of the pied piper's effect on people. When Gavin asks how the piper could have cured Lisa by playing music, Melius responds, "Cure her, no, no, no, no, he just did what the others couldn't, he took her into his own world." Although the pied piper does not literally cure her, his music indeed has a healing power. And whereas Melius desperately tries to develop a cure for the impending arrival of the plague in Hamelin, the pied piper ends up taking the children out of a sick, diseased town. Much like Disney's piper, when Demy's piper leads the children of Hamelin away, not only is he exacting revenge for the failure of the city to pay him for having rid the city of rats, but he also is saving the children from the ills of their society. In Demy, music in particular and art in general "heals" by freeing people from their immediate, often claustrophobic, surroundings, engaging them on a voyage of sorts, encouraging nomad thought. The movement and openness associated with the literal movement of traveling artists is in fact symbolic of art itself. That the children disappear with the piper at the end of the film, then, can be read figuratively: they are liberated from the prejudices and limitations of their society.

There may be a more direct allegorical reference here as well. Before the children are led out of Hamelin, the baron, Franz, and the clergy are all plotting to use the children to fight the pope's wars. The question of the church and state waging wars for their own interests and using youthful soldiers was an issue that preoccupied Demy. In *The Umbrellas of Cherbourg*, for instance, Demy looked at the tragic effects of the Algerian War on a young couple, and in his 1969 film *Model Shop*, Demy explored the consequences of the Vietnam draft on a young aspiring architect. In both cases, problematic wars interrupt love and the pursuit of creativity, a tragic fate from which the pied piper spares the children of Hamelin, taking them to a better place, perhaps the joyous land of Browning's poem.

Although situated in the fourteenth century, Demy's *Pied Piper* treats themes and issues relevant to 1960s and 1970s counterculture. As already noted, Demy was known for drawing on the real-life personas of his cast members to inform his films. Having the pop singer Donovan interpret the role of the pied piper, then, allowed Demy to play on Donovan's image as the incarnation of youth culture and flower power.[49] Much like Demy's character of the pied piper, Donovan himself believed in the transformative, "healing" power of music. In 1968, four years before *The Pied Piper* hit the screen, Donovan stated, "Pop music is helping to change the world. . . . I want to teach the world to dance, to sing again, to learn to release itself" (qtd. in Shelton). Given his public image and his own ideas about the role of music in society, Donovan was a shoo-in for the title role. Furthermore, his embodiment of the piper pushes the viewer to reread the film in light of contemporary culture.

Demy casts the artists, in this instance the pied piper and the traveling actors, as the characters who are able to move in and out of and to transcend the dynamics of political, social, and religious oppression. At the same time, the artist provides comfort to and "heals" the exploited, taking them into the enchanted world of music, art, and dance, a "trip" that momentarily removes them from their oppressive environment and frees their minds. Like the pied piper, the artist in Demy's film enchants and leads those susceptible to his or her charms to disappear into another world, far away from the moral decay represented by the Black Death.

Just as Vaucaire and Mitchell inscribe into their operetta conceptions of turn-of-the-century Bohemia, Demy incorporates into his film hippie ideals and references to the 1960s and 1970s. In his study of hippie morality and earlier forms of Bohemia, Bennett Berger foregrounds Bohemian aspects of hippie culture, most notably, for our purposes (1) the importance of self-expression and creativity; (2) the rejection of the Christian condemnation of the flesh; and (3) the notion that children, a new and innocent generation, will save the world (19). Interestingly, at Lisa's wedding celebration, the actors Matteo and Helga, along with their children, act out the *Jeu d'Adam* (*Adam's Play*), a mystery play based on the Fall. But when Helga gives birth near the end of the film, she does so without experiencing any pain. Through Helga's painless childbirth, Demy points to a prelapsarian world without sexual shame, which he associates with the Bohemian actors, who are unaffected by the plague.[50]

Demy's film ends with crosscutting between two parallel actions: that of the piper joyfully playing away as the children follow him out of Hamelin while dancing and that of Melius being burned at the stake, surrounded by authorities from the clergy, nobility, and bourgeoisie. This rather disturbing movement between joy and despair—a technique he will also use in the concluding scene of *Lady Oscar*, as we will see in the following chapter—takes the place of the unambivalent happy ending of *Hans the Flute Player* and Windust's *Pied Piper*. In the case of Demy's Hamelin, there is no going back. The children themselves are saved, but the town, we can infer, will be destroyed by the plague.[51]

We can understand this ending in at least two different and potentially overlapping ways. On the one hand, the piper leading the children away from Hamelin could allude to the idea of "dropping out." Marigay Graña notes that "after the failure of 'flower power' to vanquish the Western military combine, the hippy [sic] response was to withdraw communally to the more remote corners of the planet" (xvii). Such a reading could in fact oppose the mature and politically engaged Melius to the more naïve figure of the escapist piper. On the other hand, we can also read the conclusion in terms of the initiation of a new society: the corrupt society of Hamelin is destroyed, and the children and artists who escape the plague will initiate a new society that grants the individual all forms of freedom of expression and that embraces each other's differences. As one French critic put it, "Youth, turning its back on corruption, prepares a new world."[52] The legend of the pied piper, then, serves as a convenient vehicle to advance the notion of a youthful generation who will be saved from and who will redeem not so much the sins as the crimes of their parents and society.

DEMY AS THE PIED PIPER?

Critics who welcomed *The Pied Piper,* which had finally made its way to France, consistently commented on its contemporariness. In one interview Demy himself notes, "It's a tale, I think, that's very current."[53] Henry Chapier declares, "Donovan, his flute, his charming innocence is not the hero of a fairy tale, but the symbol of a revolutionary poet."[54] Another critic from the French weekly *Le Nouvel Observateur* remarks that "it is full of hope and adds to fairy tales for children of all ages a social message that throws boiling oil on sugar-coated, Disney-like films. Thanks to Demy, Peter Pan has become a young lefty."[55] Even the negative reviews reveal the contemporary feel of the film: "[Demy] ruined the legend. Disguised as a revolutionary poet, prophet of some May 1968 musical, the pied piper (Donovan) loses his enchanter's halo, appearing as a naïve and optimistic antiestablishment protester, in other words, a sort of happy idiot."[56] Indeed, as we have seen, Demy's *The Pied Piper* could well be read as an allegorical tale about post-1968 French society.

Critics both saw the film as a bearer of messages relevant to the present regarding racism, war, and intolerance, and found the situation of its release an ironic commentary on the French film industry. Chapier subtitles his article for the *Quotidien de Paris* "The Sabotage of a Masterpiece." He criticizes French distributors' verdict that the film was not commercial enough and their prejudice of considering film a commodity and not a work of art. At the end of his interview with Demy in *L'Humanité,* François Maurin adds his own expression of anger and puzzlement: "However, it [the film] was commercial enough for the English, for the Americans, whom it is said are greedy for dollars and who received it quite well. This makes me think that in France, we are so commercial we despise art."[57] Yoris in *Hans the Flute Player* could well have made such a statement about the people of Milkatz, and the statement would also ring true for the people of Demy's Hamelin. In *Le Point,* Robert Benayoun makes the most explicit connection between the message of the film and the circumstances of its belated distribution in France in December 1975: "What a beautiful present Demy gave us, which prophetically seems, in 1971, to defend his art, today so endangered, against the temple merchants taken in by cataclysms to the point where they stupidly are engulfed by them!"[58]

Most critics who applauded the 1975 French release of Demy's *The Pied Piper* repeated the same message regarding the commercialization of art, which leaves no room for auteur films. Their recourse to the more open examples of the British and American film industries in fact ends up making France look like Hamelin: its narrow views of art and its valorization of immediate commercial success led to the "quarantine" of Demy's film, which was only released in France after its positive reception at the festival of Paris. (In *The Pied Piper,* the piper and actors are not allowed in Hamelin at first due to a quarantine.) At the time of *Donkey Skin's* release, Demy himself already expressed his frustration about France, which he characterized as "closed" and "self-censuring" (Langlois). Little did Demy know that five years later critics would be using his film *The Pied Piper,* which French distributors did not want to release, as an allegorical tale to tell the story of the commercialization of cinema in France, with Jacques Demy playing the leading role.

4

The Queering of the French Revolution

Lady Oscar *and the Tradition of the Maiden Warrior*

It is striking to observe how much this practically accidental parenthesis in Demy's oeuvre that is *Lady Oscar* nevertheless marks a turning point. It is here that, for the first time, festival gives way to insurrection, here, too, that the heroine discovers the necessity to rebel, learns to assume her nudity and the physical reality of love, here, too—and the director did not have the power to modify the plot—the destiny of the lovers leads to death. Everything happens as if, frustrated with the progress on *A Room in Town,* Demy integrated into the commissioned *Lady Oscar* its strongest elements.

—Jean-Pierre Berthomé, *Jacques Demy et les racines du rêve*[1]

In 1973 Jacques Demy released his first film explicitly dealing with a cross-gendered character, *A Slightly Pregnant Man.* It was a box office flop, despite the casting of Marcello Mastroianni as the pregnant man and Catherine Deneuve as his wife. Demy began work on *A Room in Town* in December 1973, which was to be a musical in the tradition of *The Umbrellas of Cherbourg.* The film's backdrop concerned the historic 1955 strike in Nantes into which Demy weaves a love story between the working-class striker François Guilbaud and Edith Leroyer, a fallen aristocrat married to an abusive television salesman. After two years of looking for producers, he had to abandon the project, which would finally reach the silver screen in 1982 to critical acclaim.[2]

In the meantime, Demy was approached by Japanese producer Mataichiro Yamamoto, who had seen *The Umbrellas of Cherbourg,* to direct a film based on the popular *shōjo* manga (manga for girls) by Riyoko Ikedo titled *Berusaiyu no Bara* (*The Rose of Versailles,* serialized 1972–73; published 1982), which draws from both Asian and European folklore about maiden warriors.[3] By 1974 episodes of the manga had already been staged by the Takarazuka Revue, an all-woman Japanese musical theater troupe, and performances of *The Rose of Versailles* still ran as recently as 2006. The manga's popularity also led to an animé that aired on Japanese television in October 1979. Released in Japan a year before the film's French premiere, *Lady Oscar* was to ride the tide of Ikedo's best-selling manga.

The manga and film draw from tales about maiden warriors, much in the tradition of Mulan, whereby a girl must don the clothes of a soldier in order to maintain her father's honor and legacy and to protect king and kingdom. Oscar François de Jarjayes is born a girl, but her father, General de Jarjayes, raises her as a boy since birth, with the intention that she take his place as head of the king's Royal Guard. What makes *The Rose of Versailles* and *Lady Oscar* particularly interesting is that the action takes place during the French Revolution, and Oscar proves less obedient to father and fatherland than her predecessors. Just as the heroine's gender and sexual identity is in flux throughout the story, so is the society that upholds traditional forms of gender, sexual, and social order, which Oscar will end up challenging rather than defending.

Despite the fact that the film was a commission, the manga upon which it was to be based dealt with issues that were common currency in Demy's oeuvre, most notably challenges to class and to heteronormative notions of gender and sexuality. Through *Lady Oscar,* Demy shows a heightened interest in class not only at the level of individual characters, as in *Lola* and *The Umbrellas of Cherbourg,* but also at the level of the collective, more in line with *The Pied Piper* and especially *A Room in Town.* And whereas we can read *The Umbrellas of Cherbourg* as a story about not being able to come out of the closet, *Lady Oscar* is very much a coming out narrative. As suggested in chapter 2, like *Donkey Skin, Lady Oscar* foregrounds life-as-theater or performance; in this chapter, we will focus on how this plays out specifically in relation to gender, which affects representations of sexuality.

By situating *The Rose of Versailles* and *Lady Oscar* within the tradition of maiden warrior tales, it becomes evident that the manga and film represent queer rewritings of such narratives. In traditional versions of the maiden warrior, the heroine lives as a girl then transforms momentarily into a male soldier, only to return to the unambiguous status of "female." Lady Oscar, however, always inhabits an ambiguous gender position: she embraces and internalizes the masculine identity of a soldier, which she cannot simply shed at the end of the story.

Cross-dressing in classical examples of the maiden warrior certainly can elicit queer readings of the tales. In her discussion of temporary cross-dressing, Chris Straayer contends, "The conflict between a character's actual sex and the sex implied by the character's disguise and performance functions to create simultaneous heterosexual and homosexual interactions" (54). In other words, drag indeed prompts queer possibilities. But in the case of *The Rose of Versailles* and *Lady Oscar*, Ikeda and Demy actively queer the classical paradigm of the maiden warrior tale by maintaining the gender ambiguity of the heroine from beginning to end and by exploring alternatives to heteronormative forms of sexuality. The ways in which they construct their cross-dressed heroines are illustrative of Judith Butler's clarifications regarding her notion of gender performativity, which should not be understood simply in terms of isolated performances but rather in terms of "the ritualized repetition by which such [gender] norms produce and stabilize not only the effects of gender but the materiality of sex" (*Bodies* x; see also 95). As we will see, Oscar's identity as a masculine woman is more strongly established than that of heroines in earlier maiden warrior tales, which has implications for Oscar's sexuality.

Lady Oscar appears at the tail end of a series of French and Italian films released in the 1960s and 1970s dealing with women cross-dressing as soldiers, a trend identified by Didier Roth-Bettoni in *L'Homosexualité au cinéma* (*Homosexuality in the Cinema*, 2007). These films include Jacqueline Audry's *Le Secret du Chevalier d'Eon* (*The Secret of the Chevalier of Eon*, France, 1959; remake 1978) based on a historical character believed to be a woman cross-dressed as a knight; Umberto Lenzi's *Le avventure di Mary Read* (*The Adventures of Mary Read*, Italy, 1961), in which the eponymous heroine becomes a pirate; Mauro Bolognini's *Mademoiselle de Maupin* (France-Italy-Spain, 1966), whose heroine, disguised as a monk, gets conscripted into the king's army; Bernard Borderie's *Sept Hommes et une garce* (*Seven Guys and a Gal*, France, 1966), in which a coquettish Italian noblewoman dresses as an Austrian officer to save her French buddies during the Napoleonic Wars; Borderie's *Indomptable Angélique* (*Untamable Angelique*, France, 1967), who dresses as a page and rides the galleys to find her true love; and Ettore Fizzarotti's *Venga a fare il soldato da noi* (*Come and Be a Soldier with Us*, Italy, 1971), the only film staging a contemporary maiden warrior story, whose heroine takes advantage of being accidentally called up for military service to spy on her boyfriend.

Like the heroines of earlier maiden warrior tales, such films provide only limited challenges to patriarchal and heteronormative society. Audry's Chevalier d'Eon, for instance, lives her youth as a boy and joins the king's dragoons only to have to disguise herself as a woman, which mediates her return to her "true" gender in the film's conclusion.[4] Lenzi's Mary Read moves between masculine and feminine roles, but the film evolves into a taming of the shrew story; the maiden warrior finally is domesticated.[5] And Mauro Bolognini's Ma-demoiselle Maupin, conscripted as the soldier Théodore, leads an army captain to believe that he is in love with one of his men; but like d'Eon, such gender and sexual trouble is resolved in conformity with heteronormativity.[6] Despite this return to heteronormative order at the end of these films, the popularity of such a character in the 1960s and 1970s, in cinema as well as in *shōjo* manga, would seem to suggest that, with global changes in women's social and political roles, the maiden warrior served as a figure for writers and directors to explore what it meant for women to move out of traditional models of femininity at-tached to their apparent sex. In Roth-Bettoni's words, "Such a perturbation of the traditional order of things is only the outcome of a whole series of films that, at the turn of the 1960s and 70s, enjoyed undoing the foundations of what were believed to be the masculine and the feminine" (186).[7]

In seventeenth-century France, when Amazons and maiden warrior ico-nography and tales became popular, women had attained unprecedented cul-tural capital as arbiters of taste and as writers. In China in the 1910s and 1920s, the revival of *The Ballad of Mulan* coincided with the emergence of modern Chinese feminism, which grew out of the New Culture Movement.[8] It should come as no surprise, then, that in Western Europe as well as in Japan during the1960s and 1970s, a period in which women were challenging traditional gender roles, manga and films about maiden warriors were increasingly com-mon.

In effect, for each of these historical moments the figure of the maiden warrior represents what Marjorie Garber refers to as a "category crisis," which she describes as "a failure of definitional distinction, a borderline that becomes permeable, that permits of border crossings from one (apparently distinct) cat-egory to another: black/white, Jew/Christian, noble/bourgeois, master/servant, master/slave. The binarism male/female . . . is itself put in question or under erasure in transvestism" (16).[9] Precisely because the maiden warrior, which we could characterize as an example of "female masculinity," blurs categorical boundaries, she can become, in Judith Halberstam's words, "ambiguous, illeg-ible" (19). At the same time, such a figure denaturalizes the normal by fore-grounding the constructedness of gender. As Butler has argued, "In imitating gender, drag implicitly reveals the imitative structure of gender itself—as well as its contingency" (*Gender Trouble* 137).

Although Ikeda and Demy are both concerned with problematizing the gender norms of their respective societies, their interests also lie in the explo-ration of nonheteronormative forms of sexuality. Disagreements reign among scholars regarding the extent to which Ikeda questions heteronormativity in *The Rose of Versailles*. But as we have seen in his work, Demy often foregrounds queer couples—who take the form of "monstrous" pairings (father–daughter, animal–human)—and in *A Slightly Pregnant Man* and *Lady Oscar,* ambiguously gendered characters whose partners embrace their difference. Although class is an important theme in Ikeda's manga, Demy emphasizes class even more in the ways he rewrites the story of Lady Oscar. Garber has noted that category crises in class and race can get displaced onto gender.[10] I would argue that, especially in Demy's *Lady Oscar,* the crisis of class and gender as well as heteronormativity are all in play and come to a head in the French Revolution, which marks the end of an "Old Regime" of gender, sexuality, and class.

In order to fully take into account the ways in which Ikeda and Demy challenge their respective societies, we need to situate their accounts of Lady Oscar in relation to traditional tales and *shōjo* mangas about maiden warriors. Based on Ikeda's manga, Demy's *Lady Oscar* does not simply (nor can it) reproduce the Japanese *Rose of Versailles* on-screen. In subtle but significant ways, Demy transforms Ikeda's best-selling manga into a film that clearly merits a place within Demy's oeuvre, marking an important turning point in his own career as a queer director.[11]

THE MAIDEN WARRIOR TALE TYPE

Many studies have been carried out on what has come to be referred to as the "maiden warrior."[12] When discussing such stories, fairy-tale and folktale scholars continue to rely on the Aarne–Thompson–Uther (ATU) classification system, which, despite Uther's 2004 update, remains problematic. Torborg Lundell's 1983 critique of Aarne–Thompson's *The Types of Folktale* and Thompson's *Motif Index* regarding gender bias unfortunately still rings true.[13] Maiden warrior tales fall under several different tale types and motifs, including ATU 514 "The Shift of Sex," which entails a daughter who goes to war for a father who has no sons and accomplishes "heroic deeds"; ATU 884 "The Forsaken Fiancée: Service as Menial," a mish-mash of motifs, including "Disguise of Woman in Man's Clothes" (K1837) and "Test of a Girl Masking as Man" (H1578.1); and K1837.4 "Girl in Man's Clothes Avenges Her Father."[14] Such descriptors hardly do justice to a category of tales that gives significant agency—regardless of the final outcome—to a female character and that has such a wide diffusion, from China and the Middle East to France and the Americas. Indeed, the maiden warrior merits its own place within the pantheon of tale types.

Although the use of the term "maiden" rather than "woman" may seem problematic, many of these tales and legends concern adolescent girls transitioning into womanhood. It is perhaps because the maiden warrior finds herself in a transitional phase that her female masculinity is tolerated and even celebrated in such a culturally and historically diverse array of texts and lore. Louise Edwards characterizes the liminal state of the maiden warrior of Chinese tradition as follows:

> It is the time in a woman's life when her sexual power has yet to be realized through pregnancy and childbirth, and her sexual knowledge is limited. Virginity as a temporary state in these young women's lives adds the promise of sex to further titillate the reader. The temporariness of her lifestyle is therein also linked to her age. Once she has become a married woman her Amazon lifestyle must be forfeited or she pays the penalty of death. (253)

We might associate the maiden warrior with the tomboy, as described by Halberstam, whose female masculinity extends through childhood. For Halberstam, however, "Tomboyism is punished . . . when it appears to be the sign of extreme male identification . . . and when it threatens to extend beyond childhood and into adolescence" (60). In the case of maiden warrior tales, which emerged from medieval and early modern societies, it would seem that the tolerance (at least in fiction) for female masculinity as manifested in this particular figure extends well into adolescence, but such gender ambiguity must be renounced when the heroine fully enters into womanhood.

Dianne Dugaw and Pauline Greenhill provide insight into the shape the maiden warrior took in English cross-dressing ballads, whose audience was lower class and which conformed more or less to the following narrative sequence: (1) the heroine and hero's courtship is threatened or they are separated, (2) the heroine disguises herself as a soldier or sailor to follow her lover to war, (3) she endures various trials, and (4) she is finally reunited with her beloved.[15] Although the English cross-dressing ballad represents an important maiden warrior tradition, I would like to focus instead on the maiden warrior in Chinese and French folk and literary traditions from which authors of *shōjo* manga likely drew and that form the classical narrative upon which Ikeda and Demy's rewritings of the maiden warrior are based.

The basic narratives of the most notable examples from the Chinese and French traditions are remarkably similar. Rather than follow her lover to war, the heroine in these traditions upholds family honor by fighting in the king's army. Usually the story concerns a noble household with no sons, and the heroine—usually the youngest daughter—fulfills the function of male heir by becoming a successful knight, passing as a male, and protecting the kingdom. The king may or may not fall in love with her, and the tale ends with the daughter returning to her initial gender after having defended father and fatherland.

As several critics of the Chinese maiden warrior tradition have noted, the character is riddled with contradictions. Edwards remarks, "She is threatening to patriarchal power, with its implicit preference for meek and mild women, and yet primarily instrumental in ensuring its continued existence because the deeds she performs are undeniably consolidating of the existing Confucian social and moral order" (231). Likewise, Sufen Sophia Lai maintains, "On the surface, women warriors may appear to be unorthodox and to defy gender boundaries, but ideologically they are still well defined within the Confucian moral codes of filial piety and loyalty" (79).[16] In the premodern Chinese lore, the maiden warrior does not fit neatly into either subversive or conformist tendencies.

The prototype par excellence of maiden warrior tales in China is "The Ballad of Mulan" (fourth century C.E.). It opens with Mulan carrying out the traditional domestic work of weaving, which is associated with women's roles and femininity. But when the emperor calls for a soldier from every family, her father cannot comply, for he is too old and his son too young. Mulan thus takes it upon herself to protect family honor and goes to different markets to buy "a gallant horse . . . saddle and cloth . . . snaffle and reins . . . a tall whip" ("Ballad" 267). She rides twelve years with the emperor's army, after which she rejects his offer to be made counselor at his imperial court. She returns home, dons female garb, and surprises her messmates, who never suspected she was a girl ("Ballad" 268).[17] Edwards provides several other examples of warrior women in the Chinese tradition, all of whom perform as males out of filial duty, much in the tradition of Mulan.

Although the pre–twentieth-century maiden warrior tales may have supported traditional Confucian and patriarchal values, they have easily translated into models of female emancipation. For instance, Zheng Wang discusses the popularity of the figure of Mulan at the turn of the twentieth century in China as a symbol for anticolonial resistance and for egalitarian gender relations (21–22). In his account of the revolutionary Huang Dinghui, Wang notes that she changed her name to Mulan after joining the cause (347). As suggested by the history of Mulan in China, despite the fact that maiden warrior tales maintain a complex relationship with patriarchy, they contain the subversive potential to question the very order they ostensibly support by virtue of representing gender as performance and as a construction.

Edwards contrasts the figure of the maiden warrior in Chinese tradition to that of Western narratives, which she characterizes in terms of the "self-indulgent realization of fantasy lifestyles or attainment of romantic desires" (238). However, she focuses primarily on studies of English ballads and does not take into account the French tradition, whose Joan of Arc, much like Mulan, takes up the sword (or at least the banner) in order to protect the kingdom and uphold political and moral order. Although medieval examples of maiden warriors before and after Joan of Arc exist, seventeenth-century France was particularly prolific in the production of images of Amazons and woman warriors, a fashion that has been studied by such scholars as Ian Maclean, Joan DeJean, and Marlies Mueller, to name a few.[18]

The figure of the woman warrior took diverse forms but followed, as Christine Jones has shown, two main tendencies. They either challenged political order in the tradition of the Amazonian *frondeuses,* women who fought in the French rebellion against the monarchy called the Fronde (1648–53), or they upheld it in the tradition of the *femme forte,* the virtuous strong woman or national heroine exemplified by Joan of Arc (Jones, "Noble Impropriety" 25). This fashion gave rise, in the late seventeenth century, to several fairy tales dealing with the theme of the maiden warrior by Marie-Jeanne L'Héritier, the niece of Charles Perrault; Marie-Catherine d'Aulnoy; and Henriette Julie de Murat, whose versions of the maiden warrior straddle the two narrative tendencies of the period.

Whereas the heroine of Murat's tale "Le Sauvage" ("The Savage") cross-dresses as the knight Constantin to avoid an undesirable marriage, those of L'Héritier's "Marmoisan" and d'Aulnoy's "Belle-Belle, ou le chevalier Fortuné" ("Belle-Belle; or, The Chevalier Fortuné") do so, much in the tradition of Mulan, to uphold familial honor and political order.[19] However, the heroines' fidelity to patriarch and king is shaped in such a way as to criticize society under Louis XIV, and the tales themselves can be read as women writers' responses to contemporary debates regarding women's relation to and potential role in the public sphere.

In L'Héritier's tale, Léonore is the fourth daughter of a nobleman and twin sister of Marmoisan, the nobleman's only son. When the latter is killed trying to seduce a married woman, Léonore assumes her brother's identity and replaces her brother at court and at war. Much of L'Héritier's narrative revolves around the anxiety of the prince, the son of the king whom Marmoisan serves. He is troubled by his attraction to Marmoisan, and after hearing a rumor that Marmoisan was in fact a woman, the prince tries to test the apparent nobleman's gender through several gender-specific tests. Marmoisan's success at outwitting the prince emphasizes her recognition of the constructedness of gender and her ability to successfully maneuver within each category. However, Marmoisan's "innocent deception" (the subtitle of the tale) is finally disclosed through the revelation of the heroine's breast after she is injured in a tournament. Despite the fact that Léonore/Marmoisan is the daughter of a count and not of royal blood, the king consents to the marriage of his son to this loyal servant of the Crown due to her merit and her capability to provide solid counsel to her husband.[20]

As Joseph Harris has noted, "The heroine Léonore's gender inversion both functions as a tool of social critique for the writer and ultimately brings about a positive reestablishment of the social order portrayed within the text" (201). Although Léonore takes on the masculine identity of Marmoisan, she is quite critical of self-interested models of masculinity prevalent at the king's court, exemplified by the corrupt behavior of her twin brother. Although the tale concludes with Marmoisan transforming back into Léonore and marrying the prince, her masculine example implicitly will serve as a model for ideal courtiers and she will play an important role as her husband's counsel. Through her heroine, L'Héritier manages to save filial honor and political order, all the while subtly carving out a place of power for the female subject.

In "Belle-Belle," d'Aulnoy's heroine similarly and more obviously restores balance to a kingdom in decline. The tale concerns a king who has been "dispossessed" (*dépouillé*) of all of his wealth by the neighboring emperor Matapa. In order to recover his wealth and power, the king calls upon noble families, each of which must provide him with a knight for the cause. As in other maiden warrior tales, Belle-Belle's father is too old to fight, and he has no sons. Belle-Belle is the youngest of his three daughters, and after proving herself to a fairy, she attains the equipment and support necessary to fully transform into the accomplished knight, the Chevalier Fortuné. Over the course of the tale, several of the trials she must undergo are in fact traps set by the king's sister, who is in love with Fortuné and punishes him for not reciprocating. Fortuné's identity is finally revealed when her shirt is ripped open as she is about to be executed, and her breasts are exposed. The tale concludes with Belle-Belle marrying the prince and with the restoration of the king's wealth and power.

Adrienne Zuerner reads the tale as a commentary on the waning years of Louis XIV's monarchy, which was "plagued by economic and religious crises" (205). Opening "with a scene of masculine lack," d'Aulnoy's cross-dressed heroine restores the political and economic order of the nation. Although the tale stages a female character who puts the monarchy at risk—the dowager queen—it is another female character, along with her merry men, who supplements the king's lack (Zuerner 196–97). Despite the fact that the tale appears to uphold monarchy, it also, in Zuerner's words, "constitutes an oppositional discourse because it indicates the contradictions inhering in seventeenth-century myths of monarchical absolutism" (208).

I would like to point out in both "Marmoisan" and "Belle-Belle" that, first, these tales challenge contemporary discourses that attributed social and political disorder to women at a time when women were playing increasingly important roles within the emerging public sphere.[21] Through their cross-dressed heroines, L'Héritier and d'Aulnoy could prove women's social, political, and even martial value to the state. Second, women writers consciously played on the constructedness of gender in order to open up models of both female and male subjectivity. L'Héritier and d'Aulnoy flatten the gender hierarchy by demonstrating the weaknesses and vulnerability of conventional conceptions and models of masculinity and by foregrounding the qualities of their maiden warriors that indeed prove crucial to the maintenance of the monarchy. Like Chinese maiden warrior narratives, those by the *conteuses* end up supporting what ultimately is a patriarchal order. However, their support is conditional upon the reform of such regimes, reform that includes some kind of recognition of women's ability to contribute to public good.

Finally, both tales stage some kind of sexual tension involving members of the same sex, an inevitable outcome when a cross-dressed character becomes the object of amorous affection. In "Marmoisan," tensions between the prince and Marmoisan are foregrounded; in "Belle-Belle," it is the attraction of the dowager queen to Fortuné that is highlighted. By blurring the boundaries between male and female, not only is gender necessarily opened up and problematized—as performance, as constructedness, as detached from a male or female sexed body—but so is heterosexuality. Does the prince love the woman underneath the male disguise, or is he attracted to the knight who happens to be a woman? Is the dowager queen attracted to the knight Fortuné or the beautiful demoiselle Belle-Belle? Or both? In all cases, the maiden warrior becomes the object of desire for both male and female characters. As a figure, the maiden warrior necessarily elicits—and unveils—queer desire.

From Mulan and Joan of Arc to Marmoisan and Fortuné, the maiden knight maintains a tenuous relationship to patriarchal power, simultaneously transgressing and reaffirming paternal authority by upholding family (especially fatherly) and national honor. The same goes for her relation to gender and sexuality. The transgression is limited to the period in which the heroine reestablishes national and familial order, at the end of which she will be initiated into womanhood through marriage or the return to domestic work. In both cases, the heroine eventually must renounce her masculinity, and in some instances she will become a wife who will exercise more or less power, as subject to her husband's desires. Like a carnivalesque festival, these narratives momentarily open up the possibilities of gender and sexuality, only to reestablish gender and sexual boundaries by the end of the tale. The ways in which the maiden warrior gets shaped in the *shōjo* manga tradition, however, increasingly queers her character. This is particularly true for Ikeda's *The Rose of Versailles*, the source for Demy's *Lady Oscar*.

Critics agree that Osamu Tezuka's *Ribon no kishi* (*The Princess Knight*; in French, *Princesse Saphir*, serialized 1953–56) was the founding text for *shōjo* manga. Best known in the United States for *Astro Boy*, Tezuka worked within the genres of science fiction, adventure stories, and period romance. Regarding the latter, Susanne Phillipps notes, "In Tezuka's romantic fantasies one can see influences from three main sources: German fairy tales, from which he borrows plots; Disney characters, from which he takes stylistic features; and the Takarazuka women's revue, from which he takes scenes that he incorporates into his manga tableau" (72). Given these influences, it comes as no surprise that "Tezuka's stories are full of fairy-tale motifs" (Phillipps 72).[22]

It is difficult to determine where Tezuka found inspiration for the main plot of *The Princess Knight*. Tezuka's manga conforms in many respects to the type of maiden warrior tales discussed above. Saphir, who has both a female and a male heart but is supposed to be a girl, is raised as a boy in order to inherit her father's throne, which can only be passed down through a male heir. As in other maiden warrior tales, Saphir must identify as male for the sake of family honor as well as for the kingdom, which risks falling into the corrupt hands of Duke Duralmin. Given Tezuka's interest in the fairy-tale genre, it is not unlikely that he was familiar with the story of Mulan. Whether or not he had read other warrior maiden tales in the tradition of L'Héritier and d'Aulnoy is not clear; however, in Volume 3, when the women at court revolt against the men, another maiden warrior reference is cited, that of Joan of Arc (Tezuka 3: 24).

Although Saphir initially is presented in gender-ambiguous terms, the ways in which Tezuka integrates fairy-tale motifs into his manga emphasize the ultimately feminine nature of his heroine. For instance, he inserts a ball scene, which clearly references "Cinderella," a scene that will recur with a twist in Ikeda's *Rose of Versailles* and Demy's *Lady Oscar*. It is an important moment in the manga, for it establishes the relation between Saphir (as a woman) and Franz Charming, the prince of the neighboring kingdom. Appearing in public for the first time as a "ravishing" beauty, looking "like a movie star" (Tezuka 1: 43), Saphir ends up having to flee the ball, much like Cinderella, to avoid the revelation of her true identity. Although Saphir does not leave behind a glass slipper, Franz Charming is obsessed throughout the rest of the manga with finding the mysterious beauty who stole his heart.

Along with fairy-tale motifs, another important influence in the creation of *The Princess Knight* that Tezuka himself has recognized is that of the Takarazuka Revue, an all-woman theater troupe created in 1913 in the city of

Takarazuka, where Tezuka grew up.[23] The earliest Takarazuka performances included fairy-tale operettas such as "Hansel and Gretel" and "Jack and the Beanstalk" as well as operettas based on figures such as Cleopatra, Joan of Arc, and Christopher Columbus. From the 1920s onward, the Takarazuka Revue borrowed from European opera and Shakespeare, moving into a fare of American musicals in the 1960s and 1970s (Berlin 40–42).[24] Actresses are trained to play either male or female roles, and as critics have noted, the "*otoko-yaku* or male-impersonators in particular attract legions of female fans and have often been portrayed in the context of an 'ideal male' image" (Nakamura and Matsuo 63).[25]

Given the fan base that has emerged around the *otoko-yaku* and the tradition of romance that inflects its corpus, one might conjecture that Takarazuka theater challenges gender and sexual norms. However, the extent to which the Takarazuka Revue upholds or puts into question gender and heteronormative desire has been subject to debate. Karen Nakamura and Hisako Matsuo maintain that Takarazuka and its offspring *shōjo* manga create "asexual, agendered spaces" (59). They insist that the "female masculinity on the Takarazuka stage is fundamentally a prepubescent asexual one—a reversion to the tomboy years of freedom before adult female responsibility symbolized by the blood of menarche" (70). For her part, Jennifer Robertson points to the necessarily complicated sexual dynamics of a same-sex theater that often deals with romance, despite the revue's patriarchal managerial ideology, which insists that its performers adhere to conventional feminine gender norms outside of the theater. Robertson argues, "The Revue continues both to uphold the dominant ideal of heterosexuality and to inform a lesbian subcultural style. In this connection, the sexual tension that has marked Takarazuka from the start still frustrates the paternalistic management" (73). Much like the maiden warrior tradition, Takarazuka theater necessarily shakes the foundations of conceptions of gender and sexuality, even as directors and producers attempt to find ways to reinstate sociosexual norms.

In the same vein, Takura's manga both challenges and reinforces gender and sexual norms. *The Princess Knight* makes clear statements about gender equity: female characters at court protest the patrilineal tradition of the monarchy and insist that Saphir has the right to rule as a woman. At the same time, Takura tries to work through and sort out gender difference as the tale progresses, depriving Saphir of her male heart in an attempt to eliminate gender ambiguity, which also results in limiting queer forms of sexuality. Franz Charming loves only the female Saphir and feels no attraction to Prince Saphir, unlike male characters in other maiden warrior tales in which gender trouble brings about sexual trouble. Given the very nature of cross-dressing, however, the manga cannot fully enforce a clear distinction between male and female, nor can it purge the story of the possibility of being read in queer terms.

Whereas the characters in *The Princess Knight* visually appear prepubescent, those from Riyoko Ikeda's *Lady Oscar* are more physically mature. As Deborah Shamoon has noted, at the time *The Rose of Versailles* appeared, "shojo manga was just beginning to shift its demographic from elementary school children to high school students" (3). This shift coincided with the emergence of a new group of female *shōjo* manga writers, referred to as the Shōwa 24 or the Year 24 Group (Shōwa 24 refers to the twenty-fourth year of the Shōwa period, meaning 1949), all of whom were influenced by Tezuka's work. The group "dealt openly with politics, sexuality, and with the psychological development and interiority of the characters" (Shamoon 5). The trend was launched by Keiko Takemiya's "In the Darkroom," published in 1970, which contains "the first male-on-male kiss in *shoujo* [*sic*] manga."[26] Works that followed in its wake include Ikeda's *The Rose of Versailles*; Moto Hagio's *Thomas no Shinzō* (*The Heart of Thomas*), a love story concerning early twentieth-century German schoolmates Thomas, Juli (or Yuli), and Eric, which Hagio began publishing in 1974; and Yasuko Aoike's *Eroika yori ai wo komete* (*From Eroica with Love*, serialized 1976–79), which revolves around the gay English earl and art thief Dorian (modeled on Dorian Gray and Robert Plant), who becomes attracted to German NATO officer Klaus.

This trend in *shōjo* manga came to be known as *shōnen-ai* or "boys' love" manga, also referred to as "beautiful boys." Interestingly, in an interview in the online *Comics Journal,* Moto Hagio explains that one of the influences in her work and especially that of Keiko Takemiya was *Barazoku* or *Rose Tribe,* a Japanese gay magazine (Hagio, "Interview"). For the creation of *The Heart of Thomas,* Hagio was more directly inspired by Jean Delannoy's 1964 film *Les Amitiés particulières* (*This Special Friendship*) about a love affair at a Catholic boys school between a younger student and an upperclassman. Same-sex romance between beautiful boys became a staple in *shōjo* manga, whose audience was predominantly female.

Bounthavy Suvilay, James Welker, and Shamoon all have commented on the ways in which boys' love *shōjo* mangas use what is, for their Japanese readership, the exotic setting of a "romanticized Europe of the past" (Welker 842) in order to bring their readers into a fantasy world in which "non-heterosexual eroticism" reigns (Suvilay 4; see also Shamoon 7). With respect to prewar Japan, Shamoon maintains that same-sex romance between girls was "a socially acceptable means of delaying heterosexual courtship until girls had finished school and were available for marriage," and it was reflected in girls' magazines of the 1920s and 1930s, which would later provide the venue for *shōjo* mangas

(4). Regarding boys' love mangas, Shamoon argues that "the boy characters in these manga invite the girl readers to identify with them because of their feminine appearance, marked with ectomorphic bodies, huge eyes, and long, flowing hair" (6). She thus suggests that male same-sex romance in boys' love manga in fact is a projection of the fashion of female same-sex romances of girls' magazines. If we add the influence of Takarazuka theater to the mix, the sexual dynamics of the boys' love *shōjo* manga prove complicated indeed: it draws from a culture based in "same-sex love" between girls, a theater tradition that queers romance through cross-dressing with an all-female cast, and male gay culture. Whether or not *shōjo* mangas represent gay or lesbian or heterosexual tendencies is not at issue for me here.[27] What we can say is that boys' love *shōjo* mangas challenge gender and heterosexual norms by opening up a space of experimentation for both queer and straight readers.

The Rose of Versailles represents a fascinating example of *shōjo* manga in that it draws from Tezuka's premise about a girl being raised as a boy out of need for a male heir, which shapes Ikeda's treatment of Lady Oscar; it visually conforms to the "beautiful boys" tradition, although the story concerns the cross-dressed Oscar and her affection for Axel von Fersen and André; and just as it draws—as do all *shōjo* manga—from the Takarazuka Revue, it also significantly feeds back into it. Robertson notes that "*The Rose of Versailles* . . . is regarded by the Revue and fans alike as the most memorable and successful postwar revue to date" (74). Erica Abbitt confirms this assessment of its success: "In the twenty-five years since its inaugural performance, the stage version of *The Rose of Versailles* has achieved a total of 1,200 performances and reached an audience of nearly 3 million people" (252). Having already attained success in manga and Takarazuka form, no wonder producer Mataichiro Yamamoto wanted to transform *The Rose of Versailles* into a film.

As Shamoon explains, Ikeda initially wanted to create a manga based on the life of Marie Antoinette, having read Stefan Zweig's biography in high school (8). But in response to fan mail, Ikeda ended up privileging Oscar's role over that of Marie Antoinette, and she had André, a secondary character, evolve into a love interest for Oscar (Shamoon 11). The story follows the intertwined lives of Marie Antoinette, Hans Axel de Fersen, and Oscar François de Jarjayes, weaving into the fabric of the main narratives the lives of other characters such as Jeanne, who will carry off the Diamond Necklace Affair; Rosalie, her sister, who will befriend Oscar and marry a revolutionary; and André, the lower-class boy in love with the cross-dressed aristocrat. Although significant treatment is given to the life of Marie Antoinette, and the manga continues for sixty pages after Oscar's death to recount the executions of Louis XVI and

Marie Antoinette, I will concentrate here on the story of Lady Oscar, which is the focus of Demy's film.

Lady Oscar presents both continuities and discontinuities with earlier warrior maiden tales. As in the cases discussed above, whether we think of Mulan, d'Aulnoy's Belle-Belle, or Tezuka's Saphir, the head of household is in need of a male heir to carry on the family's military and political duties to the monarchy. Upon realizing his wife has given birth to their sixth daughter, General de Jarjayes declares, "Women do not have a place in this family where, for generations, we have commanded armies and protected kings" (Ikeda 1: 8).[28] But when he hears the boyish, hardy cry of the infant, he decides he will raise her as a boy: "She will succeed me! I'll make of her the best soldier in all of France!" (Ikeda 1: 9).[29] In earlier maiden warrior tales, the heroine in drag conceals her female identity at all times. In the case of Oscar, however, her female identity, as Shamoon observes, "is never a secret" (9). At home as well as at court, members of the French aristocracy are aware that Oscar is a woman in men's clothing; they appear to accept to some degree her gender and sexual ambiguity, which the narrator attributes to French mores of the period.[30]

At the same time, Oscar is more thoroughly masculine than her predecessors, or at least masculinity represents an integral and significant part of her identity. Raised as a boy in boys' clothes with her nursemaid's grandson André, Oscar continues donning male garb as she enters the service of the dauphine, Marie Antoinette. Even when her nursemaid insists that Oscar wear a dress the first time she meets the dauphine, Oscar responds, "I cannot wear this 'thing!'" (Ikeda 1: 63). Unlike Saphir, who devotes several hours a day to her feminine side, which includes wearing a dress, Oscar simply does not know what to do with one. At the French court, everyone accepts that Oscar is sexed as female, although the effect of her continuous ritualized performance of her masculinity suggests that both her sex and her gender are in question. Precisely because her masculinity is essential to her being, Oscar indeed proves to be a more complex and ambiguously gendered character than Marmoisan, Belle-Belle, or Saphir.

Ikeda also opens up the limits of sexuality in her depiction of Oscar. In d'Aulnoy and Tezuka, for instance, female characters only fall in love with the heroine when they are duped into believing "she" is a "he." In the case of Lady Oscar, however, women are attracted to her as an ambiguously gendered character, an ambiguity evident in the use of subject pronouns as well as the illustrations of her/him. Early in Oscar's life at court, Ikeda produces a scene in which several young ladies ogle him:

LADY 1: There is Oscar François!

LADY 2: Oh! He is always so handsome!

LADY 3: It's Oscar.

LADY 1: [*cupping her cheeks*] What coldness! He never addresses us.

LADY 2: Ah! If only he really was a man, I would do everything to be his wife!

LADY 3: Fff, well I prefer André . . .

[*Oscar looks over at them*]

LADY 3: [*covering her face with her hands*] Ah! He's looking this way!

LADY 1: But you said that you preferred André . . .

LADY 2: Hmm . . . I'm going to dream about him all night!

(IKEDA 1: 88)

Interestingly, the ladies both affirm and question Oscar's "real" sex. They consistently refer to Oscar as "he" even when suggesting Oscar is in fact a woman: "Ah! if only he really was a man." The effect of Oscar's ritualized gender performance ends up undermining any clear notion of her "true" sex. Despite or because of ambiguities related to Oscar's gender and sex, these young women continue to gaze at and fantasize about "him," and they blush when Oscar looks their way. The scene stages a queer desire that is at once both homosexual and heterosexual and neither homosexual nor heterosexual.

Such scenes recur throughout the manga, in which female characters develop schoolgirl crushes on Oscar and can only dream of marrying her. Moreover, Oscar regularly plays a manly role in several scenes with Marie Antoinette. The latter consoles herself in Oscar's arms (Ikeda 1: 155), tries to give Oscar lavish presents (1: 262), and dances with Oscar, much to Rosalie's dismay (1: 520–21). However, Ikeda sets limits to the sexual ambiguity of her character. When Jeanne de la Motte accuses the queen of having sexual relationships with her female entourage, Oscar is enraged: "What!? Me a lesbian!? I'm going to cut her in two!?"[31] Perhaps this is Ikeda's way of signaling that her depiction of Oscar fits securely within the tradition of girl same-sex love, to be distinguished from lesbianism, which, nevertheless, has been read into the manga by Japanese lesbians, as Welker has documented.[32]

At times Oscar struggles with her dual identity as masculine and feminine. In a scene that recalls the ball scene of Tezuka's *Princess Knight*, Oscar wears a dress in order to please Fersen, whom she secretly loves. Much like Cinderella, Oscar arrives out of nowhere, presenting herself as a foreign duchess, and men and women alike find her most beautiful. Immediately attracted to the duchess—but not to the ostensibly masculine woman Oscar—Fersen asks her to dance and actually tells her that she reminds him of Oscar, whom he also finds beautiful although he is puzzled by her male attire. He even asks her, "Are you Oscar?" after which, as if the clock struck twelve, Oscar flees, never to don women's clothing again (Ikeda 1: 714–22).

This first ball scene is followed later in the manga by a second one, which in many respects is the polar opposite of the first and demonstrates the extent to which Oscar fully embraces her female masculinity. Her father decides to marry her to the nobleman Girondelle, which understandably angers Oscar, who tells her father that she cannot simply become a woman, given the life she has been leading. Oscar then plans an extravagant ball and appears wearing a magnificent officer's uniform, which angers her father. Oscar proceeds to dance and flirt with Mademoiselle de Guigne, Josephine, and Flora, and the scene culminates in Oscar kissing Geneviève de Coingy on the dance floor (Ikeda 2: 66–97). This behavior does not sway Girondelle, who has a *Nouvelle Héloïse* fantasy about what his marriage to Oscar would be like, although he ends up backing down from the marriage out of love for Oscar.[33] Regarding this second ball scene, Suvilay remarks, "The heroine does not come dressed as a princess, but rather she appears with the traits of a Prince Charming, seducing men as well as women" (7).[34] Not quite feeling comfortable in the role of Cinderella, Oscar proves to be a much more confident Prince Charming.

Shamoon points to the fact that, "whereas Fersen saw her only as a man, Girodel sees Oscar only as a woman, which infuriates her" (11). André, however, is the only male protagonist who fully accepts Oscar's gender ambiguity and understands even better than Oscar who she is. When his grandmother is dismayed at Oscar's refusal to wear a dress to meet Marie Antoinette, André declares, "Grandmother, you're wasting your time! It's like that!" (Ikeda 1: 63).[35] His equivocal use of "It's like that!" marks an attempt to name the nameless, to read the unreadable. André loves Oscar as a masculine woman. This is emphasized again when Oscar prepares for the first ball. Aware that Oscar wears a dress for Fersen, André expresses both jealousy and a sense that Oscar wearing a dress is in fact an aberration. Indeed, it is abnormal: "It's a nightmare! My Oscar is going to wear a frilly dress and is going to dance with other men!?"[36] André suggests that it is when Oscar tries to pass as a feminine woman that she truly is in drag. It is precisely because André does not ask her "to compromise either her masculine or her feminine identities" that "Oscar is able to give herself completely to Andre . . . she finds true love without losing her identity to her partner" (Shamoon 12). With André Oscar never feels forced to renounce her masculinity, while André demonstrates traits of a feminine, even castrated man.

This castration manifests itself socially and physically. Not only is André of lower social standing than Oscar, but he also will lose an eye and eventually his sight. Socially and physically, then, André is in a "subordinate, dependent position" in relation to Oscar (Shamoon 12). Moreover, for most of the manga, he is the character who experiences unrequited love, a plight usually reserved for female characters. And even though André is the lower-class character, it will be Oscar who enlightens him about the plight of the people and the need for revolution. Initially desiring to understand the suffering of the people so that she can inform the queen, Oscar eventually reads works by Jean-Jacques Rousseau and Voltaire, for which her father scolds her: "These are books for the lower orders!"[37] It is through Oscar that André becomes interested in Rousseau. André as the feminine partner is emphasized as well through the implicit parallel Ikeda makes between Oscar and Fersen: just as Fersen has decided never to marry out of his love for Marie Antoinette, so Oscar decides never to marry out of her love for André. Both stories are built around impossible love, for Marie Antoinette is married to the king and André is lower class, making them inaccessible to, respectively, Fersen and Oscar.

Oscar rebels against both the sex-gender system of the Old Regime and its class and political structure. Whereas earlier maiden warriors sought to restore and reform (with respect to gender) a monarchy that privileged the upper class, Oscar instead helps topple the monarchy and renounces her title. Oscar's evolution follows in many respects that of the historical revolutionaries. Initially hoping to reform the monarchy through her own *prise de conscience,* Oscar ends up leading the siege of the Bastille with the people. Deciding she no longer wants to be the doll (*poupée*) of the monarchy, she requests to be transferred from the queen's guard to the French guards, an infantry unit consisting primarily of commoners assigned to the palace. Although the soldiers initially refuse to take orders from a woman, they end up developing a relationship with Oscar, who sympathizes with their miserable situation and protects them when necessary, using her political connections. When ordered to escort the members of the Third Estate out of the Estates General meeting, Oscar refuses, and her men are imprisoned, but they are eventually released by Marie Antoinette out of her friendship for Oscar. Later Oscar and her troops are ordered to back the German troops brought in by Louis XVI to protect the monarchy from protesters. Instead of protecting the monarchy, Oscar and her men fight alongside the people, as she renounces her title of countess. Oscar and André promise to marry after the battle, but André is killed just before Oscar leads the revolt against the Bastille, and she is then killed herself.

The fact that Ikeda shapes her maiden warrior as an agent who helps usher in the French Revolution is indeed significant. Whereas other maiden warrior tales concern the temporary suspension of a patriarchal political and familial order that privileges the upper classes, transgression in *The Rose of Versailles* is far from temporary, as symbolized by the outbreak of the French Revolution. The Old Regime's gender, sex, and class structure has been permanently altered. We must keep in mind the period in which Ikeda is writing. As Shamoon remarks in a note, "Ikeda describes the events leading to the Revolution in great detail, which in 1972 would have resonated with the student protests of the New Left [in Japan]" (16). The notion of radically transforming society—at the level of the political as well as the personal, with respect to class as well as with respect to gender—was an objective of student, worker, and civil rights movements in the 1960s and 1970s across the globe. Through her rewriting of the French Revolution, Ikeda addresses issues related to class and especially to gender and sexuality that were relevant to her generation.

DEMY'S *LADY OSCAR*

Although in her study of *The Rose of Versailles* Shamoon does an excellent job of situating the manga within the larger context of the culture and history of girls' magazines, same-sex romance, and the development of *shōjo* manga, her analysis of Jacques Demy's filmic adaptation of *The Rose of Versailles* is limited precisely because she does not situate *Lady Oscar* within Demy's oeuvre. She states, "In the film, Andre (Barry Stokes) is the strongest partner, and their conflict is not about Oscar's need for independence or her fear of losing herself in a relationship but about their class differences. Andre mockingly and smugly dictates Oscar's political awakening, but they never become social or romantic equals" (14). She goes on to argue that Catriona MacColl appears too feminine throughout Demy's film and that only a Takarazuka actress would be able to depict Oscar with the right balance of masculine and feminine traits. Ironically, it was the Japanese producers who unanimously supported MacColl for the role. After hopelessly looking for an English actress with blonde hair and blue eyes and some fencing and riding abilities who would be available after the film's Japanese release to do publicity for the cosmetic company Shiseido, one of the film's main investors, Demy presented MacColl to the producers. Demy states, "I took Catriona to the Japanese [producers]. I got a unanimous look, a smile: Okay, and that was it" (Berthomé 303).[38] One wonders if their choice was based on MacColl's "exotic"—from the perspective of a Japanese audience—appearance, one of the qualities characteristic of *shōjo* manga's heroes and heroines.

Drawing from Shamoon's analysis, one could argue that Demy's film takes away from the ways in which Ikeda's manga empowers the ambiguously gendered character Oscar. His film could be read as reinstating a patriarchal order precisely by having André mediate Oscar's transformation and by depicting Oscar as the weaker partner in the couple. At times, Demy seems to reproduce essentialist notions of gender. After killing Chantilly in a duel, a scene of Demy's invention, Oscar drinks to overcome the difficulties she has in dealing with the fact that she has taken a man's life.[39] She tells André, "Answer this riddle: now that I've learned to walk, and talk, and fight like a man, even think, and I think like a man, why can't I kill like a man?" André replies, "Because you're not a man." Such moments in the film could be read in terms of Demy disempowering Ikeda's heroine and reinforcing conventional gender norms: no matter how much Oscar performs as a man, she will never be one.

However, the reading of *Lady Oscar* proves more complex when we situate it within Demy's cinema. It becomes clear that his filmic adaptation of the manga is shaped, first, by questions of gender and sexuality that have always preoccupied Demy; second, by the recurrent theme of the closet, most explicitly treated in *The Umbrellas of Cherbourg,* which for the first time in his career moves into a "coming out" narrative; and, third, by the class issues that dominate in *A Room in Town.* Ikeda's Oscar has much more self-knowledge than Demy's heroine, who initially is in denial about sexual and class issues. Whereas in the manga Oscar seeks out answers to the questions she is already asking herself, in the film it is the lower-class André who ponders the questions Oscar fails to ask. Through her relationship with André, the aristocratic Oscar will "find herself" with respect to gender, sexuality, and class. André serves as her guide, who ushers her sexual and political "coming out." Although Demy's film presents continuities with Ikeda's manga, by granting the lower-class character André more agency and by emphasizing collective instead of individual action, Demy challenges the model of aristocratic heroism that underpins maiden warrior tales, including *The Rose of Versailles.* As such, his film both celebrates and represents the undoing of the tradition of the maiden warrior tale.

Gender as Performance

Stories within the tradition of maiden warrior tales all approach gender as performance to some degree or another. In the case of *Lady Oscar,* Demy puts increased emphasis on the performativity and constructedness of gender through the film's framing devices and through the juxtaposition between Oscar—a woman who dresses, acts, and often passes as a man—and Marie

Antoinette—who constantly performs her femininity. By foregrounding more generally life as performance in the film, Demy can denaturalize fixed gender, sexual, and class identities, whose stability is permanently shaken with the onset of the French Revolution.

What is particularly striking about the cinematography of *Lady Oscar* is the frequent use of long-shot framing to open many of the film's scenes. This technique produces the effect of a proscenium arch, making it appear as though characters emerge onto a stage, thus emphasizing the theatricality— the "unnaturalness"—of the roles they play. In *Lady Oscar*, everything from birth and death to revolution is staged through ritualized actions, which emphasizes more generally the performativity of life itself.

Lady Oscar opens with a painterly shot of the Jarjayes country manor set in a perfectly symmetrical frame. This opening shot represents the order that will come to be disrupted over the course of the film by gender and sexual play, as well as by revolution. The next image is a shot of the staircase inside the manor, to which the camera often returns over the course of the film (Figure 4.1). A site of transition, from upstairs to downstairs, the staircase is framed by two Greco–Roman statues: one of a man, to the right; and another of a woman, to the left. At the center of the shot Monsieur de Jarjayes paces back and forth, waiting to find out if his wife is about to give birth to his first son or yet another daughter. With the father walking back and forth, our eyes move with him, going from the female statue to the male statue and back again. From the very beginning of the film, then, tensions and movements between masculine and feminine are foregrounded.

In the following shot we see Monsieur de Jarjayes pacing from another perspective: he moves back and forth in front of his five daughters, who sit below a statue of a man whose genitalia are covered up by a leaf. A woman cries out, and we realize a baby is born. Jarjayes declares, "A son, at last!" But when the nurse enters the room with a baby, which she claims is a girl whose mother died in childbirth, Jarjayes replies, "My wife would not give her life for so lowly a contribution as another daughter. The child you hold is Oscar François de Jarjayes, heir to my commission as commander of the royal guards." As he pronounces these words, he stands directly next to the veiled genitalia of the statue (Figure 4.2). He then instructs the nurse to bring her grandson to the manor to serve as "my son's" companion.

The scene is a perfect illustration of what Butler refers to as "the interpellation of gender," whereby the child is, in this case, "boyed," a founding gesture that will be reiterated throughout the film in Oscar's dress and masculine training.[40] This naming initiates the process whereby Oscar's repeated performances as a boy or a man indeed "materialize" or "stabilize," to use Butler's ter-

Figure 4.1. The central staircase of the Jarjayes manor.

Figure 4.2. Monsieur de Jarjayes (Mark Kingston) declares his newborn is a boy.

minology, her identity as a man–woman, or masculine woman. Her repeated performances as a boy make Oscar's masculinity an inseparable and fixed part of her identity. The veiled genitalia of the male statue indeed announces the dissociation between one's apparent biological sex, which Oscar's father "veils" in his interpellation of Oscar as male, and one's socially recognized gender.

That Oscar's masculinity is staged is suggested at several moments in the film, especially through the shots that create the effect of a proscenium arch. In the series of images that open the segment "1767," we see a twelve-year-old Oscar emerge from behind one door, making an entrance into the dining room, and then she emerges from behind the front door of the manor, out onto an outdoor "stage" where she will engage in fencing practice with her adoptive brother, André. In a similar manner, the segment "1775" opens with the now twenty-year-old Oscar making an "entrance" from the woods as if from backstage to again fence with André (see Figures 4.3 and 4.4).[41] Through the two sequences of 1767 and 1775, we thus come to understand that Oscar's masculine training with André has been continuous throughout her youth. As such, the film conveys the sense that this is a ritual performance reiterated over time, which results in the materialization of masculinity in Oscar's body and ways of being.

Interestingly, Oscar's performance of masculinity is often juxtaposed to Marie Antoinette's performance of femininity. In the segment "1775," the film moves from the Jarjayes estate, where Oscar and André are fencing and where they receive the announcement of Oscar's position as personal guard of Marie Antoinette, to Marie Antoinette's apartment, where the young queen is preparing her own appearance as if in a dressing room backstage. Similarly, "July 1785" opens with Marie Antoinette playing the role of Rosine from Pierre-Augustin Caron de Beaumarchais's *Le Barbier de Seville* (*The Barber of Seville*, ca. 1773), which is followed by Oscar's first "performance" as head of the French Royal Guard. Whereas Marie Antoinette seeks to "look the part of the roguish maiden Rosine," Oscar, for her part, debuts as an officer in her first fully masculine role. Although her first attempt to lead her men borders on failure, her authority as officer of an all-male guard will be reaffirmed later in the film. We might read these parallel scenes in terms of the ways in which they mutually support the performative aspect of gender identity; together, they suggest not only that Oscar performs her masculinity but also that Marie Antoinette performs her femininity. Such scenes thus denaturalize masculinity and femininity—detaching them from their supposed mimetic relation to biological sex—by emphasizing performativity and the ritual reiteration of performance in the construction of gender identities.

Two particularly important moments in the staging of Oscar's gender that

Figure 4.3. A twelve-year-old Oscar walks onto the "stage" for her performance of masculinity with André.

Figure 4.4. A now twenty-year-old Oscar continues her ritual performance of masculinity.

bring out the character's inner struggles concerning her identity occur within the context of the two ball scenes, which Demy reproduces from Ikeda. In the first ball scene, Oscar seeks Fersen's affections and goes to a palace ball dressed as a woman. Like Cinderella, she makes an entrance as a beautiful unknown; no one at court recognizes her. Although she is successful in "passing" as a woman, she looks somehow unnatural in her frilly gown, even if André and Fersen find her beautiful. Her style is not in synch with the other women at court, and she understandably appears somewhat awkward and less self-assured in a role that she has never played before. As in Ikeda's manga, this scene is opposed to the second ball scene of Oscar's engagement party. Against her father's wishes, rather than dressing like a woman, Oscar makes an entrance in full officer garb in a reaffirmation of her "true"—that is to say, embodied, materialized—gender. Whereas in the first ball scene, she momentarily tries to be something she is not, in the second ball scene, she "comes out," so to say, as her true and hybrid self.

Precisely because Oscar does not cross-dress temporarily, her character could be described in terms of being "transgender." When discussing the background of the term, Susan Stryker explains, "If a *transvestite* was somebody who episodically changed into the clothes of the so-called 'other sex,' and a *transsexual* was somebody who permanently changed genitals in order to claim membership in a gender other than the one assigned at birth, then a *transgender* was somebody who permanently changed social gender through the public presentation of the self, without recourse to genital transformation" (4). Although Stryker broadens her definition of "transgender" to be more inclusive than what is suggested above, this notion of having a social gender that is distinct from one's assigned sex (although Oscar's father designates her as male at birth) is relevant to Oscar's identity. She does not fit neatly into the category of either "male" or "female." Yet, for all intents and purposes, she functions as a man in French society, an identity Oscar vindicates in the second ball scene.[42]

COMING OUT QUEER

As the two ball scenes suggest, Oscar's character evolves over the course of the film in such a way that the film could be read as a "coming out" narrative. A similar development arguably occurs with Ikeda's Oscar. Yet by making his Oscar less self-assured and less self-knowing, Demy foregrounds Oscar's timidity, even fear, of fully embracing her queer desires and her queer self, a timidity and fear not present in Ikeda's Oscar. Thus the reaffirmation of Oscar's masculinity in the second ball scene becomes pivotal in her coming out and leads her to finally embrace her transgressive relationship to the lower-class André, which becomes inseparable from embracing the cause of the French Revolution. Reminiscent of *The Umbrellas of Cherbourg*, class transgression serves as a figure for sexual transgression. However, *Lady Oscar* ends not with the heroine's concession to social pressures and the closet but, rather, with her liberation. Oscar violates the cultural taboos of her society by the end of the film, ultimately freeing herself from the social constraints that separated her from her true love. She finally comes to terms with and consummates her queer relationship to André.

The relationship between Oscar and André can be read as queer in several respects. First, the two are "suckling siblings," raised as brother and sister.[43] As such, their relationship can be construed as incestuous, which, as we have seen, serves as a figure in Demy's films for queer forms of love. Second, Oscar's gender ambiguity, the fact that in most respects she feels like a man—she walks, talks, fights, and thinks like a man—sets her relationship with André outside the norms of heterosexuality. Moreover, this relationship was never going to fulfill the reproductive demands of heteronormative society. Well before the couple meets a tragic end, Oscar makes it clear to Marie Antoinette that she never intends to have children. Finally, we can read into the "incongruity" of their class-crossing relationship another figure for transgressive sexuality.

However, Oscar has great difficulty in accepting her feelings for André. As we have seen, in the first ball scene Oscar tries to acquire Fersen's love. In Demy, Fersen does not state that it is because of her ambiguous gender identity that he rejects Oscar, as in Ikeda, but rather, it is because he is hopelessly in love with Marie Antoinette. This becomes evident in the scene in which Oscar, having left the ball, walks by a fountain and comes upon André. André forcibly embraces her and declares,

ANDRÉ: I love you Oscar.

OSCAR: You have no right.

ANDRÉ: Oh, you're wrong. I do have the right. I've loved you for my entire life and I have the right to keep on loving you. I don't pity myself because that love isn't returned. I pity you for being unable to return it. You dared all this because you knew Fersen loved another, didn't you?

OSCAR: Shut up!

ANDRÉ: And we'll both pretend that all this never happened, won't we? We'll be like those life-sized puppets in the queen's hamlet. I'll be the invisible stable boy, and you'll be the brave toy soldier.

OSCAR: I want it to be like it's always been with us.

ANDRÉ: And how sad that is for both of us, Oscar, how very sad that is. I'll never touch you again. I promise.

This dialogue asks us to read Oscar's attraction to Fersen in terms of the displacement of her affection for a taboo object (André) onto a more socially acceptable one (Fersen), which Oscar unconsciously knew would fail, as André remarks. As opposed to *The Umbrellas'* Geneviève, who "succeeded" (although she may not be happy) in displacing her affection from Guy to Roland (whom she does not seem to love), Oscar doomed to failure her attempt to conform to social norms from the start by trying to attract Fersen, whom she knew loved another. André suggests here that he knows Oscar loves him and that she is afraid to act upon this love precisely because it is taboo, but only taboo within the arbitrary social norms of pre-Revolutionary France.

The idea that Oscar is separated from André by arbitrary conventions is emphasized in the scene in which Oscar seeks out André in the Versailles stables. She tells André that she misses him, to which André responds, "Then what is this all about? Here we are, breathing the same air, both alone, missing each other." When André brings up social class, Oscar insists on their difference, stating that they are "separated by the laws I've accepted as the right laws." Whereas Oscar dwells on the way things are, André reflects on the way things could be, declaring, "A man can love whomever he wants in America." Invoking utopian possibilities, André tries to point out the arbitrariness of the laws that separate them and that bring them unnecessary suffering.

We can obviously read this dialogue as pertaining to class and the ways in which the American Revolution inspired the French Revolution. Expressing the freedoms that were gained in the American Revolution in terms of being able to love whomever one desires, however, begs a reading of the scene in terms of the vindication of a queer sexuality. Through this lens, André's words could be understood as alluding to another, more recent American Revolution that similarly influenced France: Stonewall. As Frédéric Martel explains, in France "there was no real mobilization related to sexual mores during the events of May '68" (15). In fact, the voices coming from the gay community met with repression. However, the Stonewall riots of 1969 gave impetus to French gay activists: "the concrete model that inspired homosexuals [in France] came from the United States" (Martel 17). Three years after Stonewall, Guy Hocquenghem would insist on the need "to transfer the idea of revolution to sex" in a celebrated letter published in the French weekly, *Le Nouvel Observateur* (Martel 13).

As we have seen in his own critique of France, which he viewed as a "very closed, self-censuring country with old structures" (Langlois), Demy invokes Paul Morrissey's *Trash* as a film that radically breaks with cinematic conventions, which cannot be separated from the ways in which it challenges social and sexual norms. Interestingly, the camp classic stars gay icon Joe Dallesandro as "Joe," the significant other (more or less) of "Holly," played by Holly Woodlawn, another Warhol protégé who went on to become a well-known transgender performer. Clearly Demy was interested in queer couples of all sorts throughout his career, whether we think of Monsieur Dame (Mr. Lady), a womanly man in love with Danielle Darrieux's character Yvonne in *Les Demoiselles de Rochefort,* or Marcello Mastroianni's character Marco—another female man—who believes he is pregnant with Irène's baby in *A Slightly Pregnant Man,* not to mention the numerous examples of incestuous relations that stand in for queerness in Demy's films (see chapter 2). In the spirit of Morrissey's films but depicted in much subtler tones, *Lady Oscar* represents a continuation of Demy's exploration of queer forms of sexuality.

Although an "accident," as Berthomé puts it, in his film career, *Lady Oscar* effectively serves as another vehicle for Demy to explore his preoccupation with revolutionizing gender and sexuality, of creating a world in which people are not condemned for loving each other based on arbitrary social conventions. Regarding the violent response from the French people to his own transgressive relationship with Marie Antoinette, a married woman, Fersen pensively says to Oscar, "Strange, isn't it, that a simple love between two people can be despised as hatred and war?" Fersen's lament about the hatred shown two people just for being in love anticipates André's utopian depiction of America as a place where one has the right to love whomever one desires. Such moments reveal that this film about the French Revolution is as much about liberation with respect to sexuality as it is about liberation with respect to class.

As the circumstances of the people slowly lead them to rebel, so Oscar's own evolution eventually leads to her personal rebellion, symbolized in the scene in which she draws her sword against her father. Oscar's personal revolution is mediated by André, who pushes her forward. André decides to no longer be Oscar's servant when it appears that she will not protest her father's choice of the libertine Girodet for her husband. (Demy takes the more idealistic depiction of Girondelle in Ikeda and transforms him into the debauched Girodet.) Before leaving the Jarjayes manor, André insists, "We all have the right to choose," a message Oscar eventually absorbs when she chooses not to fire upon the people later in the film. Just after the second ball scene, when Oscar affirms her transgender self, she observes Bernard giving a speech in the streets of Paris demanding a meeting of the Estates General. When the king's troops charge and disperse the protesters, André pulls Oscar out of the confusion, and Oscar informs him that she broke off her engagement with Girodet. André replies, "Then you're learning. You've already taken the first step. Now, will you have the courage to break the ties with your past? Will you come with me, Oscar?" In almost a whisper, Oscar repeats, "I can't, I can't, I can't" as she disappears, almost hiding, moving back into the shadows . . . into the closet. In the end, however, Oscar will break her ties and be united—albeit ever so briefly—with André. Whereas in *The Umbrellas* Geneviève cedes to social pressure and renounces her transgressive love, in *Lady Oscar* the heroine ends up rejecting the artificial limits to her sexuality and embraces her true feelings.

Demy himself was slowly becoming more daring as a director with respect to sexuality. In *Lady Oscar* Demy films his first same-sex kiss, which occurs, as in the manga, during the second ball scene, when Oscar appears in a beautiful white caped uniform. Looking over the ladies, Oscar chooses one with whom she dances before giving her a long kiss (Figure 4.5). In discussing temporary cross-dressing in film, Straayer argues that the kiss of a cross-dressed woman who embraces another woman "collapses actual homosexuality and implied heterosexuality" (54). Although Oscar is not a temporary cross-dresser—she, more properly speaking, is transgender—Straayer's analysis still rings true regarding the complicated reading of the kiss. And as in the case of a cross-dressed man who kisses a woman, Oscar embracing André, which happens later in the film, is a kiss that "collapses actual heterosexuality with implied homosexuality" (54). Straayer concludes that homosexual and heterosexual readings of the "bivalent kiss" concerning a cross-dresser "are not separable. The viewer experiences both simultaneously" (55).

But usually the bivalent kiss is not a final scene; the implied homosexuality is eventually negated in a heteronormative ending in temporary transvestite films. In the case of Demy, however, precisely because Oscar wears male clothing and functions like a man on a permanent basis, the homosexual or queer readings of her relationship to the woman she kisses or to André are never foreclosed upon. In fact, the kiss in *Lady Oscar* only anticipates the unveiled homosexual kiss in Demy's 1982 film *Parking*. Based on the story of *Orpheus* and Jean Cocteau's film *Orpheus*, Demy includes a same-sex kiss, this time between Orpheus and a male friend. Becoming bolder in his representation of queer desires, Demy's Orpheus proves to be a queer character who freely and openly embraces the complexities of his sexuality.

In his piece on sexuality in Demy, Raphaël Lefèvre notes the increased use of nudity in his films and describes Demy's final film, *Three Seats for the 26th,* as already noted in chapter 2, in terms of "calm audacity, absence of guilt and moral judgment: Demy tops off his career with a shaky film but with a stunning vision of love and taboos."[44] Given its daring representation of queer

Figure 4.5. Oscar kisses a lady in the second ball scene.

sexuality, *Lady Oscar* marks a significant moment in Demy's own evolution as a director. As such, we might look at Oscar as a figure for Demy himself, who "comes out" as a queer director, or director of queerness, through the film.

CLASS AND REVOLUTION

Breaking open the constraints of gender and sexuality in the film is inseparable from challenging class prejudices and oppression. Returning to Shamoon's assessment of the film, we find that she reads Demy's *Lady Oscar* in terms of disempowering Oscar. But we cannot separate Oscar—in Ikeda or Demy—from the aristocracy with which she identifies and that situates her socially as André's superior. What Shamoon sees as the disempowerment of Oscar could be read instead in terms of Demy empowering the people. This empowerment occurs, first, through the character of André, who proves much more independent and intelligent as a lower-class character than Ikeda's André, and, second, by displacing agency from the aristocratic heroine to a collective subject: the French people. Both Ikeda's manga and Demy's film have their heroines participate in the dismantling of the monarchy the traditional maiden warrior fought to uphold. However, Demy's film goes further than Ikeda's manga in its problematization of the model of aristocratic heroism the manga continues to support.

In many respects, Demy's film invites us to read into Ikeda's manga tendencies of aristocratic paternalism and noblesse oblige. Ikeda's Oscar develops on her own an awareness of class conflict in which André expresses little interest, despite his lower status. In the manga, André follows Oscar to the French guard and plays the role, essentially, of Oscar's sidekick. Demy reframes the relation by foregrounding the issue of class that divides them. When Oscar is to become Marie Antoinette's personal guard, André follows her to Versailles to work in the stables, a job Oscar's father acquired for him. When Monsieur de Jarjayes announces their new vocations, André responds, sarcastically, "I've always dreamed of working in the stables." Whereas Ikeda's lower-class André is much more self-effacing and quickly submits to Oscar, Demy's André constantly emphasizes the tensions inherent in a relationship defined according to the Old Regime social order.

Demy visually emphasizes the class divide that separates Oscar from André with respect to both their physical appearance and their duties, a divide that is instituted when they reach adulthood. (They dress and act as equals in 1767 and until the beginning of 1775, which delimits the period of their childhood.) Unlike in *The Rose of Versailles,* Demy's André never appears at court, nor is he ever dressed as elegantly as Ikeda's André. In the film, he wears only earthy browns, which presents a contrast to the crisp royal blue, white, and gold-trimmed officer's uniform that Oscar wears. Moreover, André is always positioned as Oscar's inferior in public spaces, either driving her carriage or taking care of her horses.

After they are initiated into the adult world, the only moments in the film when distinctions between them are lifted occur in the space of the stables, the site of Oscar and André's intimacy and class transgressions. Early in the film, a young Oscar and André lie together in the hay in the Jarjayes stables. After the scene of the tavern brawl, the two again find themselves waking from a drunken stupor in a stable near the tavern, and it is at the Versailles stables where Oscar seeks André's advice regarding her soldiers' failure to appear with their swords and to obey her orders. Each of these scenes anticipates the moment toward the end of the film when Oscar and André make love in the same stables where they played as children, before the artificial class structure imposed itself upon them, separating them from each other. The film comes full circle, from their union as children when class played little to no role in their relationship, to the final love scene, which occurs after Oscar renounces her family, her nobility, and the monarchy—in other words, when Oscar finally breaks through the barriers that separated her from André as well as from herself.

However, until the final scenes of the film, Oscar has a difficult time overcoming the complacency and expectations of her class in ways that are reminiscent of Geneviève in *The Umbrellas of Cherbourg.* Oscar has no awareness of the plight of the lower classes until the poor laundress Rosalie offers to sleep with Oscar to pay her rent. In disbelief, Oscar tells Rosalie, "People don't go hungry in Paris," to which Rosalie responds, "People starve in Paris." After giving Rosalie some money, Oscar scolds André for not telling her the people were starving. Noting that they pass through this same neighborhood all the time, André retorts, "Why didn't you look, why didn't you see?" As opposed to Ikeda's rather sassy aristocrat who often challenges Marie Antoinette and wants to learn more about the plight of the lower classes in order to inform the queen, Demy's Oscar defends the monarchy, much like the traditional maiden warrior. Indeed, the tavern brawl breaks out because Oscar reproaches Robespierre for speaking ill of the Crown, and then she accuses of treason another man who declared that the royal family should be amputated. Nevertheless, her heart often leads her to do the right thing. For instance, Oscar engages in a duel in defense of a commoner, which her father finds "questionable." Such scenes foreground the fact that Oscar is constantly torn between her personal sense of justice and her attachment to class, king, and father.

In Demy's film, Oscar's father embodies the patriarchal social order of the Old Regime. It is notable that Demy has Oscar's mother die after giving birth. In the manga, Oscar's mother represents an ideal image of motherhood in her femininity and her tenderness. Her character provides instances when Oscar demonstrates her very "sonly" attachment to the mother. By eliminating the mother figure, Demy can more completely associate the family with patriarchy and its connection to a larger patriarchal social order in which female heirs are deemed worthless, a theme that recurs when Marie Antoinette gives birth to her first child, a daughter, for which the royal doctor is only paid one-fourth of what he would have been paid had a son been born. Values and conflicts within the microcosm of the family reinforce and are reinforced by values and conflicts within the macrocosm of the nation.

Oscar's father is acutely aware of one's place in society and of one's duties to the Crown. When preparing Oscar and André to leave for Versailles, he states, "You will each assume responsibility for your separate stations in life." Slightly disturbed by Oscar's defense of a commoner, he later becomes furious when he learns that Oscar refused to fire on the people, who were protesting the fact that they were turned away from the Estates General and who began calling for a National Assembly. Father and daughter draw swords, and Monsieur de Jarjayes injures Oscar's hand, at which time André steps in to protect her. Just as Oscar leaves, stating, "I'll never come home again," Jarjayes continues his dinner routine, declaring, "Order must be maintained if the world is to stay the same!" We might view Monsieur de Jarjayes and André as representing the two tendencies that pull Oscar in different directions: conformism and a repressive status quo, on the one hand, and liberatory change, on the other.

Significantly, in the film Oscar and André are finally reunited in the modest stable, whereas Ikeda has them make love in Oscar's bedroom at the paternal home. The space in which their love is consummated is noteworthy in that it symbolizes the possibility of reconciliation (Ikeda) as opposed to rupture (Demy) with the family or the father. Ikeda paints a much more sympathetic picture of Monsieur de Jarjayes than Demy, and despite political tensions that come between father and daughter, they are reconciled before Oscar is killed while laying siege to the Bastille. This conciliatory take on father–daughter relations extends to class relations. Ikeda constantly blurs the boundaries between commoner and aristocrat. Jeanne de la Motte is the daughter of a noble descendant of the Valois, and her half-sister Rosalie is fully noble, discovering herself to be the bastard daughter of Madame de Polignac. Oscar's family takes the commoner Rosalie into their home, and Rosalie moves between commoners and aristocrats, having starved in the streets of Paris and attended a Versailles ball. Likewise, the noble Alain de Soissons, whose family has fallen from grace, finds himself in a unit of commoners. And the king's cousin the duc d'Orléans entertains a mixed crowd of commoners and aristocrats.

Demy instead reinforces class divisions. In the film, Jeanne claims to be a descendant of the Valois, and it remains only a claim. Rosalie is not of noble blood either and finds herself at the home of the Jarjayes only when delivering a dress to Oscar for the ball. Rather than arriving in style to court to exact revenge upon the noblewoman whose carriage killed her mother, as in the manga, Demy's Rosalie conceals herself with André's help in the trunk of Oscar's carriage, out of which she creeps to spy on the guests from outside the palace. For his part, André is confined to the stables and never wears the beautiful uniforms Ikeda's André dons. There is a clear demarcation between aristocrats and commoners in the film, and the only two characters who cross class lines are Oscar and Jeanne. In effect, the aristocracy appears less culpable in the manga than in the film.

Not unrelated to Ikeda's and Demy's respective representations of class is their depictions of individual heroism versus collective action, with Ikeda privileging the former and Demy the latter. Two episodes stand out as exemplary of these tendencies. In Ikeda, when Oscar and her men refuse to expel from the Estates General the representatives of the Third Estate, Oscar's men are imprisoned and threatened with death, and the king plans to sanction Oscar. While Oscar rallies the revolutionary Bernard to help save her men, Marie Antoinette, out of her friendship with Oscar, releases them. In a similar scene in the film, Oscar refuses to give the order to her men to fire on the people, and then her superior orders her own men to shoot her, which they refuse to carry out. When they are all thrown in jail, it is not through Oscar's aristocratic connections that she and her men are freed, but rather it is the people, led by Bernard and André, who release them.

Particularly notable is the way the fall of the Bastille is represented. In the manga, the people lack direction in defending themselves against the Bastille's cannons. Consequently, Oscar leads her men to take over the cannons and destroy the Bastille before she is heroically shot. Demy, however, represents the fall of the Bastille as a collective action in which unheroic deaths occur. In the film, Oscar and André walk together with the other protesters; members of the guard also participate, not as leaders of the people but with the people. Just as crowds begin to fill the square in front of the Bastille, royal troops begin firing at protesters, armed only with pitchforks and spears. When the shooting begins, the crowd disperses and André and Oscar become separated. Just as he was about to move away from attacking soldiers, the unarmed André is shot in the back, and—stunned—he slides, bleeding, down the city walls. When the people finally rouse the forces to push back the king's soldiers, they rush by a dying, immobile André. The Bastille is finally taken, and the crowd begins to sing and dance joyfully in the square while Oscar desperately looks for André. The film concludes with the contrasting image of collective joy and Oscar's personal despair.

Whereas Ikeda begins to problematize the traditional paradigm of the maiden warrior by having Oscar take part in the dismantling of the monarchy rather than in its defense, Demy more generally problematizes aristocratic heroism, whatever its objective, by privileging collective action. Ikeda's Oscar is the principal agent for change in the manga, with secondary characters such as Robespierre and Bernard hovering in the background and fueling her passion for justice. It is Oscar's aristocratic connections and sense of aristocratic honor that allows her to protect lower-class characters such as Rosalie or the members of the French guard, and it is Oscar and her men who lead the attack on the Bastille. Basically, Ikeda's Oscar works according to an individualistic model of heroism.

As he does in *A Room in Town*, Demy posits "the people" as the principal motor for political change, emphasized in the many shots of protesters physically opposing the king's soldiers. In fact, Demy's shooting of the protests in *Lady Oscar* anticipates the scene of the 1955 Nantes protest in *A Room in Town*. First, the fatal day is announced by the red lettering ("1789 June 17th" in *Lady Oscar;* "Nantes 1955" in *A Room in Town*). Second, both films show the people pouring out of side streets into the main square, which is also the site of power: the Bastille, in the first case; the city hall and *préfecture*, in the second.[45]

Third, Demy choreographs both confrontations by very clearly and visibly opposing the people to the agents of power, Louis XVI's soldiers and the Nantes's riot police (Figures 4.6 and 4.7). In these shots, Demy has the camera pull back to emphasize the collective, then it moves in to focus on Oscar and André, in *Lady Oscar,* and François Guilbaud and his two friends, in *Room in Town.* This strategy has the effect of reinscribing the lives of individuals within the larger narrative of history and, in particular, the history of collective action that leads to democratic reform.

But through such struggles, many individuals, as both of Demy's films show, meet a rather banal death. André is shot in the back trying to flee the soldiers as the other protesters frantically run past him, ignoring his individual fate. In *A Room in Town,* an unarmed François dies after being clubbed in the head by a riot policeman, then his two buddies carry him away from the chaotic streets in a way that recalls representations of the *Pietà.* Both films depict the struggles of the working class as a collective effort by ordinary people who die rather common deaths. And in both films, but particularly pronounced in *Lady Oscar,* Demy juxtaposes the joy of collective action with the troubling yet inevitable sacrifice of innocent people in order to further the cause.

As in several of Demy's films in which a character is not fulfilled by the end of the film, here Oscar is left out of the collective merrymaking after losing André. Demy depicts the success of the collective action, all the while recognizing the suffering of those individuals who experience loss. We see a recurrent pattern in Demy's films: at the end of *Lola,* a happy Lola drives past a de-

Figure 4.6. The people confront the king's soldiers before taking the Bastille in *Lady Oscar.*

Figure 4.7. The people confront the French riot police, the CRS (Compagnies Républicaines de Sécurité) in *A Room in Town*.

pressed Roland; at the end of *The Umbrellas*, the reunion of Guy and his family is contrasted with the lonely Geneviève; and at the end of *The Pied Piper*, the burning of Melius is juxtaposed to Hamelin's children, who skip away from the crumbling town as they sing with the pied piper. Particularly striking is the ending of *Lady Oscar*, in which queer love is finally vindicated, only to be quickly lost to a larger cause. Demy denies his audiences an unqualified happy ending, perhaps his way of communicating the very un–fairy–tale–like message that there is no such thing as happily ever after. What counts is being true to one's self and to one's ideals, even if that does not lead to a permanent state of bliss.

Whatever form it may take, the figure of the maiden warrior always reveals the constructedness of gender, even when the heroine ends up renouncing her female masculinity at the end of the tale. In all of these different forms of maiden warrior tales, gender trouble necessarily leads to sexual trouble: when borders between masculinity and femininity are blurred, so are the limits between heterosexuality and homosexuality. What makes both Ikeda's and Demy's treatment of the maiden warrior tale type distinct from similar works by other authors and directors is their heroine's refusal to renounce her masculinity as well as their active queering of the maiden warrior. In Ikeda and Demy,

Lady Oscar is a masculine woman, and she cannot simply shed her masculinity upon request: it is an integral part of her identity. Given the complex origins of the story of Lady Oscar, which grew out of the Takarazuka-inspired *shōjo* manga tradition and the Year 24 Group, the members of which sought to challenge gender and sexual norms, it comes as no surprise that Ikeda created a truly revolutionary maiden warrior tale.

Arguably, however, Demy takes this revolution even further, at least with respect to class and sexuality. With *A Room in Town* in mind, Demy rejects the model of aristocratic heroism of his source, *The Rose of Versailles*. His Lady Oscar fully renounces her aristocratic identity to join the ranks of commoners with André in scenes that visually anticipate *A Room in Town*. Oscar and André's relationship has to do with class transgression, while the film uses class transgression to signify sexual transgression. Oscar and André's relation is doubly incongruous: she is an aristocrat and he is a commoner, and he is a man in love with a manly woman. Oscar's relationship to André is as much about overcoming class prejudice as it is about Oscar's "coming out" and choosing to love whomever she wishes.

As Berthomé suggests in the passage that opens this chapter, *Lady Oscar* represents a turning point in Demy's career. Although Berthomé is correct to emphasize the importance of the film in terms of Demy's focus on insurrection and rebellion, it also represents a new daring with respect to representations of sexuality in his films. Although a same-sex kiss hardly seems revolutionary today, it still makes the news. And for the quiet and reserved director who carefully concealed his sexual orientation, *Lady Oscar* truly marks a bold move.

Epilogue

Demy's Postmodern Tales

Cinema is always the re-creation of a universe.

—Jacques Demy, "L'Art en tête"

Three years before his death, Jacques Demy was featured on the French television show "L'Art en tête."[1] The episode treated everything from Demy's appreciation of the painter Nicolas Poussin and his work with French animator Paul Grimault to a toilet paper commercial inspired by Demy's "enchanted" (*en-chanté*) films, with Demy-esque color schemes and song. Toward the end of the show, the camera focuses in on Demy, who reflects upon his films. Demy emphasizes the ways in which he conceives of his cinema as being about ordinary people and lives even when the stories are situated within the realm of fantasy or the fairy tale, which he strongly associates with his childhood. Taking *The Umbrellas of Cherbourg* as his starting point, Demy ponders:

> This universe of starry-eyed shop assistants . . . it's French society with its different social classes. . . . Starry-eyed girls or dreams of Prince Charming . . . one cannot deny this dream. It exists. Well, it's misleadingly a world of starry-eyed girls and misleadingly gay . . . people cried quite a bit . . . I'm very drawn to the everyday, reality, people's problems . . . and then the absolute dream, and I believe that it's always and continues to be these childhood memories we cart around with us, drag behind us, and which are very tenacious. Before cinema, for instance, I did puppet theater . . . I staged all the fairy tales. As an adult I made *Donkey Skin* . . . which is a

reverie, a fantasy, but it's also cinema, and this cinema, mine, the one that allows me to exist, and to dream, and then to share this great blessing, it's ultimately sharing this dream as well, that is the reward.[2]

In these reflections, Demy blends reality and fantasy, joy and sorrow, childhood and adulthood. He foregrounds what is fascinating about his cinema: the paradoxical relation his films maintain with the genre of the fairy tale.

His cinema brings apparent oppositions together to create complex fairy-tale films that both celebrate and question classical fairy-tale plots. Sometimes Demy takes us to ostensibly otherworldly places as in *Donkey Skin,* but he anchors the marvelous in realism by filming on location at the Château du Plessis-Bourré and Château de Chambord. In other films, Demy takes everyday contexts and infuses them with otherworldliness through his use of color and music. The ordinary thus appears extraordinary, and a cabaret, an umbrella shop, a gas station, even stables are transformed into sites for fairy-tale plots. These are the enchanted palaces, towers, and chambers of Demy's princes and princesses.

Demy's films also problematize the model of the male rescuer and of what a Prince Charming should be. Often failing in their attempts to "save" the heroine, Demy's Prince Charmings are not all that they are cut out to be; they tend to bring the heroine sorrow rather than happiness. Moreover, Demy takes the happy endings of tales in the tradition of Charles Perrault or Walt Disney and, hinting at the normative gender, sexual, and class values they communicate, foregrounds the possible tragic results of their effect on individuals, who might have truly found happiness through alternative paths but who give in to the lure of mainstream fairy-tale promises. Even when happiness does appear to be attained by a character who dares assume her or his singular dream against social convention, this happiness may only last a moment. Lola finds her prince but is later abandoned by him; Oscar finally accepts her true love, only to tragically lose him after their one night of bliss. In Visconti's *White Nights,* just as he loses her to the Tenant, Mario tells Natalia, "God bless you for the moment of happiness you gave me. Even a moment's worth can last a lifetime." Likewise, Demy's heroines and heroes can only cling on to that one moment of happiness, for in Demy, there is no "ever after."

In the "L'Art en tête" interview cited above, Demy focuses on cinema as dream and on childhood dreams, which are often anchored in the fairy tale and which we continue to carry with us as adults. Again Demy's notion of dream and fairy tale as well as dream as fairy tale is paradoxical. On the one hand, these dreams that are fairy tales can provide us with hope for a better future; they open up a space of freedom that allows us to imagine alternative universes, including queer ones. On the other hand, fairy tales can also be used to communicate heteronormative and bourgeois ideologies, thus setting us up for failure by inculcating us, often subconsciously, with prefabricated dreams to which we cannot conform or aspire without sacrificing our singular desires, sexualities, and identities.

As noted in chapter 1, Disney's dream theory proposes a benevolent symbolic order in which adherence to gender, sexual, and class norms is represented as painless; castration (i.e., of singular desires and identities) is concealed or denied. Demy, however, proposes a much more ambivalent notion of dream and fantasy that views the symbolic order as far from benevolent. Through his fairy-tale films, Demy reveals the ways in which people are castrated, in which they renounce a part of themselves, in order to adhere to the socially acceptable, heteronormative dreams of mass media and mainstream culture. Demy's queer enchantments encourage us to embrace our own singular, strange, marginal, and queer fantasies that may only ensure us a moment of happiness, but at least we have that moment. At the same time, they reveal the problematic underpinnings of many classical fairy-tale narratives.

In so many respects Demy's films can be considered "postmodern fairy tales," in Cristina Bacchilega's understanding of the term. Like Demy's description of his cinema, Bacchilega's characterization of postmodern tales is necessarily slippery and riddled with tensions between respect for and subversion of classical tales:

> As I read postmodern transformations of the fairy tale, I want to argue that they are doubling and double: both affirmative and questioning.... As literary texts, cartoons, movies, musicals, or soap operas, postmodern fairy tales reactivate the wonder tale's "magic" or mythopoeic qualities by providing new readings of it, thereby generating unexploited or forgotten possibilities from its repetition. As "borderline enquiries," postmodern revisions of traditional narratives do more than alter our reading of those narratives. Like meta-folklore, they constitute an ideological test for previous interpretations, and in doing so, postmodern fairy tales exhibit an awareness of how the folktale, which modern humans relegate to the nursery, almost vindictively patterns our unconscious.... Repetition functions as reassurance within the tale, but this very same compulsion to repeat the tale explodes its coherence as well-made artifice. (22–23)

The notion that postmodern tales are "doubling and double" suggests that they imitate and undermine, revel in and subvert the classical tale. As such, postmodern fairy tales function as commentaries about fairy tales as much as they are tales in and of themselves. Revealing the ideology of classical tales through rewriting, postmodern tales propose new readings, new points of view, and they tease out their "unexploited or forgotten possibilities."

Bacchilega's description of postmodern tales is useful in understanding Demy's films. As we have seen, Demy both takes delight in and "troubles"— from the perspective of gender, sexuality, and class—the classical fairy tale through his filmic re-visions. His cinematic retellings of "Cinderella" and "Sleeping Beauty," "Donkey Skin," "The Pied Piper," and maiden warrior tales play on the repressive and subversive elements existing in traditional variants of these tales, reshaping them to speak to economic and social injustices and alternative sexualities. Reading camp into and camping the classical fairy tale, foregrounding the nonheteronormative possibilities already present in the tale tradition and subverting its prevalent heteronormativity, drawing on alternative tale traditions that celebrate social and ethnic Others, undoing the tradition of aristocratic heroism in favor of a model of collective action—through such means Demy continues the fairy-tale tradition all the while stretching its possibilities to represent different forms of heroism, sexuality, and social and gender identities. His films simultaneously criticize, celebrate, and innovate the fairy-tale tradition. They move between exploiting the utopian potential of the genre and revealing the dystopia that is often the result of conventional fairy-tale plots in order to create new possibilities for the genre.

In some respects, Demy's fairy-tale films bear affinities with the ancestor of film melodrama, *le drame bourgeois,* which marked a revolutionary move toward new forms of representation.[3] In seventeenth- and eighteenth-century France, classical tragedy was a genre that mythified the aristocracy, depicting this social class as being akin to the gods of antiquity. Representations of members of the bourgeoisie and peasantry, on the other hand, were restricted to the genre of comedy, in which they were often ridiculed, and were never represented as dignified members of French society. In the second half of the eighteenth century, the playwrights Denis Diderot and Pierre-Augustin Caron de Beaumarchais lamented this state of affairs and vindicated the right of the bourgeoisie to be represented with dignity and gravitas. Their concerns gave rise to the *drame bourgeois,* which drew from the structures and mythic qualities of classical tragedy to validate and even romanticize the lives and experiences of the bourgeoisie.

In a similar manner, Demy reappropriates the fairy tale to represent with dignity and seriousness working- and lower-class, or "ordinary," people in his fantasy worlds. Unlike the tales of the Brothers Grimm, in which lower-class characters abound, the French classical tale tradition—including Perrault— tends to privilege aristocratic or upper-class characters and concerns, in which happy endings involve attaining noble or royal status. And although Disney's filmic tales are suggestive of American populism and the American work ethic, they nevertheless remain tales in which main characters recover or attain aristocratic or elite status. Such plotlines tend to devalue the lives of working and lower-class people by implying that their social position is inherently undesirable and inferior. Demy's films draw from fairy-tale and Disney aesthetics and themes to validate the dreams and lives of lower-class people, who often are able to embrace their freedoms and modest dreams in ways that characters who give in to social pressures cannot. In Demy, a happy ending might involve *not* becoming a princess but rather being true to oneself, or becoming an artist, or the owner of a gas station. Demy's interest in Gene Kelly musicals makes sense within this context: Kelly was considered the working-class dancer, as opposed to the aristocratic Fred Astaire.[4] Demy seeks a working-class marvelous in the tradition of Kelly musicals to create his cinematic fairy tales.

Demy was interested not only in validating the experiences of sailors, cabaret singers, garage owners, and hairdressers. He was also concerned with queer desires, nonheteronormative sexualities, and gender ambiguity. Although the classical fairy tale often has served to project upper-class desires or the desire to become upper class, it also has served, especially as represented by Perrault and Disney, to privilege heteronormative desires and traditional gender roles. (Although the seventeenth-century French *conteuses* often problematized gender and even sexuality, their works did not make it into the canon of twentieth-century fairy tales, nor do they have representation in Disney or other filmic works.) Demy teases out the moments in traditional tales that reveal the performativity of gender or in which sexual desire and gender prove transgressive. For instance, Lola waits for her prince but not in a state of suspended animation or imposed chastity. For her part, Donkey Skin is not the passive object of her father's desire; indeed, she accepts her "monstrous" desire for her father. In the case of the cross-dressed Oscar, her coming out coincides with the eruption of the French Revolution as she finally embraces her desire for the lower-class stable boy André, who loves her as an ambiguously gendered subject. Evident in films such as *The Umbrellas of Cherbourg* and *Lady Oscar*, moreover, transgressive class relations in Demy can serve as figures for transgressive sexual relations, all of which destabilizes and opens up the classical fairy-tale narrative.

However, all is not simply fun and games. The melodramatic overtones of many of his films suggest that Demy is keenly aware of the challenges queer subjects must face in either repressing or embracing their singularity. Both *The Umbrellas of Cherbourg* and *Donkey Skin* stage the possibility of queer sexuality and then its renunciation. And although Oscar embraces her singular desires, she loses her true love at the end of the film. At the same time that his fairy-tale films are often fueled by utopian yearnings, they also put into play those social and political forces that prevent queer characters from realizing their dreams. As such, these films are unsettling, simultaneously asking us to dream while demanding that we mourn a loss.

Demy's queer enchantments provide important insights into the genre of the fairy tale by shedding light on the ways in which gender, sexuality, and class can play out in the classical tale and by suggesting new ways the genre can represent different types of relations and worlds that go beyond heteronormativity and middle-class ideals. At the same time, taking into account the impact of the fairy tale on Demy's oeuvre means taking seriously Demy's own insistence on the importance of the fairy-tale genre to his formation as a director. Demy's cinematic tales provide us with important insights into the genre of the fairy tale—its limits, possibilities, and powers—just as the genre of the fairy tale provides us with important insights into the wonderful world of Jacques Demy.

Notes

Introduction

1   Amy Herzog nicely summarizes the ways in which Demy's films have been dismissed as "fruity" and lacking vigor by critics such as Terrance Rafferty (116).

2   I am drawing generally here from the work of Judith Butler in *Gender Trouble*.

3   For an excellent collection of essays that question the heteronormativity of the classical fairy tale, see Kay Turner and Pauline Greenhill's *Transgressive Tales: Queering the Grimms* (2012).

4   See, for instance, Berthomé, *Jacques Demy et les racines du rêve* (1982 and 1996); Taboulay, *Le Cinéma enchanté de Jacques Demy* (1996); Romney, "Happy When It Rains: Jacques Demy's Magical Realism" (2005); Billard, "Jacques Demy and His Other World" (1964); Colomb, "L'Étrange Demy-monde" (1998); Stilwell, "Le Demy-monde: The Bewitched, betwixt and between French Musical" (2003).

5   Unless otherwise indicated, with the exception of film subtitles, all translations from French are mine.

6   These terms are somewhat unstable and often intersect in their meanings. Broadly speaking, the "folktale" is considered to be a traditional fictional narrative associated with oral circulation; märchen is the German term that refers to folktales, including tales by the Brothers Grimm, some of which are considered to be "fairy tales." "Fairy tale" (*conte de fées*), a term originating in 1690s France, is a literary tale that foregrounds the marvelous, including powerful fairies with magic wands, magical means of transportation, and magnificent castles. For more in-depth definitions, see *The Greenwood Encyclopedia of Folktales and Fairy Tales*, 3 vols. (2008).

7   In 1945 Charles de Gaulle called upon the French to produce twelve million babies, which was supported by government allocations according to family size.

8   With respect to *The Umbrellas of Cherbourg*, although it would equally be the case for *Donkey Skin* and *A Room in Town*, Steve Peacock notes that the "film combines aspects and conventions from film musicals, opera, and operettas, whilst adhering to none of the above" (93).

9 Sellier discusses abstraction, especially in relation to "the cult of [cinematic] works stripped of their socio-historical contingencies" (24). I'm expanding her use of "abstraction" to include the type of metacommentary characteristic of Godard's films.

10 In his excellent study of camp and the MGM musical, Steven Cohan notes, "The studio employed a large number of homosexual, lesbian, and bisexual artists and craftspeople to collaborate on musicals, most famously but not exclusively in the Arthur Freed unit" (3). These artists infused the musical with camp aesthetics that played with and "troubled" gender and sexuality. Cohan's chapter "Dancing with Balls: Sissies, Sailors, and the Camp Masculinity of Gene Kelly" is particularly important when considering Demy's interest in Kelly himself, a costar of *The Young Girls of Rochefort* and a symbol of the sailor in the musical tradition (149–99).

11 See, for instance, Austin 15 and Sellier 28.

12 As Richard Misek has observed, "Technicolor was typically used for musicals, westerns, costume romances, fantasies, and comedies, while newsreels, documentaries, war films, and crime films remained black-and-white" (38).

13 Evident in a basic WorldCat keyword search, significantly more has been published on Godard, Truffaut, Alain Resnais, Eric Rohmer, and Claude Chabrol than on Demy or Varda, who receives only slightly more critical attention than her husband, who, however, died in 1990.

14 See, for instance, the work of Philippe Colomb.

15 See also Geneviève Sellier's *Masculine Singular* for more on the heteronormative underpinnings of the French New Wave.

16 "Je crois, enfin, il me semble, que seuls les enfants qu'on désire vraiment sont heureux."

17 For an overview of such questions in the folktale and fairy tale, see Duggan, "Conception and Birth" and Belanus and Langlois, "Monstrous Births."

18 As Holly Tucker has noted regarding the early modern period, "In most medical treatises, if there is any damage to the child at conception or in utero it is generally the fault of the mother's unbridled imagination" (101). Maternal cravings would take the form of birthmarks on the child's body (103). I am suggesting here that something similar happens, although the consequences of the impact of the imagination are not negative in Demy.

19 Other important studies on fairy tale and film worthy of mention include Jack Zipes's chapter on Walt Disney in *Fairy Tale as Myth/Myth as Fairy Tale* (72–95), Donald Haase's article on the Arabian Nights in German film (2004), Maria Tatar's explorations of Bluebeard in Hollywood films (2004), and Adriana Novoa's piece on "Sleeping Beauty" and Almodóvar's *Talk to Her* (2005).

20 Zipes draws on feminism in several of his books, including *Fairy Tales and the Art of Subversion* (1983) and *Fairy Tale as Myth/Myth as Fairy Tale* (1993). Tatar's *The Hard Facts of the Grimms' Fairy Tales* (1987) takes into account the ways in which gender norms shaped the Grimms' editorial practices. Bacchilega's *Postmodern Fairy Tales* (1997) looks at gender within the works of contempo-

rary rewritings. Haase edited the important collection *Fairy Tales and Feminism: New Approaches* (2004), and Seifert (1996), Raynard (2002), and Tucker (2003) have all contributed immensely to our understanding of gender, women, and the early modern fairy tale.

21 This search was carried out in May 2012.

Chapter 1

1 "Un chevalier (cow-boy, ex-GI) vêtu de blanc, sur son blanc destrier (Cadillac) recherche une jeune princesse (Lola) qu'il a aimée. Des maléfices innombrables (la guerre, les méchants) les ont sépararés. Le chevalier poursuivra longuement sa quête, parmi les embûches et les mauvais hasards. Enfin, les amants parviendront à se retrouver dans une sorte de grotte enchantée (le cabaret d'Eldorado) et, à jamais réunis, ils partiront ensemble dans la grande voiture blanche, vers l'Eden (américain)" (Guimard 12–13).

2 "Les gens pleuraient, c'était d'une tristesse. . . . D'ailleurs, on s'y attendait . . . on s'y attendait bien parce que Jacques et moi, on avait écrit sur la partition. 'Premier mouchoir, page 38. Deuxième mouchoir.' On avait une partition . . . il y avait des mouchoirs partout. . . . T'en amènes trop. Non, tu verras." Interview with Michel Legrand from Agnès Varda's *L'Univers de Jacques Demy*.

3 "Tous les critiques ont noté combien *Les Parapluies de Cherbourg* se situe dans la droite filiation de *Lola,* ont remarqué comment les mêmes thèmes de la séparation, de l'attente et de la fidélité à un rêve nourrissent les deux films" (Berthomé 181).

4 "Plus qu'une suite de *Lola, Les Parapluies de Cherbourg* en est le reflet inversé" (Berthomé 195).

5 English translation from Zipes, *Beauties* 51. The French reads, "Attendre quelque temps pour avoir un Epoux, / Riche, bien fait, galant et doux, / La chose est assez naturelle. / Mais l'attendre cent ans, et toujours en dormant, / On ne trouve plus de femelle, / Qui dormît si tranquillement. / La Fable semble encore vouloir nous faire entendre, / Que souvent de l'Hymen les agréables noeuds, / Pour être différés, n'en sont pas moins heureux" (Perrault 140).

6 On melodrama as "drama + melos (music)," see Nowell-Smith, "Minnelli" 114. On tears and melodrama, see Neale.

7 Many critics have noted that Demy called *Lola* "a musical without music." See, for instance, French.

8 I would like to note here that Cinderella tales within the Grimm corpus often are more complex with respect to gender than those by Perrault.

9 On Disney's Americanization of classical tales, see Stone 24–35; Zipes, *Fairy Tale as Myth* 72–95; Inge; and Wood. On the concept of rags-to-riches tales and their social contexts, see Bottigheimer.

10 Steve Neale mentions the affinities between melodrama and the *drame bourgeois,* a genre that emerged in the eighteenth century that sought to elevate bourgeois characters, previously relegated to comedy, through the sublime representation

of their sentiments and conflicts, usually played out within the arena of the family. See Neale 6.

11 "dans une voiture de rêve, une apparition, les mille et une nuits."

12 "Je rêve"; "C'est malsain."

13 Nowell-Smith remarks upon the dreamlike quality of Visconti's film, which influenced Demy: "Visconti's anti-realism goes deeper than is generally realised. *White Nights* is perhaps an extreme example of this tendency. Its spiritual descendants are to be found in the works of Jacques Demy, *Lola* and *Les Parapluies de Cherbourg*, and in Resnais's *L'Année dernière à Marienbad*" (Nowell-Smith, Visconti 131).

14 I would like to thank Elena Past for pointing out to me that characters who believe in fairy tales or *favole* are a recurrent theme in Visconti's films.

15 "Le retour du Locataire signale en quelque sorte la victoire de l'imaginaire sur le réel" (Maille).

16 "Le choix de Jean Marais pour incarner le beau ténébreux n'est pas innocent. Outre son charisme auréolé d'un lyrisme tragique, l'acteur véhicule une image de Star (donc objet de fantasme)."

17 Demy was a fan of Gene Kelly films and in one interview remarked, "Life is so difficult sometimes, and when you see *Singing in the Rain* or *On the Town*, it's so marvelous for a moment, it's like a light in your life." ("La vie est si difficile quelquefois, et quand vous voyez *Singing in the Rain* ou *On the Town*, c'est si merveilleux pour un moment, c'est comme une lumière dans votre vie." [Taboulay 35]). Demy cast Kelly as a character in *Les Demoiselles de Rochefort*.

18 Susan Hayward notes, "Before the Brigitte Bardot factor, there was Martine Carol" (165).

19 "Je l'aurais attendu très sagement."

20 "Sept ans, sept ans, tu te rends compte? Si tu savais comme je t'ai attendu, je ne pensais qu'à toi et quelque fois je te maudissais, parce que ton souvenir m'empoisonnait l'existence."

21 "Au cinéma, c'est toujours plus beau."

22 "En reprenant l'actrice, Demy prolonge donc véritablement son rôle, inscrivant en somme le film de Bresson dans son passé vivant" (Taboulay 29).

23 "C'est comme le soulier de Cendrillon. Si je trouvais une lettre pareille dans la rue je ferais battre tambour jusqu'à ce que je découvre celle qui l'a écrite."

24 In *Jacques le fataliste*, Madame d'Aisonon and her daughter (Madame D. and Agnès in the film) first meet the marquis d'Arcis (the aristocrat Jean in the film) at the Jardin du Roi, not the Bois de Boulogne.

25 "Que Dieu nous préserve des joueurs!"

26 "Mon idée est de faire cinquante films qui seront tous liés les uns aux autres ... à travers des personnages communs" (qtd. in Garson 654).

27 Jason Wilcox notes that in *Model Shop*, "the Hollywood 'dream' is revealed as a tawdry spectacle" (29).

28 Fernández-Rodríguez maintains that in feminist revisions of classical tales, "the hero is deprived to a greater or lesser extent of his mythical aura, at the same time that his function as rescuing agent is seriously questioned" (53). On the "de-mythologizing" of the male rescuer in postmodern versions of "Sleeping Beauty," see Fernández-Rodríguez 52–57.

29 McKenzie has a fascinating discussion of the function of exhibitions in France from 1948 to 1952 (66–112).

30 On the role of women's magazines in modernization efforts, see, for instance, Ross 78–105 and Weiner 21–66.

31 "I Will Wait for You" became a popular jazz standard adapted by various artists, including Bobby Darin, Frank Sinatra, Lena Horne, Oscar Peterson, Johnny Mathis, and Astrud Gilberto. Lena Horne actually performed the song, accompanied by Michel Legrand, in 1972 (Gavin 399).

32 "Mon amour, je t'attendrai toute ma vie.... Je ne peux pas, je ne peux pas, je ne peux pas." The lyrics in French are taken from Demy, *Chansons et textes chantés* 171–72, 175.

33 "La parure de la Belle au bois dormant."

34 "La caverne d'Ali Baba."

35 "Je n'ai pas le choix. Vous êtes mon roi."

36 Richard Misek provides an excellent overview of the use of color in cinema. He observes that although color was always used for musicals and fantasy genres, it was with *The Wizard of Oz* that the opposition color/black-and-white became solidified and color was "narratively motivated" (31).

37 Naomi Wood discusses the ways in which Walt Disney employed color to differentiate spaces and create associations between his characters in *Cinderella*. See Wood 31. For Rodney Hill, color is so important in *The Umbrellas* that it functions as a character in the film ("The New Wave" 39).

38 Here I would disagree with Steve Peacock, who argues that color clashes between mother and daughter increase in the film (101).

39 Demy actually found the dress first then had Bernard Evein reproduce the design for the wallpaper.

40 Often in Demy's films, white can represent the ideal, as in the case of Michel in *Lola*. But given the importance and significance of color in *The Umbrellas*, I would argue that white in this case has a negative connotation as lack or absence of color.

41 Significantly, Guy returns to the bar where he and Geneviève had gone dancing earlier in the film, where, as Peacock has noted, they clash with "the baroque depths of the room's redness" (102).

42 Herzog notes that when Roland speaks, "the score shifts into the *Lola* theme" (128). Hill also has remarked on the intertextual relation to *Lola* ("New Wave" 36).

43 "Autrefois j'ai aimé une femme, elle ne m'aimait pas, on l'appelait Lola."

44 "Tu me parles de lui comme tu parles de tes parapluies."

45 "Pourquoi l'absence est-elle si lourde à supporter?"

46 "Pourquoi Guy s'éloigne-t-il de moi, moi qui serais morte pour lui? Pourquoi ne suis-je pas morte?"

47 "Guy a pu représenter pour toi un certain idéal, mais quel avenir t'offrait-il?"

48 "Cette histoire est donc l'histoire d'un amour socialement inadmissible, d'un amour romantique et non petit-bourgeois, qui sera cassé par l'ordre de la convenance. C'est l'histoire d'un amour contrarié par la société qui préfère les couples sans amour aux couples non-conformes."

49 See also chapter 1 in Tinkcom, *Working*. Steven Cohan notes that the Arthur Freed unit was nicknamed "Freed's fairies" (47) and also comments on the unit's employment of "a large number of homosexual, lesbian, and bisexual artists and craftspeople to collaborate on musicals, most famously but not exclusively in the Arthur Freed unit" (3).

50 Cohan quotes Brett Farmer, who remarks, "In gay subcultural argot . . . the term *musical* has long been used as a coded reference to homosexuality" (1–2).

51 Jean Genet (1910–86) was an important French novelist and playwright who foregrounded homosexuality in many of his works. He met Jean Cocteau, who helped him get published and who petitioned, along with other writers, to relieve him of a life sentence. *Querelle de Brest* (1947) in particular concerns homosexuality within the milieu of sailors. (This simplifies incredibly the plot and purpose of the novel, which is richly complex.) Cocteau provided erotic illustrations for the book.

52 "C'est un mari comme vous qu'il m'aurait fallu."

53 "C'est fou comme il est sympathique."

Chapter 2

1 The French reads, "On n'épouse jamais / Ses parents / Vous aimez votre père, je comprends / Quelles que soient vos raisons / Quels que soient pour lui vos sentiments / Mon enfant / On n'épouse pas plus sa maman / On dit que traditionellement / Des questions de culture / Et de législature / Décidèrent en leur temps / Qu'on ne mariait pas / Les filles avec leur papa." See Demy, *Chansons* 92.

2 "mettait en scène le conte de Perrault sur son théâtre de guignol, avec beaucoup d'autres de Perrault et de Grimm" (Berthomé 238).

3 Raphaël Lefèvre discusses other references to incest in Demy's oeuvre, including "La Luxure," his contribution to *Les Sept Péchés capitaux* (*The Seven Deadly Sins*, 1962); *Lola*; and *Les Demoiselles de Rochefort*.

4 Bernard Bastide traced versions of Charles Perrault's tales in French cinema from 1897 to 1912 and found five versions each of "Cinderella" and "Little Thumbling," four versions of "Puss-in-Boots," three versions each of "Bluebeard" and "Sleeping Beauty," but only one each of "Little Red Riding Hood," "Riquet with the Tuft," "The Fairies," and "Donkey Skin" ("Présence de Perrault" 32). In

1929 Alberto Calvacanti filmed a version of "Little Red Riding Hood" with Jean Renoir playing the wolf, but it was not until 1970 that "Donkey Skin" would again make it to the screen.

5 See "Le Livret de Peau d'âne" in *Le Livre: Bibliographie moderne*. The text of Vanderburch and company's *féerie* was published and republished in 1838, 1863, 1867, and 1883. The Bibliothèque Nationale lists an 1808 version, but the 1838 edition is advertised as "represented for the first time in Paris in 1838" (599), which could mean it had been circulating earlier in the provinces. In Paris it was performed at the Théâtre de la Porte Saint-Martin and at the Théâtre de la Gaïté, both popular venues for French vaudeville at this time.

6 Capellani has the king's men brush the donkey in order to make it defecate gold coins. Not a part of Perrault's tale, this detail likely was taken from the fairy-tale extravaganza. Capellani also depicts the king as crying, and in the extravaganza he likewise cries when he is upset by a situation, such as his daughter rejecting a possible mate.

7 Most versions are based on the apocryphal 1781 prose version of the tale. I examined editions from 1843, 1858, 1867, 1884, 1886, 1901, 1905, 1910, and 1923, all of which explicitly recount the story of incest.

8 My numbers are based on an inexhaustive search of the Bibliothèque Nationale's catalog.

9 For different versions of "Donkey Skin," see Straparola's "Tebaldo" and Basile's "The Bear" in Zipes, *Great Fairy-Tale Tradition* 27–38. For Basile's "The She-Bear," see also Nancy Canepa's 2007 translation of his *Tale of Tales* (177–83).

10 For a brief comparison of versions of "Donkey Skin" by Straparola, Basile, and Perrault, see Duggan, *Salonnières* 149.

11 Pulju argues that despite the French Communist Party's attempt to open up notions of gender, work, and family at a time when women had attained the right to vote and had played key roles during the war, "the desire for normalcy (another effect of the war) and the need for population growth would trump the factors heralding change" (99).

12 "Si on demande à une petite fille à qui tu vas te marier plus tard elle dira que 'Papa,' si elle a cinq ou six ans et qu'elle aime bien son père." See Varda, *L'Univers de Jacques Demy*.

13 Demy states, "Je voulais différencier les deux châteaux: d'un côté le sang royal, le sang bleu, conservateur; et de l'autre cette espèce de prince un peu révolutionnaire et tout cet univers rouge" ("I wanted to differentiate the two castles: on the one hand, royal blood, blue blood, conservative; and on the other, a prince who is somewhat revolutionary and this red universe" [qtd. in Berthomé 241]).

14 The French reads, "Le végétal et l'animal montent encore à l'assaut de la pierre dans le château du roi bleu" (Berthomé 243).

15 On the use of stags in the princess's bedroom, see Berthomé 240.

16 The white cat throne could be a reference to Marie-Catherine d'Aulnoy's tale "La Chatte blanche" ("The White Cat," 1698). For an English version of the tale, see

Zipes, *Beauties* 515–44.

17 I'm drawing generally here from the work of Claude Lévi-Strauss, who views the prohibition of incest (as defined by specific societies) as the foundation for "culture." See, for instance, 3–29.

18 By the time she made *Donkey Skin*, Seyrig had already attained international acclaim for her role in Alain Resnais's *L'Année dernière à Marienbad* (*Last Year at Marienbad*, 1961), and she also had starred in Truffaut's *Baisers volés* (*Stolen Kisses*, 1968) and Luis Buñuel's *La Voie lactée* (*The Milky Way*, 1969).

19 "J'ai voulu ce clin d'oeil à Cocteau . . . car il a été le seul en France à toucher au cinéma fantastique. C'est en souvenir de lui, de 'La belle et la bête' que je voulais si fort Jean Marais." See "Jacques Demy: 'J'ai attendu neuf ans.'"

20 Regarding preculture or "savage" humans, Rousseau characterizes them as follows: "There were families, but there were no nations. There were domestic languages, but there were no popular ones. There were marriages but there was no love at all. Each family was self-sufficient and perpetuated itself exclusively by inbreeding. . . . They became husband and wife without ceasing to be brother and sister" ("Essay" 45–46). For the French, see Rousseau, *Essai* 525–26.

21 In some respects the valorization of the "beast" in Cocteau and Demy brings to mind Angela Carter's "The Tiger's Bride," in which the heroine turns into a beast rather than the beast into a prince, suggesting another nonnormative form of sexuality shared between hero and heroine. See Carter 154–69.

22 See, for instance, Harry Benshoff's *Monsters in the Closet: Homosexuality and the Horror Film*.

23 Susan Hayward, for instance, remarks that Belle is "so terribly disappointed at the end of the film when the Beast . . . transforms into Prince Charming" (47).

24 "Tout est arrangé, ma chèrie, j'épouse votre père. Tâchez de lui faire bonne figure."

25 With respect to the form nonnormative sexuality takes in Cocteau, Eynat-Confino contends, "It is in *The White Paper*, which preceded the writing of *The Infernal Machine* by four years, that the explicit connection between nonnormative sexuality and the stigma of the monster is made. As noted above, nonnormative sexuality was already represented in Cocteau's play *Orpheus* (1926); incest will be represented in his novel *Les Enfants terribles* [1929] (translated by Rosamond Lehmann in 1955 as *Children of the Game*); and incest, bisexuality and homosexuality in *The Infernal Machine*. Two years later, incest is intimated in his play *Les Parents Terribles* (translated by Charles Frank in 1956 as *Intimate Relations*)" (96).

26 For a brief summary of Hocquenghem's contribution to the reframing of homosexual desire, see Dean and Lane 18–19.

27 In "Certain Neurotic Mechanisms in Jealousy, Paranoia, and Homosexuality," Freud discusses homosexuality in terms of "fixation on the mother," which can eventually make of "rivals of the earlier period . . . the first homosexual love-objects," one of the foremost rivals being the father. See Freud, *Sexuality* 157–59.

28 In *Les Demoiselles*, Monsieur Dame is in love with Solange, but he does not re-

alize she is the daughter of Yvonne, a woman he had loved. Unbeknownst to Solange, Monsieur Dame is the father of her half-brother, Boubou, and, as such, represents a father figure in relation to her character.

29 In her piece "Help! Me, S/he, and the Boss," Vivian Labrie examines incest in *Three Seats for the 26th* from the very different perspective of bureaucratic culture and reads incest as a figure for relations within the workplace, interestingly linking the discussion to relevant folktales.

30 "Audace tranquille, absence de culpabilité et de jugement moral: Demy achève sa carrière avec un film bancal mais sur une étonnante vision de l'amour et des tabous." See Lefèvre.

31 In fact, a disturbing accusation emerged in 2004 when Benjamin Castaldi, the son of Yves Montand's adopted daughter Catherine Allégret (daughter of Simone Signoret), published *Maintenant il faudra tout se dire* (*Now We Must Tell Ourselves Everything*, 2004), in which he declared that Montand sexually violated Allégret when she was a child. Allégret followed up with her own memoir, *Un Monde à l'envers* (*The World Upside Down*, 2004), describing incidents in which he sexually molested her and even tried to rape her. See, for instance, John Lichfield's summary of the media event in *The Independent*.

32 The association between money and feces has a long history in philosophy, psychoanalysis, and folklore. Wayne Andersen notes, "[Sigmund] Freud collected a number of folktales in which gold and feces are equated" (163). Freud notably discusses the association in his essay on the "wolfman" (see, for instance, Freud, *Wolfman* 280–81). For the purposes of my argument here, however, I insist on the distinctions between the two.

33 Berthomé notes the Louis XV dresses of the princess and her mother and the Henri II costume of the prince (245).

34 On the resemblance between Jean Harlow and the Lilac Fairy, see Berthomé 247.

35 The English is a modified translation from the film's subtitles. In the French, the sound "fée," which means "fairy," is repeated in "fairy guitar," in "Or-*phée*," or "Orpheus," and in "*faits* divers," or "news items."

36 The official wedding film can be seen on http://www.ina.fr/video/4223827001. It was broadcast on *Les Actualités françaises* May 9, 1956.

37 Another possible intertext here would be the red (associated with the prince) and blue (associated with Aurora) in Disney's *Sleeping Beauty*. Cocteau's Orphic trilogy includes *The Blood of a Poet*, *Orpheus*, and *The Testament of Orpheus*.

38 The scene in which Snow White comes upon the dwarfs' cottage is an important change to the tale by the Grimms. In the version collected by the Grimms, the home of the dwarfs is quite tidy, whereas in Disney the cottage of the seven dwarfs is a complete mess. Snow White starts cleaning with the help of the animals, but initially she spends time teaching them how to clean properly. When the dwarfs return home, she makes them all wash up before dinner, which is quite a comical scene. Disney significantly dwells on the notion of cleanliness in two rather long and entertaining scenes.

39 "Quand j'ai écrit la scène où l'on voit Peau d'âne pétrir la pâte et chanter la chan-

son du cake d'amour, j'ai revu Blanche-Neige confectionnant une tarte aidée par les oiseaux" (qtd. in Berthomé 242).

40 I am drawing very generally here from the work of Luce Irigaray. See, for instance, "Le Marché des femmes" (*Ce Sexe* 167–85); for the English version, see "Women on the Market" (*This Sex* 170–91). For a similar discussion of woman as exchange value and woman as use value, see Jean-Joseph Goux, "Sexual Difference and History" in *Symbolic Economies* 213–44. See also Gayle Rubin for a discussion of female labor and a discussion of the exchange of women that questions the universality of models proposed by, for instance, Claude Lévi-Strauss.

41 See Sontag 54 and Wilde, *Miscellanies* 177.

42 Mary Elizabeth Storer first identified this "fairy-tale vogue" in her 1928 *Un Épisode littéraire à la fin du XVIIe siècle: La Mode des contes de fées (1685–1700)*. For a succinct overview of the sociocultural context of this 1690s literary trend, during which Perrault along with Marie-Catherine d'Aulnoy, Marie-Jeanne L'Héritier de Villandon, and Henriette Julie de Murat penned volumes of fairy tales, see Zipes, *Beauties* 1–9.

43 I have demonstrated elsewhere (*Salonnières* 139–64) that Perrault was critical of worldly women and was proposing a model of bourgeois domesticity in which women were to play the roles of mother and wife, and not that of self-fashioning socialite.

44 Although there is ample evidence that Demy was familiar with tales by Charles Perrault and the Brothers Grimm, I have not found any evidence of familiarity with d'Aulnoy. Interestingly, though, Cocteau names the double of the Beast and Prince "Avenant" in *Beauty and the Beast*, the name of d'Aulnoy's character from "Beauty with Golden Hair."

45 Although Christine Jones uses the concept "aesthetic of frivolity" to talk about the aesthetics of the 1690s *conteuses*, the focus on beautiful, fashionable, and worldly women that the concept qualifies is relevant with respect to Demy's Lilac Fairy and princess.

46 "Vous, à cette heure! Vous savez que j'ai horreur qu'on me surprenne. Je ne suis pas prête." The translation is mine.

47 The Lilac Fairy first tells the princess, "Ne pleurez pas mon enfant. Les larmes abîment et creusent le visage." She then states, "Décidément, je porte très mal le jaune!" and after changing into lilac, "Oui, c'est mieux." English translations are mine.

48 "Y penses-tu? dans ce négligé! ... Je reposais encore, lorsque tes cris de détresse sont venus troubler mon sommeil ... mes cheveux sont dans un désordre.... Ma toilette" (Vanderburch, "Peau d'âne" 616).

49 "Ma chère Lilia, retiens bien ceci: quelque chagrin qu'une femme éprouve, elle ne doit jamais négliger sa toilette.... On se pare d'abord, et l'on pleure ensuite, et pas trop encore, rien ne ternissant l'éclat des yeux comme les larmes" (Vanderburch, *Peau d'âne* 17).

50 "Amour, amour, je t'aime tant."

51 Deneuve appears on the cover of the April 30, 1968 issue of *Look,* and the inside piece begins with "Catherine Deneuve, the most beautiful actress in France"
("Catherine Deneuve" 62). Le Gras also cites *Look* magazine with respect to Deneuve (28). *Look* magazine had a circulation of well over 7.5 million in 1969,
only to close shop in 1971. See "Cowles Closing *Look*" 34.

52 The connection between Demy's Lilac Fairy and Disney's stepmother could
be explained by the fact that Demy constructs his Lilac Fairy as a Jean Harlow
type, who was popular in the 1930s, the period in which Disney produced *Snow
White.* As Inge points out, Disney and his collaborators grounded the characters
of the film in 1930s American culture (141). At the same time, Demy had seen
Disney's *Snow White* numerous times. In an interview with Bernard Bastide, Agnès Varda emphasized Demy's love of *Snow White,* and as an adult "he continually obtained 16mm copies of Walt Disney's animated versions of these [fairy-
tale] titles, which we would watch at Noirmoutier, Jacques especially" ("il n'a eu
de cesse de se procurer des copies 16mm de ces titres en dessin animé de Walt
Disney, que nous regardions à Noirmoutier, lui surtout" [Bastide, "Plus que les
contes" 257]). The island of Noirmoutiers is where Demy and Varda commonly
vacationed with their children.

53 "Le Dandy doit aspirer à être sublime, sans interruption; / Il doit vivre et dormir
devant un miroir" (5 verso).

54 Baudelaire, however, viewed woman as being the opposite of the dandy: "La
femme est le Contraire du Dandy. / Donc elle doit faire horreur.... La femme est
naturelle, c'est à dire [*sic*] abominable" ("Woman is the Contrary of the Dandy.
/ Thus she must be loathed.... Woman is *natural,* that is to say, abominable" [5
recto]).

55 Richard Dyer discusses such a strategy in Jean Genet, in which distinctions between narcissism, exhibitionism, and voyeurism get blurred (69).

56 The Lilac Fairy desires the king and thus functions as the princess's rival. For her
part, the princess pursues the prince, but, as the film suggests, she would prefer
her father, who has been forbidden (by, ironically, the Lilac Fairy).

57 For a French version of "L'Ile de la félicité," see Aulnoy, *Contes I* 9–26. For an
English version, see "The Island of Happiness" in Zipes, *Beauties* 299–308. On
the utopian aspects of the tale, see Duggan "Feminine Genealogy."

58 With respect to Cocteau, Walter Strauss has examined the ways in which Cocteau blends aspects of Narcissus in his versions of Orpheus in his article "Jean
Cocteau: The Mask of Orpheus and Narcissus." On Cocteau as dandy, see Fontenot 166. Erik Aschengreen notes that Apollinaire's circle considered Cocteau
"un dandy intelligent mais ennuyeux" ([28] Aschengreen 73).

59 On the problematics of narcissism as a queer trope and the relation of the concept to psychoanalysis, see Steven Bruhm's book *Reflecting Narcissus.*

60 "C'est [France] un pays très fermé, très auto-censuré, aux structures vieilles, où
un film comme 'Trash' de Paul Morrissey (assistant de Warhol) est finalement
impensable.... Si dans les films de Warhol, les acteurs sont si admirables dans
leur improvisation, c'est parce qu'ils se connaissent, je veux dire aussi biblique-

ment, et cela leur permet de sortir d'eux-mêmes, de vaincre leur pudeur et leur honte" (Langlois).

61 Glyn Davis characterizes Morrissey's cult films in terms of "queer camp" (60).

Chapter 3

1 "C'est la fin d'un scandale. On peut voir enfin en France ce film délicieux tourné il y a quatre ans par Jacques Demy, d'après la légende très librement adaptée de 'Hans le joueur de flûte.'"

2 "Persuadé que ce beau film n'était pas assez commercial, on préférait indéfiniment ajourner le verdict du public, en oubliant à la fois la popularité d'un Donovan auprès de la jeune génération, et celle de Jacques Demy depuis 'les Parapluies de Cherbourg.'"

3 Chapier remarks, "Now, the audience's standing ovation at the Théâtre de Chaillot, as well as the praise by the most severe critics, were of a kind to ease this appalling situation that had already gone on too long" ("Or, l'ovation du public au théâtre de Chaillot, ainsi que les éloges des critiques les plus sévères, étaient de nature à 'décrisper' cette affligeante situation qui n'avait que trop duré").

4 For Fincelius's version of the legend, see Mieder, *Pied Piper* 33; for the Grimms' "The Children of Hamelin, see Mieder, *Pied Piper* 38–39; and for Browning's poem, see Mieder, *Pied Piper* 83–90.

5 Lang published an adaptation of Marelles's version of the piper in 1890 in *The Red Fairy Book*. See Mieder, *Tradition* 58. In the preface to the collection, first published in 1888, in which appeared his version of "The Rat Catcher," Charles Marelles explains that he had been told this legend in his youth. Interestingly, Marelles's version includes the moment when the rat catcher begins to play with his back toward the church, and like Mérimée and Gautier, an old white rat, here named Blanchet, is the last to drown in the river. (Blanchet comically gives the rat catcher a headcount—999,999 rats—before leaping to his death.) With these specific elements being found in Mérimée, Gautier, and Marelles, the last claiming his source had not read Mérimée, it is possible that the German legend had made its way to France via Alsace and entered into the French oral tradition. Marelles's version also includes a lame boy who cannot follow the troop of children through the mountain pass, which is present in English versions of the tale by Richard Verstegan (1605) and by Robert Browning (1842).

6 By the end of the nineteenth century, Mérimée's version of "The Pied Piper" made it into school textbooks, evident in the 1898 textbook *L'Ecole moderne*.

7 As Mieder has documented, the historical window dates "from around 1300," it "was restored in 1572 but is now lost" (*Tradition* 46).

8 Wilson explains that in medieval society, for instance, "art had been seamlessly integrated into the social institutions of religion" (15). In the early modern period, art was supported through patronage. In the post-Revolutionary period, the artist no longer had state or aristocratic support and lived according to the whims of a market economy.

9   Wilson notes that when "Gautier and Alexandre Dumas travelled through Spain in the 1840s they often wore gypsy costumes as if to make the willed identification more real" (140).

10 Massenet explains that his friend Emile Bergerat, Gautier's future son-in-law at this point, took him to visit the writer. Massenet remarks, "He [Gautier] developed for me the two following subjects: *The Rat Catcher* and *The Daughter of the King of Aulnes*. Regarding the latter subject, the memory of Schubert terrified me, and we agreed that we would propose to the director of the Opéra *The Rat Catcher*" ("il me développa les deux sujets suivants: *le Preneur de rats* et *la Fille du roi des Aulnes*. Pour ce dernier sujet, le souvenir de Schubert m'épouvanta, et il fut convenu que l'on ferait au directeur de l'Opéra l'offre du *Preneur de rats*" [Massenet 85]).

11 "un personnage d'aspect singulier, moitié saltimbanque, moitié musicien" (Gautier 192).

12 In his biography of Massenet, Demar Irvine notes that Ganne was "conductor for the balls at the Paris Opéra" (269) and ran the Louis Ganne orchestra at the Monte Carlo Opéra (283). Regarding Monte Carlo, Donald Grout observes that after 1870 it "was the scene of some notable premieres," along with the Opéra-Comique and the Brussels Théâtre de la Monnaie (474).

13 Hammerstein changed the venue of the Manhattan Opera House in 1910 through an agreement with the Metropolitan Opera House: in exchange for $1.2 million, he would agree to not produce grand operas for ten years. He initiated the new policy by opening with *Hans the Flute Player* (see "Fairy Tale Set to Music"). For a contemporary review of the operetta, see "'Hans the Flute Player.'"

14 "Tout au commerce! / Tout au travail!" (Vaucaire and Mitchell 6).

15 "Je vous rappelle que nous n'avons pas de temps à perdre. Le temps, c'est de l'or! . . . Avant un an, nous aurons accaparé, monopolisé les céréales des deux mondes! . . . Nous amassons, Messieurs! Nous entassons! nous accumulons!" (Vaucaire and Mitchell 14).

16 "Paresseux, vagabond! propre à rien!" (Vaucaire and Mitchell 18).

17 "Votre administration mercantile a tué toutes ces belles oeuvres. L'Art est mort! l'idéal s'est envolé!" (Vaucaire and Mitchell 20).

18 "La mendicité est interdite dans le duché de Milkatz!" (Vaucaire and Mitchell 39).

19 "Je viens d'un pays, d'un pays lointain / Où l'art et l'amour se donnent la main" (Vaucaire and Mitchell 47).

20 "Il m'a lassé parler d'amour!" (Vaucaire and Mitchell 59).

21 "C'est de la sorcellerie, et le complice d'un sorcier, ça se brûle comme un cotret!" (Vaucaire and Mitchell 61).

22 "C'est un rival flambé!" (Vaucaire and Mitchell 63).

23 Mary Gluck begins her study on *Popular Bohemia* with a question posed by many nineteenth-century artists and critics: "What is the function of the artist in a commercial culture?" (1). For another view of the relation between the arts

and the bourgeoisie under the Third Republic highlighting the positive role the bourgeoisie played in the development of the arts, see Young.

24   Whitney Stewart notes that Walt Disney drew from *The Green Fairy Book* by Lang for "The Three Little Pigs" (1933), so it certainly is possible that he also looked at Lang's *The Red Fairy Book* for his version of "The Pied Piper" (Stewart 54).

25   Michael Barrier remarks, "In the months just after he made *Three Little Pigs*, Walt Disney took up the challenge of human characters again and made five Silly Symphonies with them. The third of those cartoons, *The Pied Piper* . . . was easily the most ambitious of the new cartoons because its central figures, the Piper and Hamelin's Mayor, most resembled real human beings in how they were drawn" (109). One might add that in Disney's desire to make the characters resemble real human beings, he also may have chosen to structure the film around a genre—the operetta—that was acted out by people, not imaginary creatures. Less realistic than *The Pied Piper*, Disney's *Old King Cole* (1933) similarly drew from vaudeville.

26   With respect to the legend of the pied piper, Demy's film proves to be the only variant of the legend that explicitly associates the Black Death with the story of the infamous rat catcher. The very first manifestations of the legend concern 130 children who disappear from Hamelin, led away by a strange man. It was not until 1565 that a second story about a rat catcher who rids the city of rats, is refused pay, and takes his revenge by leading the children away was grafted onto the first, providing an explanation for the disappearance of the children. It should be noted that in all versions of the legend before Demy, the rats in the city threaten food supplies and are a general menace, but they are not associated with the plague. Some scholars, however, have speculated that the legend of the pied piper indeed refers to the disappearance of children during the period of the bubonic plague—a logical hypothesis given the importance of rat catchers at that time. See Mieder, *Tradition* 46–49 and *Pied Piper* 8–9.

27   As Kayser's *The Grotesque in Art and Literature* makes clear, the concept of the grotesque changes in meaning over time and across geographical borders, from its first use in fifteenth-century Italy to what it comes to signify in nineteenth-century France and Germany.

28   In an interview for *Le Journal du cinéma*, Demy talks about how he wanted *The Pied Piper* to be more realistic than *Donkey Skin*: "I did a lot of research on the Middle Ages to be absolutely precise, in effect, about the historical facts or about the ways to treat the plague and for example find remedies" ("j'ai fait beaucoup de recherches sur le Moyen Age pour être absolument précis, enfin sur des faits historiques ou sur des manières de traiter la peste et par exemple trouver des remèdes"). See "Jacques Demy sur le tournage du film."

29   "Jarry a écrit une sorte de canevas où la tyrannie était saisie, pour ainsi dire, à l'état pur, dans sa monstruosité effrayante—si effrayante qu'on ne pouvait réagir autrement que par des bouffées de rire libératrices. . . . La dérision, le grotesque, la trivialité montraient le pouvoir dans ce qu'il a de plus bas et de plus saugrenu" (Delaperrière 55–56).

30 Critics often make mention of the Id-like nature of Ubu, and I would suggest a similar nature in Hamelin's authority figures. Brian Nelson states, for instance, "As an embodiment of unbridled indulgence of appetites, Ubu is an image of the destructive potential of the human personality itself, of the disruptive Freudian *Id*" (207).

31 Patrick O'Neill notes, "The grotesque . . . operates precisely by exaggeration rather than understatement, by surprise rather than insinuation" (158).

32 Whether we think of *Histoire de la folie à l'âge classique* (*History of Madness*, 1962), *Surveiller et punir: Naissance de la prison* (*Discipline and Punish: Birth of the Prison*, 1975), or *Histoire de la sexualité* (*History of Sexuality*, Volume 1, 1976), Foucault is always interested in the strategies and tactics deployed by different social and political institutions to maintain control over the body politic. He incessantly examines battles between secular and religious institutions and between medical and criminal authorities in the definition of crime, madness, and forms of sexuality, which ultimately have to do with each institutional apparatus's ability to exercise authority over a population.

33 Swan indeed was eaten in this period. Melitta Adamson explains, "Throughout the Middle Ages the swan was not just admired for its majestic appearance but also eaten. Especially in Britain and France it was considered a delicacy" (39).

34 For an overview of swan maiden tales, see Haase, *Encyclopedia* 934–35.

35 In *The Plague*, the character Dr. Bernard Rieux, much like Melius, realizes early on the danger posed by the dead rats. I would like to thank Victor Figueroa for bringing the parallels between Camus and Demy to my attention.

36 Interestingly, Kayser considers vermin to be a grotesque animal due to its status as "unclean and unworthy of being sacrificed. It belongs not to God but to the evil powers" (182).

37 I'm drawing here from Harpham's comments on the grotesque, where he cites Goya: "The Sleep of Reason Produces Monsters." See Harpham, "Grotesque" 463–64.

38 In his entry on "The Plague of Our Time: Societal Responses to AIDS" for the *Encyclopedia of AIDS*, Mervyn Silverman evokes the Black Death and leprosy to make comparisons with the social response to AIDS, noting the lack of response to the epidemic by the Reagan and H. W. Bush administrations due to "distain" and "apathy" for the gay community, initially believed to be the only affected group. Some religious leaders proclaimed AIDS was "God's retribution for the sinful acts of homosexuals" (23).

39 Roxane Hamery observes, "The scene of the travelling theater and the scaffolding that fits tightly around the cathedral under construction, the circularity of the movements of the tracking shots that often end up leading back to the point of departure, foreground the image of the city as prison" ("La scène du théâtre ambulant et les échafaudages qui enserrent la cathédrale en construction, la circularité de ses mouvements qui aboutissent très souvent à un retour au point de départ, appuie l'image de la ville comme prison").

40 See, for instance, Deleuze and Guattari 25–27 and Massumi's foreword xii–xiv.

The notion of "smooth spaces" is expressed in part by the image of the desert, which appears without boundaries and heterogeneous and which is in constant flux or becoming: "The sand desert has not only oases, which are like fixed points, but also rhizomatic vegetation that is temporary and shifts location according to local rains, bringing changes in the direction of the crossings . . . there is no line separating earth and sky; there is no intermediate distance, no perspective or contour" (Deleuze and Guattari 421).

41 Deleuze makes it clear that nomadism can occur without movement in the often cited passage on Nietzsche: "But the nomad is not necessarily one who moves: some voyages take place *in situ,* are trips in intensity. Even historically, nomads are not necessarily those who move about like migrants. On the contrary, they do not move; nomads, they nevertheless stay in the same place and continually evade the codes of settled people" ("Nomad Thought" 149).

42 It should be noted that Demy was probably influenced by Bergman's *Sawdust and Tinsel* (1953), which is structured around a circus caravan that crosses open fields to enter a close-minded bourgeois town, only to leave again to move out into open space at the end of the film. Bergman returns more or less to this structure in *The Seventh Seal,* a film that strongly influenced Demy's *The Pied Piper.*

43 Jack Wild, nominated for an Academy Award for his role as the artful dodger in the 1968 screen version of *Oliver,* was in fact already twenty years old by 1972, when he played Gavin. However, his small stature, his love interest clearly being thirteen years old, and, at the time, his association with *Oliver* clearly suggest his character was meant to be an adolescent.

44 Berthomé notes, "Demy and Mark Peploe in fact considerably reworked Andrew Birkin's initial screenplay in order to include aspects that interested them. In particular, they completely modified the structure by interlacing into the principal plot secondary stories that gave it much more complexity. They further developed the role of the Jew Melius, which was only hinted at in the first version" ("Demy et Mark Peploe remanient en fait considérablement le premier scénario d'Andrew Brikin afin d'y introduire les aspects qui les intéressent. Surtout, ils en modifient complètement la structure en entrelaçant dans la trame principale des intrigues secondaires qui lui donnent une complexité beaucoup plus grande, développant en particulier le rôle du juif Melius qui n'était qu'esquissé dans la première version" [262]).

45 Here Demy draws in particular from Bergman's *The Seventh Seal.* Along with the theme of itinerant actors and pilgrimage to the Holy Land, Bergman's film treats the subject of religious intolerance that leads to the burning at the stake of a woman accused of being a witch.

46 The entry on "The Black Death" in *Medieval Jewish Civilization: An Encyclopedia* provides more specific information on the waves of massacres in Germany as they moved from Rothenburg and Frankfurt to Mainz, Trier, and Cologne (Roth 114–16).

47 On the National Front's electoral platform of 1973, see Mayer 16. On the "murderous summer" of 1973, see Silverstein 159.

48 I should clarify that Hargreaves only cites unemployment as a factor in France freezing Algerian immigration.

49 It should be noted that Donovan was already on board for the project when producers Lieberman and Puttnam approached Demy to direct the film.

50 The ending recalls that of *The Seventh Seal*, in which the actors Mia and Jof and their child are spared from the plague.

51 After Melius is burned, Franz shows signs of the plague on his face, meaning that the plague has indeed begun to spread.

52 "La jeunesse, tournant le dos à la corruption, prépare un monde nouveau" (Remond 73).

53 "C'est un conte je crois très actuel" (Maurin).

54 "Donovan, sa flûte, son innocence de charme n'est pas le héros d'un conte de fées, mais le symbole du poète révolutionnaire" (Chapier, "Joueur").

55 "Il contient plein d'espoirs et ajoute au conte de fées pour gosses de tout âge un message social qui jette de l'huile bouillante sur les sucreries à la Disney. Grâce à Demy, Peter Pan devient un (jeune) homme de gauche" ("Le Joueur de flûte").

56 "[Demy] a dénaturé la légende. Travesti en poète révolutionnaire, prophète de quelque mai 1968 musical, le joueur de flûte (Donovan) perd son auréole d'enchanteur pour apparaître comme un contestataire candide et optimiste, c'est-à-dire une sorte d'imbécile heureux" ("Joueur," *Valeurs Actuelles*).

57 "Il était tout de même assez commercial pour les Anglais, pour les Américains qu'on dit avares de dollars et qui l'ont sorti très bien. Cela me fait penser qu'en France on est si commerçant qu'on méprise l'art" (Maurin).

58 "Quel beau cadeau nous fait Demy qui semble prophétiquement, en 1971, plaider pour son art, aujourd'hui si menacé, contre tous les marchands du temps épris de cataclysmes au point de s'y engloutir stupidement!" (Benayoun).

Chapter 4

1 "Il est frappant de constater combien, paranthèse quasi accidentelle dans l'oeuvre de Demy, *Lady Oscar* en marque cependant un tournant. C'est là que pour la première fois l'émeute se substitue à la fête, là aussi que l'héroïne découvre la nécessité de la révolte, apprend à assumer sa nudité et la réalité physique de l'amour. Là surtout que—et le réalisateur n'avait aucun pouvoir pour modifier l'intrigue—le destin des amants débouche sur la mort. Tout se passe comme si, frustré de la réalisation d'*Une Chambre en ville*, Demy en avait intégré les éléments les plus forts dans la commande qu'on lui proposait" (Berthomé 343). In his 1987 piece on *Lady Oscar* for *Cahiers du cinéma*, Michel Chion likewise remarks on the similarities between *Lady Oscar* and *A Room in Town*, which was released some three years later and whose screenplay had been written by 1974 (54–55).

2 In 1983 the film was nominated for several César Awards, including best picture and best director. It won the Prix Méliès.

3 On the background regarding the commission for *Lady Oscar*, see "Film Jacques

Demy" and Berthomé 298–301.

4   When the Chevalier d'Eon's parents try to dissuade her from becoming a dragoon, she responds with a line that anticipates the reaction of Lady Oscar to her father's desire that she marry: "Look at me, I was taught to ride horseback and to go about in all kinds of weather, to kill deer with a knife, and bears with a hunting spear, to fight like a musketeer, damn it! and to swear like a gentleman.... And why this wonderful education? to tell me one day enough of this mascarade?"

5   Lenzi's heroine interestingly is a skilled and notorious fighter and thief *as a woman;* thus the moments when she cross-dresses are continuous with her behavior when appearing as female. However, the film works to reestablish gender norms by the end of the film, which concludes with the image of Mary having become a true lady.

6   More than the other films within this tradition, Bolognini focuses on the way gender trouble elicits sexual trouble. In some respects this is not surprising. Bolognini worked closely on several films with Piero Pasolini, who was openly gay and thus may have been more sensitive to such questions. Interestingly, certain scenes of *Mademoiselle de Maupin* suggest that Demy may have been familiar with Bolognini's film. One of the opening shots of the character Magdeleine on a swing resembles the scene in *Lady Oscar* where Marie Antoinette similarly swings in a Fragonard-like pastoral setting; and for the second ball, Oscar dons a beautiful white uniform, not unlike the one Théodore wears in Bolognini's film.

7   "Une telle perturbation de l'ordre traditionnel des choses n'est pourtant que l'aboutissement de toute une série de films qui, au tournant des années 1960/1970, s'amusent à saper les fondements de ce que l'on croit savoir du masculin et du féminin."

8   On the importance of the figure of Mulan in the May Fourth Movement and the New Culture Movement, see Wang 20–22 and 347.

9   Lisa Brocklebank looks at the notion of cross-dressing as "category crisis" specifically in the context of the seventeenth-century French fairy-tale writers Madame d'Aulnoy, Madame de Murat, and Charles Perrault.

10 Garber maintains, "Category crises can and do mark displacements from the axis of *class* as well as from *race* onto the axis of gender ... the sumptuary laws that regulated dress for each social class in medieval and Renaissance Europe quickly came as well to regulate and reify dress codes for men and women. Once again, transvestism was the specter that rose up—both in the theater and in the streets—to mark and overdetermine this crisis of social and economic change" (17).

11 Demy maintains in an interview with Saïd Ould Khelifa that *Lady Oscar* sold well and was a success in Japan. But because the Japanese producers asked too much from Gaumont, the French distributors abandoned the film. Demy admits, "I'm a bit saddened because it's a film [French] people don't see" ("Je suis un peu triste car c'est un film que l'on ne voit pas" [Khelifa 10]).

12 Important studies include Dianne Dugaw, *Warrior Women and Popular Balladry, 1650–1850* (1989); Catherine Velay-Vallantin, *La Fille en garçon* (1992); and

Christine Jones, "Noble Impropriety: The Maiden Warrior and the Seventeenth-Century *conte de fées*" (2002). There is a plethora of books and articles on the maiden or woman warrior in European, Native American, and Chinese literature and folklore that would be too numerous to cite here.

13　Lundell characterizes the gender bias in terms of "selective labeling" (i.e., the use of "search" for heroines vs. "quest" for heroes), "misleading plot summaries" (the more forceful qualities of heroines are played down), and "focus on male character instead of heroine" (i.e., a tale in which the princess is central gets classified as "The Prince as Bird"). See Lundell 240–46.

14　See, for instance, Christine Jones's entry on "Cross-dressing" (1: 241–43) and D. L. Ashliman's entry on "Soldier" (3: 891) in *The Greenwood Encyclopedia of Folktales and Fairy Tales*. See also Jacques Barchilon's discussion of tale types and motifs regarding a maiden warrior tale by Marie-Catherine d'Aulnoy (359–60).

15　See Greenhill "'Neither a Man nor a Maid'" and Dugaw 92–93. Dugaw provides a sequence of five narrative elements. I condensed here the distinction Dugaw makes between trials of valor and trials of love.

16　Lan Dong similarly states, "These female combatants' successes on the battlefield or in the martial world are carefully characterized without either challenging or threatening the dominant male-centered rule. Instead, heroic women's achievements are lauded with a particular emphasis on these heroines who are loyal subjects, filial daughters, wise mothers and wives, or lady knights-errant with integrity and virtue" (*Mulan's Legend* 13).

17　In "Writing Chinese America into Words and Images," Dong maintains that "The Ballad of Mulan" is based on a historical figure, who issued from the Xianbei, a formerly nomadic group, who eventually "established a unified regime in north China in the year 386"; Dong notes that "it was not uncommon for Xianbei women to be skillful at riding and archery" (219).

18　See, for instance, Maclean 155–232; DeJean 24–42; and Mueller.

19　For French versions of "Marmoisan," see Velay-Vallantin 17–54; for "Belle-Belle, ou le chevalier Fortuné," see d'Aulnoy, *Contes II* 215–69; for "Le Sauvage," see Murat 2: 1–65. For an English version of "Belle-Belle" and "The Savage," see Zipes, *Great Fairy-Tale Tradition* 174–205 and 205–19, respectively.

20　The narrator relates, "The king preferred that his son give himself over to the advice of a cherished wife, whose sentiments aspired only to virtue, than to those of some ambitious favorite" ("Le roi aimait mieux qu'il s'abandonnât aux conseils d'une épouse chérie, dont tous les sentiments semblaient n'aspirer qu'à la vertu, qu'à ceux de quelque favori ambitieux" [Velay-Vallantin 53–54]). L'Héritier seems to be criticizing the practice of French kings marrying foreign princesses, several of whom were viewed as pursuing their own ambition, the most notable being perhaps Marie de Médici, wife of Henri IV and mother of Louis XIII, and Anne d'Autriche, wife of Louis XIII and mother of Louis XIV, who was the target of political pamphlets during the Fronde. In his reading of the tale, Joseph Harris makes a parallel between the king's wife in the tale and Louis XIV's wife, the unpopular Madame de Maintenon (202).

21 See, for instance, Duggan, *Salonnières*, "Boileau and Perrault: The Public Sphere and Female Folly" 121–64.

22 Suvilay similarly notes that the manga is "influenced by Western fairy tales and the graphics of the Fleischer Brothers and Disney" ("influencé par les contes de fées occidentaux et le graphisme des frères Fleischer et de Disney" [2]).

23 Natsu Onoda Power notes that Tezuka lived next door to two sisters who were Takarazuka performers, and his mother was a fan. Tezuka acknowledged his debt to Takarazuka in the creation of the character Saphir, and Takarazuka's influence can also be observed in the style and props in his *shōjo* manga (Power 115–16).

24 Benito Ortolani also notes that, in its early years, the Takarazuka Revue staged fairy-tale operettas and nursery tales (272).

25 On the popularity of the *otoko-yaku*, see also Brau 80.

26 See in particular James Welker's remarks cited by Dirk Deppey in his blog entry (Deppey).

27 Critics seem divided. Shamoon, for instance, focuses on the heterosexual readings of the stories; Nakamura and Matsuo insist on the asexual nature of same-sex relations (59); Suvilay argues that female readers live out by proxy a heterosexual relation as a means to circumvent Japanese patriarchy (4); and Welker looks at the ways in which boys' love manga liberates "readers not just from patriarchy but from gender dualism and heteronormativity" (843).

28 "Les femmes n'ont pas leur place dans cette famille où depuis des générations nous commandons des armées et protégeons les rois." I have used the French translation of *The Rose of Versailles* (*La Rose de Versailles*. 3 vols., 2002–5); there is no available English translation.

29 "Elle va me succéder! Je ferai d'elle le meilleur soldat de toute la France!"

30 The narrator states at one point, "In this period in high society . . . among women it was fashionable to have close female friends . . . without a homosexual connotation. Among them, some cross-dressed as men to exude an ambiguous charm" ("A cette époque dans la haute société . . . parmi les dames il était de bon ton d'avoir des amies très proches . . . sans connotation homosexuelle. Parmi elles, certaines se travestissaient en homme pour dégager un charme ambigu" 1: 307). Here Ikeda alludes to the Japanese tradition of female same-sex romance.

31 "Comment!? Moi lesbienne!? Je vais la couper en deux!?" (Ikeda 1: 632).

32 Interestingly, Nakamura and Matsuo found that, with respect to Takarazuka theater, lesbians they interviewed did not view romance in Takarazuka plots in terms of lesbian desire; instead, they felt Takarazuka was asexual (65). Welker, however, states, "Members of the Japanese lesbian community have . . . pointed to boys' love and other gender-bending manga as strong influences on them in their formative years, specifically naming Ikeda Riyoko's *The Rose of Versailles* . . . and Takemiya Keiko's *The Song of the Wind and the Trees*" (843).

33 In Jean-Jacques Rousseau's *La Nouvelle Héloïse*, the daughter of a baron, Julie, is in love with her commoner tutor, Saint-Preux. After Julie feels obligated to marry Monsieur de Wolmar, Saint-Preux is later brought back into the house-

hold. Ikeda's Girondelle is basically saying he does not mind being the husband of a wife who pines over her lower-class servant.

34 "L'héroïne ne s'y rend pas habillée en princesse, mais paraît sous les traits d'un prince charmant séduisant aussi bien les hommes que les femmes."

35 "Grand-mère, tu perds ton temps! C'est comme ça!"

36 "C'est un cauchemar! Mon Oscar va porter une robe pleine de froufrous et va danser avec d'autres hommes!?"

37 "Ce sont des lectures du peuple!" (Ikeda 1: 880).

38 Demy states, "J'amenais Catriona aux Japonais. J'ai eu un regard unanime, un sourire: D'accord, et c'était ça."

39 In the manga, Oscar is challenged to a duel by Monsieur de Guémené, but nothing comes of it when Oscar is consigned to her estate.

40 Butler explains, "In that naming, the girl is 'girled,' brought into the domain of language and kinship through the interpellation of gender. But that 'girling' of the girl does not end there; on the contrary, that founding interpellation is reiterated by various authorities and throughout various intervals of time to reinforce or contest this naturalized effect. The naming is at once the setting of a boundary, and also the repeated inculcation of a norm" (*Bodies* 7–8).

41 At one point Oscar and André manoeuver around a statue of Diana the huntress, a figure that blends masculine and feminine traits, symbolizing Oscar's own complex gender.

42 My discussion of Oscar as being transgender bears affinities with Lewis Seifert's discussion of the abbé de Choisy, whose cross-dressing also was not simply a temporary state but an integral part of his gender identity. See Seifert, *Manning* 210–41.

43 Charlotte Garson makes this observation, noting that "the heroine and her suckling brother end up uniting" ("l'héroïne et son frère de lait finiront par s'unir"), which recalls the incestuous relation in *Donkey Skin* and anticipates that of *Three Seats for the 26th* (657–58).

44 "Audace tranquille, absence de culpabilité et de jugement moral: Demy achève sa carrière avec un film bancal mais sur une étonnante vision de l'amour et des tabous."

45 With respect to *A Room in Town*, Bill Marshall notes, "The space of the city moves slightly eastward from that of *Lola,* to the area associated with political power, in medieval times the cathedral and the ducal castle, now the city hall and *préfecture*" (30).

Epilogue

1 The show's title plays on the double meaning of *en tête*, which can mean "leading" or "first" as well as "in mind."

2 "Cet univers de midinettes ... c'est la société française avec ses classes différentes. ... Midinettes ou les rêves de Prince Charmant ... on ne peut pas empêcher ce

rêve. Il existe. Bon, c'est faussement un univers de midinettes, et faussement gai … on a pleuré pas mal. … Je suis très attiré par le quotidien, la réalité, les problèmes des gens … et puis le rêve absolu, et je crois que c'est toujours et encore ces enfances qu'on trimballe avec soi, derrière soi qui sont très tenaces. Avant le cinéma j'ai fait, par exemple, du guignol … j'ai monté tous les contes de fées. Adulte … j'ai fait *Peau d'âne* … qui est une rêverie, c'est un fantasme, mais c'est ça le cinéma, et ce cinéma, le mien, celui qui me permet d'exister, et de rêver et puis de partager la grande grâce, c'est que finalement déjà on partageait ce rêve aussi, ça c'est la récompense" ("L'Art en tête").

3   As Alan Williams argues, "Domestic melodramas" in film "owe little to the stage melodrama and much to the older French tradition of the *drame bourgeois*" (128).

4   "Gene Kelly reflected more of the working-class, common man in the roles he played as opposed to the upper-class image imparted by the often tuxedo-clad Astaire" (Oboler 253).

Filmography of Jacques Demy

Feature-Length Films

Trois Places pour le 26 (Three Seats for the 26th, 1988)

Starring: Yves Montand (himself), Mathilda May (Marion), Françoise Fabon (Marie-Hélène de Lambert), Patrick Pierry (Toni Fontaine), Catriona McColl (Betty Miller)

Written and directed: Jacques Demy

Music: Michel Legrand

Choreography: Michael Peters

Production design: Bernard Evein

Costume design: Rosalie Varda

Cinematography: Jean Penzer

Sound: André Hervée

Editing: Sabine Mamou

Parking (1982)

Starring: Francis Huster (Orphée), Keïko Ito (Eurydice), Laurent Malet (Calaïs), Jean Marais (Hades), Marie-France Pisier (Persephone)

Written and directed: Jacques Demy

Music: Michel Legrand

Production design: Patrice Mercier

Costume design: Rosalie Varda

Cinematography: Jean-François Robin

Sound: Bernard Ortion

Editing: Sabine Mamou

Une Chambre en ville (*A Room in Town*, 1982)

Starring: Dominique Sanda (Edith Leroyer), Richard Berry (François Guilbaud), Danielle Darrieux (Margot Langlois), Michel Piccoli (Edmond Leroyer), Fabienne Guyon (Violette), Jean-François Stévenin (Dambiel), Jean-Louis Rolland (Ménager)

Written and directed: Jacques Demy

Music: Michel Colombier

Production design: Bernard Evein

Costume design: Rosalie Varda

Cinematography: Jean Penzer

Sound: André Hervée

Editing: Sabine Mamou

La Naissance du jour (*Break of Day*, made for TV, 1979)

Starring: Danièle Delorme (Colette), Jean Sorel (Vial), Dominique Sanda (Hélène Clément), Orane Demazis (Sido), Guy Dhers (Villebeuf)

Written and directed: Jacques Demy

Music: Felix Mendelssohn, directed by Laurent Petitgérard

Production design: Hubert Monloup

Costume design: Rosalie Varda

Cinematography: Jean Penzer

Sound: Auguste Galli

Editing: Anne-Marie Cotret

Lady Oscar (1979)

Starring: Catriona MacColl (Oscar François de Jarjayes), Barry Stokes (André Grandier), Christina Böhm (Marie Antoinette), Terence Budd (Louis XVI), Jonas Bergström (Hans Axel von Fersen), Anoushka Hempel (Jeanne de la Motte)

Written and directed: Jacques Demy

Screenplay: Jacques Demy and Patricia L. Knop

Music: Michel Legrand

Production design: Bernard Evein

Costume design: Jacqueline Moreau

Cinematography: Jean Penser

Sound: Anthony Jackson

Editing: Paul Davies

L'Événement le plus important depuis que l'homme a marché sur la lune (*A Slightly Pregnant Man*, 1973)

Starring: Catherine Deneuve (Irène de Fontenoy), Marcello Mastroianni (Marco Mazetti)

Written and directed: Jacques Demy

Music: Michel Legrand

Production design: Bernard Evein

Costume design: Gitt Magrini

Cinematography: Andréas Winding

Sound: Louis Hochet

Editing: Anne-Marie Cotret

The Pied Piper (1972)

Starring: Donovan (pied piper), Jack Wild (Gavin), Cathryn Harrison (Lisa), Donald Pleasence (the baron), John Hurt (Franz), Michael Hordern (Melius), Roy Kinnear (the mayor), Peter Vaughan (the bishop), Diana Dors (Frau Poppendick)

Directed: Jacques Demy

Written: Andrew Birkin, Jacques Demy, Mark Peploe

Music: Donovan

Production design: Assheton Gorton

Costume design: Vangy Harrison

Cinematography: Peter Suschitzky

Sound: Tony Jackson

Editing: John Trumper

Peau d'âne (*Donkey Skin*, 1970)

Starring: Catherine Deneuve (first queen and Donkey Skin), Jean Marais (the king, her father), Jacques Perrin (Prince Charming), Delphine Seyrig (Lilac Fairy)

Written and directed: Jacques Demy

Music: Michel Legrand

Production design: Jim Léon, Jacques Dugied

Costume design: Augusto Pace, Gitt Magrini

Cinematography: Ghislain Cloquet

Sound: André Hervée

Editing: Anne-Marie Cotret

Model Shop (1969)

Starring: Anouk Aimée (Lola), Gary Lockwood (George Matthews)

Directed: Jacques Demy

Written: Jacques Demy, Adrian Joyce, Jerry Ayres

Music: The Spirit

Production design: Antony Mondello

Costume design: Riga Riggs, Gene Ashman

Cinematography: Michel Hugo

Editing: Walter Thompson

Les Demoiselles de Rochefort (*The Young Girls of Rochefort*, 1967)

Starring: Catherine Deneuve (Delphine Garnier), Françoise Dorléac (Solange Garnier), Jacques Perrin (Maxence), Gene Kelly (Andy Miller), Danielle Darrieux (Yvonne Garnier), Michel Piccoli (Simon Dame), Georges Chakiris (Etienne), Grover Dale (Bill)

Written and directed: Jacques Demy

Music: Michel Legrand

Choreography: Norman Maen

Production design: Bernard Evein

Costume design: Jacqueline Moreau

Cinematography: Ghislain Cloquet

Sound: Jacques Maumont

Editing: Jean Hamon

Les Parapluies de Cherbourg (*The Umbrellas of Cherbourg*, 1964)

Starring: Catherine Deneuve (Geneviève Emery), Nino Castelnuovo (Guy Foucher), Anne Vernon (Madame Emery), Marc Michel (Roland Cassard), Ellen Farner (Madeleine)

Written and directed: Jacques Demy

Music: Michel Legrand

Production design: Bernard Evein

Costume design: Jacqueline Moreau

Cinematography: Jean Rabier

Editing: Anne-Marie Cotret

Awards: Palme d'or, Cannes Film Festival, 1964; Louis Delluc Prize, 1964

La Baie des anges (*Bay of Angels*, 1963)

Starring: Jeanne Moreau (Jacqueline Demestre), Claude Mann (Jean Fournier)

Written and directed: Jacques Demy
Music: Michel Legrand
Production and costume design: Bernard Evein
Cinematography: Jean Rabier
Sound: André Hervée
Editing: Anne-Marie Cotret
Awards: special mention, New York Film Critics Circle, 2001

Lola (1961)
Starring: Anouk Aimée (Lola), Marc Michel (Roland Cassard), Jacques Harden (Michel), Alan Scott (Frankie), Elina Labourdette (Madame Desnoyers), Annie Dupéroux (Cécile Desnoyers)
Written and directed: Jacques Demy
Music: Michel Legrand
Production and costume design: Bernard Evein
Cinematography: Raoul Coutard
Editing: Anne-Marie Cotret
Awards: BAFTA (British Academy of Film and Television Arts), 1963; special mention, New York Film Critics Circle, 2001

Short Films

"La Luxure." Episode in *Les Sept Péchés capitaux* (*The Seven Deadly Sins,* 1962)
Starring: Jean Dessailly (the father), Jean-Louis Trintigant (Bernard), Micheline Presle (the mother), Laurent Terzieff (Jacques)
Written and directed: Jacques Demy

Ars (1959)
Written and directed: Jacques Demy

La Mère et l'enfant (*Mother and Child,* 1958)
Directed: Jacques Demy
Screenplay, adaptation, and commentary: Jacques Demy and Jean Masson
Music: Jean Sebastian Bach, performed by Jean-Pierre Rampal
Cinematography: Serge Rapoutet
Editing: Guy Michel-Ange

Musée Grévin (1958)

Starring: Michel Serrault (museum visitor), Ludmila Tcherina (herself), Jean
 Cocteau (himself), Jean-Louis Barrault (himself)

Directed: Jacques Demy

Assistant director: Charles Nughe

Music: Jean Françaix

Editing: Guy Michel-Ange

Le Bel Indifférent (*The Handsome Indifferent One*, 1957)

Starring: Jeanne Allard (C), Angelo Bellini (Emile)

Written and directed: Jacques Demy

Music: Maurice Jarre

Production design: Bernard Evein

Costume design: Jacqueline Moreau

Cinematography: Marcel Fradetal

Sound: Jean-Claude Marchetti

Editing: Denise de Casabianca

Le Sabotier du val de Loire (*The Clogmaker from the Loire Valley*, 1955)

Written and directed: Jacques Demy

Works Cited

*Can be found through the Ciné-Ressources' digital archive of *Revues de Presse* at the Cinémathèque française, which often do not include page numbers.

Abbitt, Erica Stevens. "Androgyny and Otherness: Exploring the West through the Japanese Performative Body." *Asian Theatre Journal* 18.2 (2001): 249–56.

Adamson, Melitta Weiss. *Food in Medieval Times.* Westport: Greenwood Press, 2004.

Allan, Robin. *Walt Disney and Europe.* Bloomington: Indiana UP, 1999.

Alphabet des contes des fées: Peau d'âne. Paris: Pellerin et Cie., 1866.

Andersen, Wayne V. *Freud, Leonardo da Vinci, and the Vulture's Tail: A Refreshing Look at Leonardo's Sexuality.* New York: Other Press, 2001.

Angelides, Steven. *A History of Bisexuality.* Chicago: Chicago, 2001.

Aoike, Yasuko. *From Eroica with Love.* 15 vols. La Jolla: CMX, 2004–10.

Aschengreen, Erik. *Jean Cocteau and the Dance.* Trans. Patricia McAndrew and Per Avsum. Copenhagen: Glydendal, 1986.

Ashliman, D. L. "Soldier." *The Greenwood Encyclopedia of Folktales and Fairy Tales.* Ed. Donald Haase. Westport: Greenwood Press, 2008. 3: 890–91.

Audry, Jacqueline, dir. *Le Secret du chevalier d'Eon.* Gray-film, 1959. Editions René Chateau vidéo, 2009.

Aulnoy, Marie-Catherine de. *Contes I.* Introd. Jacques Barchilon. Ed. Philippe Hourcade. Paris: Société des Textes Français Modernes, 1997.

———. *Contes II.* Introd. Jacques Barchilon. Ed. Philippe Hourcade. Paris: Société des Textes Français Modernes, 1998.

Austin, Guy. *Contemporary French Cinema: An Introduction.* 1996. Manchester: Manchester UP, 2008.

Babuscio, Jack. "Camp and the Gay Sensibility." *Camp Grounds: Style and Homosexuality.* Ed. David Bergman. Amherst: U of Massachusetts P, 1993. 19–38.

Bacchilega, Cristina. *Postmodern Fairy Tales: Gender and Narrative Strategies.* Philadelphia: U of Pennsylvania P, 1997.

Bakhtin, Mikhail. *Rabelais and His World.* Trans. Hélène Iswolsky. Bloomington: Indiana UP, 1984.

"Ballad of Mulan." *The Shorter Columbia Anthology of Traditional Chinese Literature.* Ed. Victor H. Mair. New York: Columbia UP, 2000. 267–69.

Barchilon, Jacques. "Adaptations of Folktales and Motifs in Madame d'Aulnoy's *Contes*: A Brief Survey of Influence and Diffusion." *Marvels & Tales* 23.2 (2009): 353–64.

Barrier, Michael. *Hollywood Cartoons: American Animation in Its Golden Age.* Oxford: Oxford UP, 2003.

Bastide, Bernard. " 'Plus que les contes, ce qui m'intéresse c'est la mythologie lorsqu'elle entre dans la vie quotidienne des gens.' Entretien avec Agnès Varda." *Contes et légendes à l'écran.* Ed. Carole Aurouet. Condé-sur-Noireau: Corlet, 2005. 256–61.

———. "Présence de Perrault dans le cinéma français des premiers temps (1897–1912)." *Contes et légendes à l'écran.* Ed. Carole Aurouet. Condé-sur-Noireau: Corlet, 2005. 24–33.

Batchelor, David. *Chromophobia.* London: Reaktion Books, 2000.

Baudelaire, Charles. *Mon Coeur mis à nu.* Ed. Claude Pichois. Geneva: Droz, 2001.

Beaver, Harold. "Homosexual Signs (In Memory of Roland Barthes)." *Critical Inquiry* 8.1 (1981): 99–119.

Becker, Svea, and Bruce Williams. "What Ever Happened to *West Side Story*? Gene Kelly, Jazz Dance, and Not So Real Mean in Jacques Demy's *The Young Girls of Rochefort.*" *New Review of Film and Television Studies* 6.3 (2008): 303–21.

Belanus, Betty J., and Janet L. Langlois. "Monstrous Births, Motifs T550–T557." *Archetypes and Motifs in Folklore and Literature: A Handbook.* Ed. Jane Garry and Hasan El-Shamy. Armonk: M. E. Sharpe, 2005. 425–31.

*Benayoun, Robert. "*La Peste* selon Demy." *Le Point* 12 Jan. 1976. N. pag.

Benshoff, Harry M. *Monsters in the Closet: Homosexuality and the Horror Film.* Manchester: Manchester UP, 1997.

Berger, Bennett M. "Hippie Morality—More Old Than New." *Society* 5.2 (1967): 19–27.

Bergman, Ingmar, dir. *Sawdust and Tinsel.* 1953. Criterion Collection, 2007.

———, dir. *The Seventh Seal.* 1957. Criterion Collection, 1999.

Berlin, Zeke. "The Takarazuka Touch." *Asian Theatre Journal* 8.1 (1991): 35–47.

Berthomé, Jean-Pierre. *Jacques Demy et les racines du rêve.* 1982. Nantes: L'Atalante, 1996.

Billard, Ginette. "Jacques Demy and His Other World." *Film Quarterly* 18.1 (1964): 23–27.

Bleich, Erik. *Race Politics in Britain and France: Ideas and Policymaking since the 1960s.* Cambridge: Cambridge UP, 2003.

Bolognini, Mauro, dir. *Mademoiselle de Maupin.* Film Servis, 1966.

Borderie, Bernarnd, dir. *Indomptable Angélique.* Cinéphonic, 1967.

———, dir. *Sept Hommes et une garce.* Dean Film, 1966.

Bottigheimer, Ruth B. "Straparola's *Piacevoli Notti*: Rags-to-Riches Fairy Tales as Urban Creations." *Merveilles & Contes* 8.2 (1994): 281–96.

Brassart, Alain. *L'Homosexualité dans le cinéma français*. Paris: Nouveau Monde, 2007.

Brau, Lorie. "The Women's Theatre of Takarazuka." *The Drama Review* 34.4 (1990): 79–95.

Brocklebank, Lisa. "Rebellious Voices: The Unofficial Discourse of Cross-Dressing in d'Aulnoy, de Murat, and Perrault." *Children's Literature Association Quarterly* 25.3 (2000): 127–36.

Browning, Robert. "The Pied Piper of Hamelin." *The Pied Piper: A Handbook*. Ed. Wolfgang Mieder. Westport: Greenwood Press, 2007. 83–90.

Bruhm, Steven. *Reflecting Narcissus: A Queer Aesthetic*. Minneapolis: U of Minnesota P, 2001.

Butler, Judith. *Bodies That Matter: On the Discursive Limits of "Sex."* New York: Routledge, 1993.

———. *Gender Trouble: Feminism and the Subversion of Identity*. New York: Routledge, 1990.

Camus, Albert. *La Peste*. Paris: Gallimard, 1972.

Canepa, Nancy, trans. *Giambattista Basile's The Tale of Tales, or Entertainment for Little Ones*. Detroit: Wayne State UP, 2007.

Carter, Angela. *Burning Your Boats: The Collected Short Stories*. Introd. Salman Rushdie. London: Penguin, 1997.

"Catherine Deneuve." *Look* 30 Apr. 1968: 62–67.

*Chapier, Henry. "'Le Joueur de flûte' de Jacques Demy. Le Sabotage d'un chef d'oeuvre." *Quotidien de Paris* 5 Nov. 1976. N. pag.

Chion, Michel. "Le Théâtre de la reine." *Cahiers du cinéma* (Feb. 1987): 54–56.

Clark, John R. *The Modern Satiric Grotesque and Its Traditions*. Lexington: UP of Kentucky, 1991.

Clum, John M. *Something for the Boys: Musical Theater and Gay Culture*. New York: St. Martin's Press, 1999.

Coates, Paul. *Cinema and Colour: The Saturated Image*. New York: Palgrave Macmillan, 2010.

Cohan, Steven. *Incongruous Entertainment: Camp, Cultural Value, and the MGM Musical*. Durham: Duke UP, 2005.

Colomb, Philippe. "L'Étrange Demy-monde." *Q comme queer : les séminaires Q de 1996–1997*. Ed. Marie-Hélène Bourcier. Paris: Cahiers GKC, 1998. 39–47.

"Cowles Closing *Look* Magazine after 34 Years." *New York Times* 17 Sept. 1971: 1+.

Danks, Adrian. "Living Cinema: The 'Demy Films' of Agnès Varda." *Studies in Documentary Film* 4.2 (2010): 159–72.

Davis, Glyn. "Camp and Queer and the New Queer Director: Case Study—Gregg Araki." *New Queer Cinema: A Critical Reader*. Ed. Michele Aaron. New Brunswick: Rutgers UP, 2004. 53–67.

Dean, Tim, and Christopher Lane. "Homosexuality and Psychoanalysis: An Introduction." *Homosexuality and Psychoanalysis.* By Dean and Lane. Chicago: U of Chicago P, 2001. 3–42.

DeJean, Joan. *Tender Geographies: Women and the Origins of the Novel in France.* New York: Columbia UP, 1991.

Delannoy, Jean, dir. *Les Amitiés particulières (This Special Friendship).* Lux Compagnie Cinématographique de France and Progéfi, 1964.

Delaperrière, Maria. "L'Irrésistible fascination du pouvoir." *Revue de littérature comparée* 329.1 (2009): 55–69.

Deleuze, Gilles. "Nomad Thought." *The New Nietzsche.* Ed. David B. Allison. Cambridge: MIT Press, 1985. 142–49.

Deleuze, Gilles, and Félix Guattari. *A Thousand Plateaus.* Trans. and introd. Brian Massumi. 1980. New York: Continuum, 2004.

Demy, Jacques. "L'Art en tête." 23 May 1987. <http://www.ina.fr/art-et-culture/cinema/video/CPC87004652/jacques-demy.fr.html>. 3 March 2013.

——, dir. *La Baie des anges (Bay of Angels).* 1963. Ciné Tamaris and ARTE, 2008.

——, dir. *Le Bel indifférent (The Handsome Indifferent One).* 1957. Ciné Tamaris and ARTE, 2008.

——, dir. *Une Chambre en ville (A Room in Town).* 1982. Ciné Tamaris and ARTE, 2008.

——. *Chansons et textes chantés.* Paris: Editions Léo Scheer, 2004.

——, dir. *L'Evénement le plus important depuis que l'homme a marché sur la lune (A Slightly Pregnant Man).* 1973. Ciné Tamaris and ARTE, 2008.

——, dir. *Lady Oscar.* 1979. Ciné Tamaris and ARTE, 2008.

——, dir. *Lola.* 1961. Ciné Tamaris and ARTE, 2008.

——, dir. "La Luxure." Ciné Tamaris and ARTE, 2008.

——, dir. *Model Shop.* 1969. Ciné Tamaris and ARTE, 2008.

——, dir. *Les Parapluies de Cherbourg (The Umbrellas of Cherbourg).* 1964. Ciné Tamaris and ARTE, 2008.

——, dir. *Parking.* 1982. Ciné Tamaris and ARTE, 2008.

——, dir. *Peau d'âne (Donkey Skin).* Ciné Tamaris and ARTE, 2008.

——, dir. *The Pied Piper.* 1972. Ciné Tamaris and ARTE, 2008.

——. "Rencontre avec Jacques Demy." Interview with Saïd Ould Khelifa. Nov. 1986. *Album* [accompanies DVD set]. Ciné Tamaris and ARTE, 2008. 3–11.

——, dir. *Trois Places pour le 26 (Three Seats for the 26th).* 1988. Ciné Tamaris and ARTE, 2008.

Deppey, Dirk. "Mar. 27, 2007: The First Draft of History (Some Revisions Might Be Necessary." *Journalista.* The News Weblog of *The Comics Journal.* <http://archives.tcj.com/journalista/?p=321>. 1 Feb. 2011.

Diderot, Denis. *Jacques le fataliste.* 1796. Paris: Bordas, 1993.

Dong, Lan. *Mulan's Legend and Legacy in China and the United States*. Philadelphia: Temple UP, 2011.

———. "Writing Chinese America into Words and Images: Storytelling and Retelling of *The Song of Mu Lan*." *The Lion and the Unicorn* 30 (2006): 218–33.

Doty, Alexander. *Making Things Perfectly Queer: Interpreting Mass Culture*. Minneapolis: U of Minneapolis P, 1993.

Dugaw, Dianne. *Warrior Women and Popular Balladry, 1650–1850*. Cambridge: Cambridge UP, 1989.

Duggan, Anne. "Conception and Birth, Motifs T500–T599." *Archetypes and Motifs in Folklore and Literature: A Handbook*. Ed. Jane Garry and Hasan El-Shamy. Armonk: M. E. Sharpe, 2005. 419–24.

———. "Feminine Genealogy, Matriarchy, and Utopia in the Fairy Tale of Marie-Catherine d'Aulnoy." *Neophilologus* 82.2 (1998): 199–208.

———. *Salonnières, Furies, and Fairies: The Politics of Gender and Cultural Change in Absolutist France*. Newark: U of Delaware P, 2005.

Dyer, Richard. *Now You See It: Studies on Lesbian and Gay Film*. New York: Routledge, 1990.

Eder, Bruce. "Bretaigne Windust." *All Movie Guide*. 6 July 2010. <http://www.allmovie. com/artist/bretaigne-windust-117038/bio>. 3 March 2013.

Edwards, Louise. "Women Warriors and Amazons of the Mid Qing Texts *Jinghua Yuan* and *Honglou Meng*." *Modern Asian Studies* 29.2 (1995): 225–55.

Elsaesser, Thomas. "Tales of Sound and Fury: Observations on the Family Melodrama." *Monogram* 3 (1972): 2–15.

Eynat-Confino, Irène. *On the Uses of the Fantastic in Modern Theatre: Cocteau, Oedipus, and the Monster*. New York: Palgrave, 2008.

"Fairy Tale Set to Music. 'Hans the Flute Player' to be Manhattan's Opening Bill." *New York Times* 18 Sept. 1910. N. pag.

Farmer, Brett. "The Fabulous Sublimity of Gay Diva Worship." *Camera Obscura* 20.2 (2005): 165–95.

Fernández-Rodríguez, Carolina. "The Deconstruction of the Male-Rescuer Archetype in Contemporary Feminist Revisions of 'The Sleeping Beauty.'" *Marvels & Tales* 16.1 (2002): 51–70.

Fischlin, Daniel. "Queer Margins: Cocteau, *La Belle et la Bête*, and the Jewish Differend." *Textual Practice* 12.1 (1998): 69–88.

Fizzarotti, Ettore Maria, dir. *Venga a fare il soldato da noi*. Mondial Televisione Film, 1971.

Fontenot, Andrea. "The Dandy Diva." *Camera Obscura* 23.1 (2008): 165–71.

Foucault, Michel. *Histoire de la folie à l'âge classique*. 1962. Paris: Gallimard, 1976.

———. *Histoire de la sexualité. La volonté de savoir*. Paris: Gallimard, 1976.

———. *Surveiller et punir: Naissance de la prison*. Paris: Gallimard, 1975.

French, Philip. "*Lola*." *The Observer* 18 Sept. 2010. Web 23 Mar. 2012.

Freud, Sigmund. *Sexuality and the Psychology of Love*. Introd. Philip Rieff. New York: Touchstone, 1997.

———. *The "Wolfman" and Other Cases*. New York: Penguin, 2003.

Gaines, Jane M. "Dream/Factory." *Reinventing Film Studies*. Ed. Christine Gledhill and Linda Williams. London: Arnold, 2000. 100–113.

Garber, Marjorie. *Vested Interests: Cross-Dressing and Cultural Anxiety*. 1992. New York: Routledge, 1997.

Garson, Charlotte. "Jacques Demy en ses oeuvres complètes." *Etudes* 409 (Dec. 2008): 653–62.

Gautier, Théophile. *Entretiens, souvenirs et correspondance*. Ed. Emile Bergerat. Preface Edmond de Goncourt. Paris: G. Charpentier, 1879.

Gavin, James. *Stormy Weather: The Life of Lena Horne*. New York: Atria, 2009.

Genet, Jean. *Querelle de Brest*. Illus. Jean Cocteau. Paris: Morihien, 1947.

Gide, André. *Traité du Narcisse, suivi de La Tentative Amoureuse*. 1891. Lausanne: Mermod, 1946.

Gluck, Mary. *Popular Bohemia: Modernism and Urban Culture in Nineteenth-Century Paris*. Cambridge: Harvard UP, 2005.

Godard, Jean-Luc. *A Bout de souffle (Breathless)*. 1960. Criterion Collection, 2007.

———. *Une Femme est une femme*. 1961. Criterion Collection, 2004.

Godfrey, Sima. "The Dandy as Ironic Figure." *SubStance* 36 (1982): 21–33.

Goux, Jean-Joseph. *Symbolic Economies: After Marx and Freud*. Ithaca: Cornell UP, 1990.

Graña, Marigay. "Preface." *On Bohemia: The Code of the Self-Exiled*. By Graña. New Brunswick: Transaction Publishers, 1990. xv–xviii.

Greenhill, Pauline. " 'Neither a Man nor a Maid': Sexualities and Gendered Meanings in Cross-Dressing Ballads." *Journal of American Folklore* 108.428 (1995): 156–77.

Greenhill, Pauline, and Sidney Eve Matrix, eds. *Fairy Tale Films: Visions of Ambiguity*. Logan: Utah State UP, 2010.

Grimm, Joseph, and Wilhelm Grimm. *The Complete Tales of the Brothers Grimm*. Trans. and introd. Jack Zipes. 3rd ed. New York: Bantam, 2003.

Grout, Donald Jay. *Short History of Opera*. New York: Columbia UP, 2003.

Guimard, Paul. "Préface." *Jacques Demy et les racines du rêve*. By Jean-Pierre Berthomé. Nantes: L'Atalante, 1996. 11–13.

Haase, Donald. "*The Arabian Nights*, Visual Culture, and Early German Cinema." *Fabula* 45.3–4 (2004): 261–74.

———, ed. *Fairy Tales and Feminism: New Approaches*. Detroit: Wayne State UP, 2004.

———, ed. *The Greenwood Encyclopedia of Folktales and Fairy Tales*. 3 vols. Westport: Greenwood Press, 2008.

Hagio, Moto. *The Heart of Thomas*. mangareader.net. <http://www.mangareader.net/heart-of-thomas/1/>. 3 March 2013.

———. "The Moto Hagio Interview Conducted by Matt Thorn. Part Three of Four." *The Comics Journal*. 11 Mar. 2010. <http://www.tcj.com/history/the-moto-hagio-interview-conducted-by-matt-thorn-part-three-of-four/>. 3 March 2013.

Halberstam, Judith. *Female Masculinity*. Durham: Duke UP, 1998.

Hamery, Roxane. "La Géographie urbaine de Jacques Demy." *Place publique: La Revue urbaine* 13 (2008). Nantes/Saint-Nazaire. <http://www.revue-placepublique.fr/Sommaires/Sommaires/Articles/dvddemy.html>. 3 March 2013.

"'Hans the Flute Player' Is Full of Melody. Light Opera Comique Charms Audience at Manhattan." *New York Times* 21 Sept. 1910. N. pag.

Hargreaves, Alec G. *Immigration in Post-War France: A Documentary Anthology*. London: Methuen, 1987.

Harpham, Geoffrey Galt. *On the Grotesque: Strategies of Contradiction in Art and Literature*. 1982. Aurora: Davies Group, 2006.

Harris, Joseph. *Hidden Agendas: Cross-Dressing in 17th-Century France*. Tübingen: Gunter Narr Verlag, 2005.

Hay, Sylvie. "Film Jacques Demy." *Télévision Française 1*. 1 Oct. 1978. <http://www.ina.fr/art-et-culture/cinema/video/CAA7801340801/film-jacques-demy.fr.html>. 3 March 2013.

Hayward, Susan. *French National Cinema*. 1993. New York: Routledge, 2005.

Herzog, Amy. *Dreams of Difference, Songs of the Same: The Musical Moment in Film*. Minneapolis: U of Minnesota P, 2009.

Hill, Rodney. "*Donkey Skin (Peau d'âne)*." *Film Quarterly* 59.2 (2006): 40–44.

———. "The New Wave Meets the Tradition of Quality: Jacques Demy's *The Umbrellas of Cherbourg*." *Cinema Journal* 48.1 (2008): 27–50.

House, Jim, and Neil MacMaster. "'Une Journée portée disparue': The Paris Massacre of 1961 and Memory." *Crisis and Renewal in France, 1918-1962*. Ed. Kenneth Mouré and Martin S. Alexander. New York: Berghahn Books, 2002. 267–90.

Ikeda, Riyoko. *La Rose de Versailles*. 3 vols. Brussels: Kana, 2002-5.

Inge, M. Thomas. "Walt Disney's *Snow White*: Art, Adaptation, and Ideology." *Journal of Popular Film & Television* 32.3 (2004): 132–42.

L'Institut national de l'audiovisuel. "Mariage de Grace Kelly avec Rainier de Monaco." *ina.fr*. 23 June 2010. <http://www.ina.fr/video/4223827001>. 3 March 2013.

Irigaray, Luce. *Ce Sexe qui n'en est pas un*. Paris: Minuit, 1977.

———. *This Sex Which Is Not One*. Trans. Catherine Porter. Ithaca: Cornell UP, 1985.

Irvine, Demar. *Massenet. A Chronicle of His Life and Times*. Portland: Amadeus Press, 1994.

"Jacques Demy: 'J'ai attendu neuf ans pour faire "Peau d'âne" mais c'est mon adieu aux films roses.'" *France-Soir* 19 Dec. 1970. N. pag.

"Jacques Demy sur le tournage du film *Le Joueur de flûte*." *Le Journal du cinéma* 1 Oct. 1971. N. pag.

Jarry, Alfred. *Ubu roi*. 1896. Paris: Gallimard, 2002.

Jobs, Richard Ivan. "Youth Movements: Travel, Protest, and Europe in 1968." *American Historical Review* 114.2 (2009): 376–404.

Jones, Christine. "Cross-dressing." *The Greenwood Encyclopedia of Folktales and Fairy Tales*. Ed. Donald Haase. Westport: Greenwood Press, 2008. 1: 241–43.

———. "Noble Impropriety: The Maiden Warrior and the Seventeenth-Century *conte de fées*." Diss. Princeton University, 2002.

———. "The Poetics of Enchantment (1690–1715)." *Marvels & Tales* 17.1 (2003): 55–74.

*"Le Joueur de flûte." *Valeurs Actuelles* 12 Jan. 1976. N. pag.

*"'Le Joueur de flûte' de Jacques Demy." *Le Nouvel Observateur* 12 Jan. 1976. N. pag.

Kayser, Wolfgang. *The Grotesque in Art and Literature*. Trans. Ulrich Weisstein. 1957. New York: Columbia UP, 1981.

Labrie, Vivian. "Help! Me, S/he, and the Boss." *Undisciplined Women: Tradition and Culture in Canada*. Ed. Pauline Greenhill and Diane Tye. Montreal: McGill-Queen's UP, 1997. 151–66.

Lai, Sufen Sophia. "From Cross-Dressing Daughter to Lady Knight-Errant: The Origin and Evolution of Chinese Women Warriors." *Presence and Presentation: Women in the Chinese Literati Tradition*. Ed. Sherry J. Mou. New York: St. Martin's Press, 1999. 77–107.

*Langlois, Gérard. "Jacques Demy. 'Peau d'âne': La Féerie existe-t-elle?" *Lettres françaises* 23 Jan. 1970. N. pag.

Lefèvre, Raphaël. "Jacques Demy et le sexe." *Critikat.com* 24 July 2012. <http://www.critikat.com/Jacques-Demy-et-le-sexe.html>. 3 March 2013.

Le Gras, Gwénaëlle. "Soft and Hard: Catherine Deneuve in 1970." *Studies in French Cinema* 5.1 (2005): 27–35.

Lenzi, Umberto, dir. *The Adventures of Mary Read*. Romana Film, 1961.

Lévi-Strauss, Claude. *Les Structures élémentaires de la parenté*. Paris: Mouton, 1967.

Lichfield, John. "Book Claims Yves Montand Had Secret Affair with His Stepdaughter." *The Independent* 7 May 2004. <http://www.independent.co.uk/news/world/europe/book-claims-yves-montand-had-secret-affair-with-his-stepdaughter-562521.html>. 3 March 2013.

Lindeperg, Sylvie, and Bill Marshall. "Time, History, and Memory in *Les Parapluies de Cherbourg*." *Musicals: Hollywood and Beyond*. Ed. Bill Marshall and Robynn Stilwell. Exeter: Intellect, 2000. 98–106.

"Livret de Peau d'âne, Le." *Le Livre: Bibliographie moderne* 1.5 (1880): 415.

Lundell, Torborg. "Folktale Heroines and the Type and Motif Indexes." *Folklore* 94.2 (1983): 240–46.

Maclean, Ian. *Woman Triumphant: Feminism in French Literature, 1610–1652*. Oxford: Clarendon Press, 1977.

Maille, Nicolas. "Fantaisie nocturne: *Nuits blanches*." *Critikat.com* 22 December 2009. <http://www.critikat.com/Nuits-blanches.html>. 3 March 2013.

Marelles, Charles, comp. *Affenschwanz et cetera. Variantes orales de contes populaires français et étrangers.* Brunswick: George Westermann, 1888.

Marshall, Bill. *The French Atlantic: Travels in Culture and History.* Liverpool: Liverpool UP, 2010.

Martel, Frederic. *The Pink and the Black: Homosexuals in France since 1968.* Trans. Jane Marie Todd. 1996. Stanford: Stanford UP, 1999.

Massenet, Jules. *Mes Souvenirs (1848–1912).* Paris: Pierre Lafitte, 1912.

*Maurin, François. "Jacques Demy: Trois projets en suspens." *L'Humanité* 22 Nov. 1975. N. pag.

Mayer, Nonna. "The French National Front." *The New Politics of the Right: Neo-Populist Parties and Movements in Established Democracies.* Ed. Hans-Georg Betz and Stefan Immerfall. London: Macmillan, 1998. 11–25.

Mayne, Judith. "Dietrich, *The Blue Angel,* and Female Performance." *Seduction and Theory: Readings of Gender, Representation, and Rhetoric.* Ed. Dianne Hunter. Champaign: U of Illinois P, 1989. 28–46.

McKenzie, Brian Angus. *Remaking France: Americanization, Public Diplomacy, and the Marshall Plan.* 2005. New York: Berghahn Books, 2008.

Mérimée, Prosper. *Chronique du règne de Charles IX.* 1829. Paris: Calmann Lévy, 1890.

———. "Le Preneur de rats." *Contes et récits du XIXe siècle.* Ed. Armand Weil and Emile Chénin. 2nd ed. Paris: Larousse, 1913. 52–53.

———. "Le Preneur de rats." *L'Ecole moderne. Morale, enseignement civique, Langue française, histoire, géographie, arithmétique, géométrie, sciences usuelles et agriculture. Livre du maître. Cours élémentaire tome IV. Huitième, neuvième et dixième mois. (Mai, juin et juillet).* Ed. A. Seignette. Paris: Paul Dupont, 1898. 198–200.

Mieder, Wolfgang. *The Pied Piper. A Handbook.* Westport: Greenwood Press, 2007.

———. *Tradition and Innovation in Folk Literature.* Lebanon: UP of New England, 1987.

Millar, Daniel. "*Les Dames du Bois de Boulogne.*" *The Films of Robert Bresson.* New York: Movie Magazine, 1969. 33–41.

Misek, Richard. *Chromatic Cinema: A History of Screen Color.* Oxford: Blackwell, 2010.

Modleski, Tania. "Time and Desire in the Woman's Film." *Cinema Journal* 23.3 (1984): 19–30.

Monaco, James. *The New Wave: Truffaut, Godard, Chabrol, Rohmer, Rivette.* 1976. New York: Harbor Electronic Publishing, 2004.

Mueller, Marlies. "The Taming of the Amazon: The Changing Image of the Woman Warrior in Ancien Régime." *Papers on French Seventeenth-Century Literature* 42 (1995): 199–232.

Murat, Henriette Julie de. *Histoires sublimes et allégoriques.* 2 vols. Paris: Delaulne, 1699.

Murger, Henry. *Scènes de la vie de Bohème.* Paris: Michel Lévy, 1861.

Nakamura, Karen, and Hisako Matsuo. "Female Masculinity and Fantasy Spaces:

Transcending Genders in the Takarazuka Theatre and Japanese Popular Culture." *Men and Masculinities in Contemporary Japan: Dislocating the Salaryman*. Ed. James E. Roberson and Nobue Suzuki. New York: Routledge, 2002. 59–76.

Neale, Steve. "Melodrama and Tears." *Screen* 27.6 (1986): 6–23.

Nelson, Brian. "Alfred Jarry: The Art of the Grotesque." *Groteske Moderne—Moderne Groteske. Festschrift für Philip Thomson/Festschrift for Philip Thomson*. Ed. Franz-Josef Deiters, Axel Fliethmann, and Christiane Weller. St. Ingbert: Röhrig Universitätsverlag, 2011. 205–12.

Neupert, Richard. *A History of the French New Wave*. 2002. Madison: U of Wisconsin P, 2007.

Novoa, Adriana. "Whose Talk Is It? Almodovar and the Fairy Tale in *Talk to Her*." *Marvels & Tales* 19.2 (2005): 224–48.

Nowell-Smith, Geoffrey. *Luchino Visconti*. London: Martin Secker & Warburg, 1973.

———. "Minnelli and Melodrama." *Screen* 18.2 (1977): 113–18.

Oboler, Howard. "Fred Astaire: The Perfect Leap from Stage to Screen." *Playbills to Photoplays: Stage Performers Who Pioneered the Talkies*. Ed. Brenda Loew. Bloomington: New England Vintage Film Society, 2010. 244–59.

O'Neill, Patrick. "The Comedy of Entropy: The Contexts of Black Humour." *Canadian Review of Comparative Literature/Revue canadienne de littérature comparée* 10.2 (1983): 145–66.

Ortolani, Benito. *The Japanese Theatre: From Shamanistic Ritual to Contemporary Pluralism*. Princeton: Princeton UP, 1995.

Ozon, François, dir. *8 Femmes*. 2002. Universal, 2003.

Pace, David. "Beyond Morphology: Lévi-Strauss and the Analysis of Folktales." *Cinderella: A Casebook*. Ed. Alan Dundes. Madison: U of Wisconsin P, 1988. 245–58.

Pasachoff, Naomi E., and Robert J. Littman. *A Concise History of the Jewish People*. Oxford: Rowman and Littlefield, 2005.

Peacock, Steve. *Colour*. Manchester: Manchester UP, 2010.

Perrault, Charles. *Contes*. Ed. Jean-Pierre Collinet. Paris: Gallimard, 1981.

———. *Complete Fairy Tales*. New York: Dodd, Mead, 1961.

Petrie, Duncan, ed. *Cinema and the Realms of Enchantment*. London: British Film Institute, 1993.

*"'The Pied Pipper [*sic*] of Hamelin': Le Pipeau enchanté." *France-Soir* 22 Feb. 1975. N. pag.

Phillipps, Susanne. "Characters, Themes, and Narrative Patterns in the Manga of Osamu Tezuka." *Japanese Visual Culture: Explorations in the World of Manga and Anime*. Ed. Mark W. MacWilliams. New York: M.E. Sharpe, 2008. 68–90.

Power, Natsu Onoda. *God of Comics: Osamu Tezuka and the Creation of Post-World War II Manga*. Jackson: UP of Mississippi, 2009.

Pulju, Rebecca J. *Women and Mass Consumer Society in Postwar France*. Cambridge: Cambridge UP, 2011.

Rank, Otto. *The Myth of the Birth of the Hero*. 1909. New York: Vintage Books, 1964.

Raynard, Sophie. *La Seconde Préciosité: Floraison des conteuses de 1690 à 1756*. Tübingen: Gunter Narr Verlag, 2002.

Rees-Robert, Nick. *French Queer Cinema*. Edinburgh: Edinburgh UP, 2008.

Remond, Alain. "Le Joueur de flûte: La Terrible Candeur des enfants." *Télérama* (31 Dec. 1975): 73.

Robertson, Jennifer. "The Politics of Androgyny in Japan: Sexuality and Subversion in the Theater and Beyond." *American Ethnologist* 19.3 (1992): 419–42.

Romney, Jonathan. "Happy When It Rains: Jacques Demy's Magical Realism." *Modern Painters* 2005: 41–47.

Ross, Kristin. *Fast Cars, Clean Bodies: Decolonization and the Reordering of French Culture*. Cambridge: MIT Press, 1996.

Roth, Norman, ed. *Medieval Jewish Civilization: An Encyclopedia*. New York: Routledge, 2003.

Roth-Bettoni, Didier. *L'Homosexualité au cinéma*. Paris: La Musardine, 2007.

Rousseau, Jean-Jacques. *Essai sur l'origine des langues*. Paris: Le Graphe, 1967.

———. "Essay on the Origin of Languages." *On the Origin of Language*. Trans. John H. Moran. New York: Ungar, 1966. 1–74.

Rubin, Gayle. "The Traffic in Women: Notes on the 'Political Economy' of Sex." *Toward an Anthropology of Women*. Ed. Rayna R. Reiter. New York: Monthly Review Press, 1975. 157–210.

Seifert, Lewis C. *Fairy Tales, Sexuality and Gender in France, 1690–1715: Nostalgic Utopias*. Cambridge: Cambridge UP, 1996.

———. *Manning the Margins: Masculinity and Writing in Seventeenth-Century France*. Ann Arbor: U of Michigan P, 2009.

Seigel, Jerrold. *Bohemian Paris: Culture, Politics, and the Boundaries of Bourgeois Life, 1830–1930*. 1986. Baltimore: Johns Hopkins UP, 1999.

Sellier, Geneviève. *Masculine Singular: French New Wave Cinema*. Trans. Kristin Ross. Durham: Duke UP, 2008.

Shamoon, Deborah. "Revolutionary Romance: The Rose of Versailles and the Transformation of Shojo Manga." *Mechademia 2: Networks of Desire*. Ed. Frenchy Lunning. Minneapolis: U of Minnesota P, 2007. 3–17.

Shelton, Robert. "Donovan Brings His Message in Word and Song." *New York Times* 26 Oct. 1968: 28.

Sherman, Sharon R., and Mikel J. Koven, eds. *Folklore/Cinema: Popular Film as Vernacular Culture*. Logan: Utah State UP, 2007.

Shiel, Mark. "The Southland on Screen." *The Cambridge Companion to the Literature of Los Angeles*. Ed. Kevin R. McNamara. Cambridge: Cambridge UP, 2010. 145–56.

Silverman, Mervyn. "The Plague of Our Time: Societal Responses to AIDS." *Encyclopedia of AIDS: A Social, Political, Cultural, and Scientific Record of the HIV Epidemic*. Ed. Raymond A. Smith. Chicago: Fitzroy Dearborn Publishers, 1998.

22–24.

Silverstein, Paul A. *Algeria in France: Transpolitics, Race, and Nation.* Bloomington: Indiana UP, 2004.

Smith, Timothy B. "Assistance and Repression: Rural Exodus, Vagabondage and Social Crisis in France, 1880–1914." *Journal of Social History* 32.4 (1999): 821–46.

Sontag, Susan. "Notes on 'Camp.'" 1964. *Camp: Queer Aesthetics and the Performing Subject.* 1999. Ed. Fabio Cleto. Ann Arbor: U of Michigan P, 2002. 53–65.

Stanton, Domna. *The Aristocrat as Art: A Study of the Honnête Homme and the Dandy in Seventeenth- and Nineteenth-Century French Literature.* New York: Columbia UP, 1980.

Starzmann-Gaillard, Gerald. "Regarding the Front National." *Neo-Nationalism in Europe and Beyond: Perspectives from Social Anthropology.* Ed. André Gingrich and Marcus Banks. New York: Berghahn Books, 2006. 177–96.

Sternberg, Josef von, dir. *The Blue Angel.* 1930. New York: Kino Video, 2001.

Stewart, Whitney. *Who Was Walt Disney?* New York: Penguin, 2009.

Stilwell, Robynn J. "Le Demy-monde: The Bewitched, betwixt and between French Musical." *Popular Music in France from Chanson to Techno.* Ed. Steve Cannon and Hugh Dauncey. Aldershot: Ashgate, 2003. 123–38.

Stone, Kay. *Some Day Your Witch Will Come.* Detroit: Wayne State UP, 2008.

Storer, Mary Elizabeth. *Un Épisode littéraire à la fin du XVIIe siècle: La Mode des contes de fées (1685–1700).* Paris: Champion, 1928.

Straayer, Chris. *Deviant Eyes, Deviant Bodies: Sexual Re-Orientation in Film and Video.* New York: Columbia UP, 1996.

Strauss, Walter A. "Jean Cocteau: The Mask of Orpheus and Narcissus." *Religiologiques* 15 (Spring 1997). <http://www.religiologiques.uqam.ca/>. 3 March 2013.

Stryker, Susan. "(De)Subjugated Knowledges. An Introduction to Transgender Studies." *The Transgender Studies Reader.* Ed. Susan Stryker and Stephen Whittle. New York: Routledge, 2006.

Suvilay, Bounthavy. "L'Héroïne travestie dans le shōjo manga: Entre création d'un genre et revendication féministe." *Image & Narrative* 7 (Oct. 2003). <http://www. imageandnarrative.be/inarchive/graphicnovel/bounthavysuvilay.htm>. 3 March 2013.

Taboulay, Camille. *Le Cinéma enchanté de Jacques Demy.* Paris: Cahiers du cinéma, 1996.

Tatar, Maria. *The Hard Facts of the Grimms' Fairy Tales.* Princeton: Princeton UP, 1987.

———. *Secrets beyond the Door: The Story of Bluebeard and His Wives.* Princeton: Princeton UP, 2004.

Tezuka, Osamu. *Princesse Saphir.* 3 vols. Paris: Soleil Manga, 2005.

Thompson, Stith. *Motif Index of Folk Literature: A Classification of Narrative Elements in Folktales, Ballads, Myths, Fables, Mediaeval Romances, Exempla, Fabliaux, Jest-Books, and Local Legends.* Bloomington: Indiana UP, 1960.

Tiffin, Jessica. *Marvelous Geometry: Narrative and Metafiction in Modern Fairy Tale.* Detroit: Wayne State UP, 2009.

Tinkcom, Matthew. *Working Like a Homosexual: Camp, Capital, Cinema.* Durham: Duke UP, 2002.

———. "Working Like a Homosexual: Camp Visual Codes and the Labor of Gay Subjects in the MGM Freed Unit." *Cinema Journal* 35.3 (1996): 24–42.

Tucker, Holly. *Pregnant Fictions: Childbirth and the Fairy Tale in Early-Modern France.* Detroit: Wayne State UP, 2003.

Turner, Kay, and Pauline Greenhill, eds. *Transgressive Tales: Queering the Grimms.* Detroit: Wayne State UP, 2012.

Uther, Hans-Jörg. *The Types of International Folktales: A Classification and Bibliography.* 3 vols. Helsinki: Suomalainen Tiedeakatemia, Academia Scientiarum Fennica, 2004.

Vanderburch, Emile, Charles Clairville, and Laurencin. "Peau d'âne. Féerie en neuf tableaux." *La France dramatique au dix-neuvième siècle.* Paris: J. N. Barba; Delloye; Bezou, 1838. 599–641.

Vanderburch, Emile, Laurencin, and Charles Clairville. *Peau d'âne. Féerie en quatres actes et vingt tableaux.* Paris: Tresse, 1883.

Varda, Agnès, dir. *Les Demoiselles ont eu 25 ans.* Fravidis, 1993.

———, dir. *Jacquot de Nantes.* 1991. Ciné Tamaris, 2008.

———, dir. *Les Plages d'Agnès.* Ciné Tamaris and ARTE, 2008.

———, dir. *L'Univers de Jacques Demy.* 1995. Ciné Tamaris, 2003.

Vaucaire, Maurice, and Georges Mitchell. *Hans, le joueur de flûte. Opéra-comique en trois actes.* Music Louis Ganne. Paris: G. Ricordi, 1906.

Velay-Vallantin, Catherine. *La Fille en garçon.* Carcassonne: Garae/Hesiode, 1992.

Vidal, Mary. *Watteau's Painted Conversations.* New Haven: Yale UP, 1992.

Wang, Zheng. *Women in the Chinese Enlightenment: Oral and Textual Histories.* Berkeley: U of California P, 1999.

Watts, Steven. *The Magic Kingdom: Walt Disney and the American Way of Life.* 1997. Columbia: U of Missouri P, 2001.

Weiner, Susan. *Enfants Terribles: Youth and Femininity in the Mass Media in France, 1945–1968.* Baltimore: Johns Hopkins UP, 2001.

Welker, James. "Beautiful, Borrowed, and Bent: 'Boys' Love' as Girls' Love in *Shōjo Manga.*" *Signs* 31.3 (2006): 841–70.

Wilcox, Jason. "Looking at *Lola*, Looking at Cinema." *CineAction* Summer 2005: 24–37.

Wilde, Oscar. "The Disciple." *The Complete Works of Oscar Wilde.* Ed. Bobby Fong and Karl Beckson. 4 vols. Oxford: Oxford UP, 2000. 172–73.

———. *Miscellanies.* London: Methuen, 1908.

Williams, Alan Larson. *Republic of Images: A History of French Filmmaking.* Cambridge: Harvard UP, 1992.

Wilson, Elizabeth. *Bohemians: The Glamorous Outcasts.* London: I. B. Tauris, 2000.

Windust, Bretaigne, dir. *The Pied Piper of Hamelin.* 1957. Alpha Video, 2002.

Wood, Naomi. "Domesticating Dreams in Walt Disney's *Cinderella.*" *The Lion and the Unicorn* 20.1 (1996): 25–49.

Young, Robert J. "Cultural Politics and the Politics of Culture in the Third French Republic: The Case of Louis Barthou." *French Historical Studies* 17.2 (1991): 343–58.

Zapperi, Roberto. *The Pregnant Man.* Trans. Brian Williams. New York: Harwood, 1991.

Zipes, Jack, ed. *Beauties, Beasts, and Enchantments: Classic French Fairy Tales.* New York: New American Library, 1989.

———. *Breaking the Magic Spell: Radical Theories of Folk and Fairy Tales.* 1979. Lexington: U of Kentucky P, 2002.

Zipes, Jack. *The Enchanted Screen: The Unknown History of Fairy-Tales Films.* New York: Routledge, 2011.

———. *Fairy Tales and the Art of Subversion.* 1983. 2nd ed. New York: Routledge, 2006.

———. *Fairy Tale as Myth/Myth as Fairy Tale.* Lexington: UP of Kentucky, 1994.

———, ed. *The Great Fairy-Tale Tradition. From Straparola and Basile to the Brothers Grimm.* New York: Norton, 2001.

Zuerner, Adrienne E. "Reflections on the Monarchy in d'Aulnoy's *Belle-Belle ou le chevalier Fortuné.*" *Out of the Woods: The Origins of the Literary Fairy Tale in Italy and France.* Ed. Nancy L. Canepa. Detroit: Wayne State UP, 1997. 195–217

INDEX

www.ingramcontent.com/pod-product-compliance
Lightning Source LLC
Chambersburg PA
CBHW070330270326
41926CB00017B/3830